THE
ENCYCLOPEDIA
OF
RESTAURANT
FORMS

**A Complete Kit of Ready-To-Use
Checklists, Worksheets and Training Aids
for a Successful Food Service Operation**

Douglas Robert Brown

Published By:
ATLANTIC PUBLISHING GROUP, INC

THE ENCYCLOPEDIA OF RESTAURANT FORMS

A Complete Kit of Ready-To-Use Checklists, Worksheets and Training Aids for a Successful Food Service Operation with Companion CD-Rom

BY DOUGLAS ROBERT BROWN

Published By: **ATLANTIC PUBLISHING GROUP, INC**
ATLANTIC PUBLISHING COMPANY • 1210 S.W. 23rd Place • Ocala, FL 34474-7014
800-541-1336 • http://www.atlantic-pub.com • sales@atlantic-pub.com

SAN Number :268-1250

Member American Library Association
Copyright 2004, All Rights Reserved

Library of Congress Cataloging-in-Publication Data: Brown, Douglas Robert, 1960-
The encyclopedia of restaurant forms : a complete kit of ready-to-use checklists, worksheets and training aids for a successful food service operation with companion CD-ROM / Douglas Robert Brown.-- 1st ed.
p. cm.
Includes bibliographical references and index.
ISBN 0-910627-29-0 (alk. paper)
1. Restaurant management. I. Title.
TX911.3.M27B7597 2004
647.95'068--dc22

2003024261 CIP

WARNING DISCLAIMER

This book is designed to provide information in regard to the subject matter covered. It is sold with the understanding that the publisher and author are not engaged in rendering legal, accounting or other professional services. If legal or other expert assistance is required, the services of a competent professional should be sought.

It is not the purpose of this manual to reprint all the information that is otherwise available to the author and/or publisher but to complement, amplify and supplement other texts.

Every effort has been made to make this manual as complete and as accurate as possible. However, there may be mistakes both typographical and in content. Therefore, this text should be used only as a general guide and not as the ultimate source of information.

The purpose of this manual is to educate and entertain. The author and the publisher shall have neither liability nor responsibility to any person or entity with respect to any loss or damage caused to or alleged to be caused directly or indirectly by the information contained in this book.

Table of Contents

Chapter 1
Food Safety

Chapter 2
Kitchen Management

Chapter 3
Bar & Beverage Management

Chapter 4
General Management

Chapter 5
Menu Management

Chapter 6
Employee Training

Chapter 7
Human Resource Management

Chapter 8
Inventory Control

Chapter 9
Financial Management

Chapter 10
Catering/Banquet Management

Chapter 11
Hotel Management

We recently lost our beloved pet "Bear," who was not only our best and dearest friend but also the "Vice President of Sunshine" here at Atlantic Publishing. He did not receive a salary but worked tirelessly 24 hours a day to please his parents. Bear was a rescue dog that turned around and showered myself, my wife Sherri, his grandparents Jean, Bob and Nancy and every person and animal he met (maybe not rabbits) with friendship and love. He made a lot of people smile every day.

We wanted you to know that a portion of the profits of this book will be donated to The Humane Society of the United States and/or a local animal shelter.

–Douglas & Sherri Brown

REMEMBERING A FRIEND

The human-animal bond is as old as human history. We cherish our animal companions for their unconditional affection and acceptance. We feel a thrill when we glimpse wild creatures in their natural habitat or in our own backyard.

Unfortunately, the human-animal bond has at times been weakened. Humans have exploited some animal species to the point of extinction.

The Humane Society of the United States makes a difference in the lives of animals here at home and worldwide. The HSUS is dedicated to creating a world where our relationship with animals is guided by compassion. We seek a truly humane society in which animals are respected for their intrinsic value, and where the human-animal bond is strong.

Want to help animals? We have plenty of suggestions. Adopt a pet from a local shelter, join The Humane Society and be a part of our work to help companion animals and wildlife. You will be funding our educational, legislative, investigative and outreach projects in the U.S. and across the globe.

Or perhaps you'd like to make a memorial donation in honor of a pet, friend or relative? You can through our Kindred Spirits program. And if you'd like to contribute in a more structured way, our Planned Giving Office has suggestions about estate planning, annuities, and even gifts of stock that avoid capital gains taxes. Maybe you have land that you would like to preserve as a lasting habitat for wildlife. Our Wildlife Land Trust can help you. Perhaps the land you want to share is a backyard—that's enough. Our Urban Wildlife Sanctuary Program will show you how to create a habitat for your wild neighbors.

So you see, it's easy to help animals. And The HSUS is here to help.

THE HUMANE SOCIETY OF THE UNITED STATES ©

The Humane Society of the United States
2100 L Street NW
Washington, DC 20037
202-452-1100
www.hsus.org

Introduction

For the new and veteran food service operators alike, this book is essentially a unique "survival kit," packed with tested advice, practical guidelines and ready-to-use materials for all aspects of your job, gleaned from food service operators and consultants from around the country.

The Encyclopedia of Restaurant Forms focuses on the issues, situations and tasks that you face daily in your management role as leader, manager, arbitrator, evaluator, chairperson, disciplinarian and more; from working with difficult customers and employees to ensuring the profitability of your operation.

Included in this book are hundreds of easy-to-implement tools, forms, checklists, templates and training aids to help you get your operation organized and easier to manage, while building your bottom line! The material may be used as is or readily adapted for any food service application. For example, you'll find a practical form to use to interview employees, a template to develop an employee schedule and checklists to examine the food service operation and prepare a budget. All of this tested, ready-to-use help is organized for quick access into 11 sections, with a companion CD-ROM.

This manual will arm you with the right information to help you do your job. Keep it on your desk for constant reference. The many valuable forms contained in this work may be easily printed out and customized from the companion CD-ROM.

Good reading and good luck!

Sincerely,

Douglas R. Brown

Acknowledgements

Many people helped to make this book possible. Some were inspirational and some provided valuable information, while others provided editorial talent, encouragement and support. Without the assistance of the individuals listed below, this book would never have become a reality. I sincerely thank all these fine people and organizations:

- Sherri Lyn Brown
- Halowell & Jean E. Brown
- Bruce & Vonda Brown
- Kim Hendrickson
- Ed Manley; IFSEA
- Robert Baker
- Diana Toomalatai
- Katerina Toomalatai
- Kastania Toomalatai
- Hal & Charlanne Brown
- Lynn & Jim Durante
- Robert M. & Nancy Frazier
- Dr. Joseph E. Gelety
- Richard Mead, CPA

- Meg Buchner; Megadesign
- Jackie Ness
- Mr. Ed Larson; Superior Products
- National Restaurant Association
- The Small Business Administration
- The Internal Revenue Service
- The U.S. Department of Labor
- Ocala Public Library
- University of Florida Library
- Central Florida Community College & Library
- Gizmo Graphics Web Design; www.gizwebs.com

Cover, design and interior graphics by Meg Buchner of Megadesign
www.mega-designs.com • e-mail: megadesn@mchsi.com

CHAPTER 1

Every restaurant employee must be thoroughly familiar with basic food safety and sanitation procedures. The forms in this chapter provide the fundamental methods that must be followed in order to control food contamination, the spread of infectious diseases and personal safety practices.

Food Safety

General Kitchen Sanitation Compliance Checklist

FOOD PRODUCTION AREA

- ☐ Equipment, appliances, walls and screens are clean in food service area.

- ☐ Food preparation equipment is cleaned and sanitized after every use. This would include choppers, mixers and can openers.

- ☐ Frozen food is thawed using the proper thawing procedures.

- ☐ Cutting boards are sanitized properly after each use and when alternating between raw and cooked foods.

- ☐ Prior to preparation, fruits and vegetables are thoroughly washed.

- ☐ Foods are cooked properly and internal temperatures checked.

- ☐ Foods that are potentially hazardous are held at the correct temperature. Hot foods at 140°F or above; cold foods at 41°F or below. Frozen food must be at or below 0°F at all times.

- ☐ Steam tables or food warmers are used properly and not used to reheat or prepare food.

- ☐ Food service employees do not touch cooked food with bare hands.

- ☐ The food preparation area is not used by employees for smoking or eating. All beverage containers and cups are covered and contain some type of drinking straw.

- ☐ Employees who are ill are sent home or restricted to activities where he or she does not come into contact with food.

- ☐ Employees are wearing hair restraints.

- ☐ Employees wash their hands thoroughly after using the bathroom, after coughing or sneezing, after handling garbage, or after any activity that could cause food contamination.

- ☐ The kitchen has an easily accessible, clean sink specifically for handwashing with soap and disposable towels. A sign with proper handwashing procedures is posted near the sink.

- ☐ Lighting has covers or bulbs that will not shatter.

- ☐ In holding areas, food temperatures are checked regularly with a clean, sanitized thermometer.

- ☐ Uncovered glassware and dishes of food items are not stacked.

DISHWASHING AREA

- ☐ A high-temperature dishwashing machine is used, with wash-cycle water temperatures over 140°F, and rinse-cycle water temperatures over 160°F.

- ☐ A low-temperature dishwashing machine is used with a chemical agent. Manufacturer's specifications are adhered to for proper temperature and chemical concentration.

- ☐ For manual washing, a three-compartment sink is used. The sink has a bleach sanitizing solution or iodine, and chemical strips are used to verify the sanitizing solution's strength.

- ☐ Glassware and dishes are not stacked while wet.

- ☐ Glassware or dishes that are cracked or chipped are immediately discarded.

- ☐ Clean dishes, glassware, utensils and pots and pans do not have any food residue.

General Kitchen Sanitation Compliance Checklist

CHEMICAL & NON-FOOD STORAGE

☐ Dirty water is discarded after use. All mops, brooms and cleaning equipment are cleaned and put away.

☐ The storage area is easily accessible, and clean with no refuse or food residue.

☐ Toxic materials are in the proper container and clearly labeled.

REFRIGERATORS & FREEZERS

☐ Shallow containers are used for cooked foods in the refrigerator.

☐ Air can circulate freely throughout the freezer or refrigerator. Food should not be stored too closely.

☐ Freezers and refrigerators are clean and free from debris.

☐ Freezers are at a temperature of 0°F or lower. Refrigerators are at a temperature of 41°F or lower.

☐ Any frozen food with freezer burn or spoilage is immediately discarded.

☐ Frozen foods are stored in their original container, or are properly packaged, labeled and dated, using the "first in, first out" method.

☐ Proper storage order is observed with prepared foods on the top shelves.

☐ Raw items, meat and eggs are stored below thawed or cooked foods.

☐ Refrigerated foods are well-wrapped, labeled and dated, using the "first in, first out" method.

☐ Seven days is the maximum holding time for refrigerated leftovers. At 45°F, food can only be held for four days.

TRASH & REFUSE AREA

☐ Trash receptacles do not leak and are clean and in good condition.

☐ Exterior dumpsters and all trash receptacles are securely covered.

FOOD TRANSPORTATION

☐ Service trays are used once and then thoroughly washed and sanitized.

☐ Carts used to transport food are clean and well-maintained.

☐ Dairy items or eggs are transported in a cart at 41°F or lower. If coolers are used, they are packed with ice.

DRY FOOD STORAGE

☐ Storage and food handling areas are clean with no insects or rodent droppings.

☐ Food packages are tightly sealed.

☐ Labeled, clean containers are used for dry bulk food items.

☐ Unprotected or exposed water or sewer lines are not in or near food storage areas.

☐ Food is stored on shelves at least 4 inches from the floor for proper cleaning.

☐ The food storage shelves are clean and well-organized without debris or empty boxes.

☐ Foods are properly dated and shelved, using the "first in, first out" method.

☐ Dented cans are discarded.

☐ All shelving units are at least 4 inches from walls, so rodents, bugs and other pests cannot nest between walls and shelves.

☐ Food items have a separate storage area from cleaning agents, pesticides and other toxic substances.

General Food Safety & Sanitation Checklist

Check each item when completed.

EMPLOYEES

○ Employees have a designated area for storing all personal items, which is separate from food preparation areas.

○ An area is designated for non-food items such as for recipes and non-food tools.

○ Employees practice proper handwashing between tasks, at a designated handwashing sink, with soap and single-use paper towels.

○ Employees preparing food wear clean uniforms or aprons.

○ Hair restraints are worn and no jewelry is allowed (except a wedding band). No false nails or nail polish is allowed.

○ Employees do not eat, drink, smoke or chew gum in the food preparation areas.

○ Employees with any illness are sent home. Any cuts, wounds or abrasions are bandaged and gloves are worn over the bandage.

RECEIVING FOOD

○ Receiving trucks meet standards of cleanliness and food safety storage.

○ Food is received by designated employee and checked for acceptable condition, date and temperature.

○ Once food is received, it is noted on invoice and put away immediately.

○ Any damaged or open item will not be accepted including dented or rusted cans.

○ Food is covered, labeled and stored, using the "first in, first out" system.

○ Cross-contamination is avoided by storing raw meats and un-rinsed vegetables away from ready-to-eat food.

FOOD

○ Food is thawed properly in the refrigerator or under running water.

○ Bulk food receptacles are clean and clearly labeled. Scoops with handles are used and stored separately.

○ Ice scoops are not stored in ice.

○ Cross-contamination is not possible between foods and food contact surfaces or staff and chemicals.

○ If possible, pasteurized eggs are used rather than raw eggs.

○ Food is cooked or reheated to the proper temperature (above 165°F).

○ Food is cooled in quick-chill manner such as in a shallow pan in ice or on the top shelf of the walk-in freezer.

○ Potentially hazardous foods are prepared according to safety standards.

EQUIPMENT

○ Freezer and refrigerators: Record area/temperature readings

Freezer 1 _____ / _____

Freezer 2 _____ / _____

Refer 1 _____ / _____

Refer 2 _____ / _____

Refer 3 _____ / _____

○ Equipment is cleaned and maintained according to a set schedule per manufacturer's specifications.

○ Hand sinks are easily accessible, clean and in good condition.

○ Towels that are in use for wiping are replaced every 4 hours. They are stored in sanitizer solution (200ppm) in labeled buckets.

○ Refrigerators are stocked to allow adequate air circulation. Water should not be pooled on bottom shelf, and condensers should be clear and visible.

○ Thermometers are available for all cold-holding equipment. Every thermometer is accessible, in good repair and calibrated regularly (ice water 32°F; boiling water 212°F).

○ The gaskets are clean and in excellent condition.

○ Preparation equipment is clean and well-maintained including range, deep fat fryer, oven, grill and broiler. Equipment with small parts are in good condition without cracks or leaks.

○ The ice machine is sanitized, clean and free from rust, mildew, scale and deposits. The water filters are properly tagged.

○ Beverage machines are cleaned and sanitized daily, including soda gun and holster, and soft drink nozzles are cleaned inside.

○ Glass mats are cleaned/sanitized daily.

○ Equipment not in use and spare parts are stored in separate area and cannot contaminate food or harbor pests.

DISHWASHING

○ Employees wash their hands at hand-wash sinks, regularly using proper handwashing techniques.

○ A three-compartment sink is used with separate compartments for pre-scrape, wash and rinse.

○ The three-compartment sink uses the correct temperature water and sanitizer @ _____ (200ppm).

○ Clean utensils are stored properly (upside down) and away from contamination and dirty utensils.

General Food Safety & Sanitation Checklist

FACILITY

○ The plumbing is in good condition with no leaking pipes, slow drains or leaking faucets. Pipes are 2 inches above drains.

○ All fixtures, walls, ceilings and ventilation are clean and in good repair.

○ Floors are clean and in good condition, and floor mats are pressure-cleaned regularly.

○ Lighting is adequate and shatter-proof.

○ Break areas and wash stations are clean and free from clutter.

○ Maintenance is done regularly and repairs made in a timely manner.

RESTROOMS

○ Sinks are clean and stocked with soap and single-use paper towels. Hot water is at or above 110°F.

○ Handwashing signs are posted.

○ The facilities have adequate supplies and are disinfected, clean and in good repair.

CHEMICAL STORAGE

○ Chemicals are labeled, stored in designated areas (away from food), with material safety data sheets (MSDS).

FIRE & SAFETY

○ Fire extinguishers are available, charged, tagged and mounted, and employees have been instructed how to use them properly.

○ Extension cords are not used.

○ CO_2 tanks are stored upright and secured.

○ Bulletin boards with tacks or pins are not used in food preparation, washing or storage areas.

PEST CONTROL

○ There is no evidence of insects, rodents or birds (such as droppings).

○ The building is pest-proof, with sealed doors, working fly fans and no exterior holes or cracks.

○ Traps are tamper-proof and secured.

○ The pest-control operator manual has pesticide lists, map of traps and emergency contacts list.

GARBAGE & REFUSE

○ The dumpsters are clean and the lids are closed.

○ The outside premises are clean, free from trash and debris.

○ The grease bin and surrounding area is maintained and clean.

○ The recycle bins and surrounding area is maintained and clean.

○ When washing or degreasing trash cans, food bins or other equipment, wastewater does not run into storm drains.

○ Garbage and waste food cans have plastic liners, and are pressure-cleaned and disinfected.

GENERAL

○ Employees have been properly trained in food protection and Hazcom procedures. All training is documented.

○ Health permits are current and prominently posted.

○ A food-safety-certified manager is on the premises at all times.

○ Water quality is checked annually and reports are on file.

○ Cleaning tools such as mops and brooms are stored separately from food, dishes and utensils.

○ The mop sink is easily accessible and clean, with hot and cold water. Mop heads are air-dried upside down and clean.

DATE: **SUPERVISOR:**

NOTES/COMMENTS:

Comprehensive Food Facility Compliance Checklist

Circle Yes or No for every applicable item.

 RECEIVING

Y N 1. Food is received only from previously approved vendors.

Y N 2. Food deliveries are inspected immediately for proper condition and temperature, with potentially hazardous foods delivered at a temperature of 41°F.

Y N 3. Frozen foods delivered in frozen state with no evidence of thawing or refreezing.

Y N 4. Raw or frozen clams, mussels, scallops and oysters have a temperature below 45°F and are properly labeled, with labels maintained onsite for at least 90 days.

Y N 5. Deliveries are rejected if the food is not at the proper temperature or in unacceptable condition.

Y N 6. Food is promptly placed in proper storage locations, with refrigerated and frozen foods stored immediately.

 STORAGE

Y N 1 All food is stored away from chemicals, vermin, insects, etc., and cannot be contaminated.

Y N 2. All food is properly labeled using the "first in, first out" system, including prepackaged and bulk foods.

Y N 3. Shelving for food storage is at least 6 inches from floor and walls.

Y N 4. Items to be returned and damaged goods are stored separately.

Y N 5. Proper layering is used in refrigerated storage, with raw meat and fish stored below and away from ready-to-eat foods (produce, vegetables, beverages).

Y N 6. All food in storage is properly covered and sealed.

Y N 7. Contaminated food is promptly discarded.

 PREPARATION

Y N 1. Frozen foods thawed properly using an acceptable method:

In a refrigerator.

In a microwave.

Under cold, running water.

As part of the cooking process.

Comprehensive Food Facility Compliance Checklist

PREPARATION, CONT.

Y N   2. Hot foods (which can be potentially hazardous) are cooled quickly by the following methods before placement in a refrigerator or freezer:

With a rapid, cool stirring device.

Stirring while in an ice bath.

In a blast chiller.

Adding ice to the food.

In shallow, iced pans.

Separating food into smaller portions.

Y N   3. Separate sinks are available and used only for food preparation activities—not handwashing or janitorial use.

Y N   4. Potentially hazardous foods do not have sulfite added.

Y N   5. Potentially hazardous foods are cooked thoroughly with proper internal temperatures:

Poultry–165°F (comminuted poultry, game birds, stuffed meats, stuffed pasta and reheated foods).

Beef–155°F (ground beef, other comminuted meats and foods containing comminuted meat).

Pork–155°F.

Eggs–145°F (food containing raw eggs and other cooked, potentially hazardous food).

SERVING

Y N   1. All prepackaged foods are labeled properly with name, list of ingredients, net weight and name and address of manufacturer.

Y N   2. Any food returned from customers uneaten is discarded (not reused or reserved).

Y N   3. Food and utensils in self-service areas, such as salad bars, buffets, snack counters and beverage dispensers, are protected from contamination by customers (e.g., sneezing, coughing and handling).

Y N   4. Bare hands are not used for food service and serving utensils, such as spoons, tongs and ladles, are provided.

Comprehensive Food Facility Compliance Checklist

 TEMPERATURES

| Y | N | 1. Hot, potentially hazardous foods kept at or above 140°F. |

Y N 1. Hot, potentially hazardous foods kept at or above 140°F.

Y N 2. Cold, potentially hazardous foods kept at or below 41°F.

Y N 3. The danger zone for potentially hazardous foods is 42°–140°F. When cooling or reheating foods, the time spent in this temperature range is kept to a minimum.

Y N 4. Properly calibrated thermometers are visible in the warmest part of each refrigeration and freezer unit.

Y N 5. If serving potentially hazardous food, a metal probe-type thermometer is used to check temperature prior to service.

Y N 6. Thermometers are sanitized before and after each use.

Y N 7. Thermometers are calibrated regularly.

Y N 8. While in use, tongs, scoops, spoons, ladles or other serving utensils for potentially hazardous foods are kept at or below 41°F or above 140°F, or in a dipper well that has clean water continually provided.

 DISHWASHING

Y N 1. Plates, glasses and silverware are sanitized by mechanical dishwasher according to manufacturer specifications. If manually washed, they are sanitized by one of the following methods: 100ppm chlorine for 30 seconds; 25ppm iodine for 60 seconds; 200ppm quaternary ammonium for 60 seconds; or 180°F water for 30 seconds.

Y N 2. All mechanical dishwashers are provided with dual integral drainboards.

Y N 3. During operation of dish machines, the correct temperature is maintained as well as proper amounts of sanitizer and chemicals.

Y N 4. When sanitizing utensils, a test strip or thermometer is used to check effectiveness.

Y N 5. A three-compartment (preferred) or two-compartment sink is available for utensil washing.

Y N 6. All compartments can fully submerge the largest utensil in use.

Y N 7. Utensils are maintained and clean.

Y N 8. Utensils used in the kitchen or for serving are regularly cleaned and sanitized.

Y N 9. Only commercial-grade utensils that are certified by an American National Standards Institute (ANSI)-accredited program are used.

Y N 10. Utensils are stored away from any possible contamination including dirt, rodents, insects and chemicals.

Y N 11. Single-use customer utensils are used only once and disposed.

Comprehensive Food Facility Compliance Checklist

 RESTROOMS

Y	N	1	Restroom facilities are provided for employees.
Y	N	2.	Restroom facilities are provided for customers.
Y	N	3.	Toilet stalls have self-closing, locking doors.
Y	N	4.	Restroom facilities are not used for storage of food, utensils, equipment or supplies.
Y	N	5.	Restroom facilities have adequate supplies such as toilet paper, single-use sanitary towels (or air dryer) and sanitizing hand cleanser.
Y	N	6.	A handwashing sink has pressurized hot and cold water.
Y	N	7.	Restroom facilities have adequate ventilation.

 HANDWASHING

Y	N	1.	A separate handwashing sink is located in, or adjacent to, restrooms and kitchens.
Y	N	2.	The handwashing sink has adequate supplies including single-service sanitary towels (or air dryers) and sanitizing hand cleanser.
Y	N	3.	The handwashing sink has pressurized hot and cold water.
Y	N	4.	The handwashing sink is easily accessible at all times.
Y	N	5.	A separate handwashing sink is used exclusively for handwashing in food prep areas and is conveniently located.

 CHEMICALS & CLEANING

Y	N	1.	Chemicals are labeled properly.
Y	N	2.	Chemicals are not stored in food preparation area.
Y	N	3.	The only pesticides used have been specifically approved for food facility usage.
Y	N	4.	All chemicals, pesticides and hazardous materials are used properly. Employees have access to MSDS information on all chemicals.
Y	N	5.	Cleaning supplies and equipment are stored in a separate area away from food preparation, food storage, dishwashing and utensil storage areas.
Y	N	6.	A separate janitorial sink has hot and cold water with a back-flow prevention device.
Y	N	7.	All mops, buckets, brooms and other cleaning equipment is kept away from food and utensils.

Comprehensive Food Facility Compliance Checklist

 LIGHTING

Y N 1. In food preparation and utensil cleaning areas, lighting has a minimum intensity of 20 footcandles (fc).

Y N 2. In dining and other areas, lighting has a minimum intensity of 10 fc, but intensity of at least 20 fc available during cleaning operations.

Y N 3. Food preparation, food storage and utensil cleaning areas have shatterproof light covers installed and are in good repair.

 PEST INFESTATION

Y N 1. Rodents, insects and other vermin are not in the building.

Y N 2. Building does not have cracks or openings where rodents and insects can enter, and any droppings and dead insects are cleaned up.

Y N 3. All building entrances have air curtains or tight-fitting, self-closing doors. All windows are protected by screens.

Y N 4. Any fumigation or pest control is done by a licensed pest control operator.

 GARBAGE

Y N 1. Garbage is removed frequently and proper facilities are provided for disposal and storage.

Y N 2. Garbage containers have tight-fitting lids, do not leak and are rodent-proof.

Y N 3. Before being placed in the dumpster, all garbage is in securely fastened plastic bags.

 EMPLOYEES

Y N 1. Employees wear clean uniforms or approved clothing.

Y N 2. Employees only use tobacco products in designated areas, away from food preparation, storage and service.

Y N 3. Employees wash hands thoroughly and frequently. Hands are washed after engaging in any activity that may cause contamination including working between raw food and ready-to-eat foods, after coughing or sneezing, after touching soiled equipment or utensils and after using restrooms.

Comprehensive Food Facility Compliance Checklist

EMPLOYEES, CONT.

Y N 4. Ill employees are sent home or do not come to work.

Y N 5. Employees practice safe food-handling procedures and have been trained in food safety.

Y N 6. Employees check temperatures of potentially hazardous foods during storage, preparation and serving. Employees also check utensil-cleaning chemical levels, water temperatures and water pressures.

Y N 7. A separate employee changing area is provided, apart from toilets, food storage, food preparation, utensil cleaning and utensil storage areas.

PLUMBING

Y N 1. Water supply has been tested and comes from an approved source.

Y N 2. Adequate amounts of hot and cold water are available.

Y N 3. Sewage and wastewater is disposed properly into a sewer or septic system.

Y N 4. All equipment that discharges waste, such as prep sinks, steam tables, salad bars, ice machines, ice storage bins, beverage machines, display cases or refrigeration/freezer units, have a floor sink or funnel drain provided for indirect waste drainage.

Y N 5. Receptacles for indirect waste are accessible and cleaned regularly.

Y N 6. Plumbing is clean, in good repair and operating properly.

Y N 7. A licensed company cleans out grease interceptors and septic tanks regularly.

SIGNAGE

Y N 1. Restrooms have handwashing signs posted and clearly visible.

Y N 2. Handwashing sinks have signage with proper handwashing procedures posted and clearly visible.

Y N 3. "No smoking" signs are clearly visible throughout the facility, especially in food preparation, food storage, utensil cleaning and utensil storage areas.

Y N 4. A Choking First Aid poster is visible and readily accessible to employees (in facilities with sit-down dining).

Comprehensive Food Facility Compliance Checklist

 FACILITY

Y	N	1.	Facility is fully enclosed, clean and well-maintained.
Y	N	2.	The building meets all applicable building and fire codes.
Y	N	3.	Exterior premises is clean and well-maintained.
Y	N	4.	All equipment is clean, well-maintained and meets applicable ANSI-accredited certification program standards.
Y	N	5.	No unused, out-dated or broken equipment is on the premises.
Y	N	6.	Cooking equipment and high-temperature dish machines have ventilation and exhaust systems installed over areas of operation.
Y	N	7.	In food preparation and storage areas, flooring is level, non-skid, durable, non-absorbent and easily cleaned.
Y	N	8.	In janitorial facilities, restrooms and employee changing areas flooring is smooth, non-skid, durable, non-absorbent and easily cleaned.
Y	N	9.	In food preparation, food storage areas, janitorial facilities, restrooms and employee changing areas, walls and ceilings are smooth, durable, non-absorbent and easily cleaned.
Y	N	10.	The health department has approved all construction, remodeling and new equipment installation prior to work.
Y	N	11.	All soiled linens are held in a clean container, and a linen storage area is provided.
Y	N	12.	Tobacco permit is valid, up to date and posted in a prominent location (if applicable).
Y	N	13.	Health permit is valid, up to date and posted in a prominent location.

Comprehensive Sanitation Compliance Checklist

DATE: _____ TIME: _____ EMPLOYEE(S): _____

JANITORIAL ROOM

Is it clean and neat?	Yes No
Are buckets empty and stored upside down?	Yes No
Are there rodent or insect droppings visible?	Yes No
Are all toxic materials (including pesticides) in their original containers and clearly labeled?	Yes No

DISHWASHING AREA

	MAIN KITCHEN	AUX KITCHEN
Wash cycle temperature	_____ °F	_____ °F
Rinse cycle temperature	_____ °F	_____ °F
Are there any obstructions or contaminents in the jets and nozzles (such as food particles)?	Yes No	Yes No
Is the dishwashing equipment cleaned daily to remove food particles, chemicals and debris?	Yes No	Yes No
Is the proper amount or level of detergent and/or sanitizer being used consistently in the wash cycle?	Yes No	Yes No
Do separate employees remove and store clean tableware?	Yes No	Yes No
Do dishwashing employees practice proper handwashing between handling soiled tableware and sanitized ware?	Yes No	Yes No
Do employees pre-scrape and flush dishes and utensils prior to washing?	Yes No	Yes No
Once dishes and utensils are cleaned and sanitized, are they stored in a clean, dry location (off the floor)?	Yes No	Yes No
Are utensils and tableware toweled properly?	Yes No	Yes No

Notes or Concerns:

_____
_____
_____
_____
_____
_____
_____
_____
_____
_____
_____
_____
_____
_____
_____
_____
_____
_____
_____
_____
_____
_____
_____
_____
_____
_____
_____
_____
_____
_____
_____
_____

Comprehensive Sanitation Compliance Checklist

DATE: _____ TIME: _____ EMPLOYEE(S): _____

SERVICES AREA	MAIN KITCHEN Yes No	AUX KITCHEN Yes No	Notes or Concerns:
Are floors, tables and chairs clean and dry in the dining area?	Yes No	Yes No	
Is the floor being swept or cleaned while food is being served or when customers are eating?	Yes No	Yes No	
Is the temperature correct in the dining area for customer comfort?	Yes No	Yes No	
Does the dining area have any unpleasant odors?	Yes No	Yes No	
Are the dishes and silverware clean, sanitized and stored correctly to prevent contamination?	Yes No	Yes No	
Are condiment containers clean and in good repair?	Yes No	Yes No	
Are menus clean and in good repair, without food marks or stains?	Yes No	Yes No	
Are food warmers or steam tables used to re-heat prepared foods?	Yes No	Yes No	
Is food being held in the hot-holding equipment at or above 140°F?	Yes No	Yes No	
Is cold food being held at 41°F or lower?	Yes No	Yes No	
Are cold- and hot-holding cabinets equipped with thermometers?	Yes No	Yes No	
Are tongs or other serving utensils available and used to pick up rolls, bread, butter pats, ice or other food to be served?	Yes No	Yes No	
Are tableware towels clean, dry and only used for wiping food spills?	Yes No	Yes No	
Are servers wearing proper uniforms that are clean and in good condition?	Yes No	Yes No	
Do servers show any signs of illness, such as coughing or wiping their noses?	Yes No	Yes No	
Do servers handle drinking glasses and silverware properly, without touching glass tops or silverware blades?	Yes No	Yes No	

The Encyclopedia of Restaurant Forms

Comprehensive Sanitation Compliance Checklist

DATE: _____ TIME: _____ EMPLOYEE(S): _____

	MAIN KITCHEN	AUX KITCHEN

PERSONAL SANITATION

	MAIN KITCHEN	AUX KITCHEN
Are all employees involved with food handling properly dressed in clean uniforms or attire?	Yes No	Yes No
Are employees wearing jewelry other than a wedding band?	Yes No	Yes No
Are employees wearing hair restraints?	Yes No	Yes No
Do employees have a noticeable odor (such as strong perfume or body odor)?	Yes No	Yes No
Do employees have properly groomed hands, without fingernail polish and with short, clean fingernails?	Yes No	Yes No
If employees have any wounds, are they properly covered and free of infection?	Yes No	Yes No
Do employees show any signs of illness, such as sneezing or coughing?	Yes No	Yes No
Do employees scratch their head, face or body?	Yes No	Yes No
Are employees seen eating in food preparation or serving areas?	Yes No	Yes No

GENERAL SANITATION

	MAIN KITCHEN	AUX KITCHEN
Are cleaning supplies and chemicals stored separately from the food preparation and service areas?	Yes No	Yes No
Is prepared food held correctly (at the correct temperature and in the proper containers?	Yes No	Yes No
Are clean, sanitary towels available?	Yes No	Yes No
Are frozen foods thawed correctly, either in the refrigerator, under cold, running water or thawed during the cooking process?	Yes No	Yes No
Is a separate sink available for food preparation that is not used for handwashing or cleaning?	Yes No	Yes No

Notes or Concerns:

_____
_____
_____
_____
_____
_____
_____
_____
_____
_____
_____
_____
_____
_____
_____
_____
_____
_____
_____
_____
_____
_____
_____
_____
_____
_____
_____
_____
_____
_____
_____
_____

Comprehensive Sanitation Compliance Checklist

DATE: _____ TIME: _____ EMPLOYEE(S): _____

	MAIN KITCHEN	AUX KITCHEN	Notes or Concerns:

GENERAL SANITATION (continued)

	MAIN KITCHEN	AUX KITCHEN
Is preparation equipment cleaned and sanitized between and after each use, or at the end of the day?	Yes No	Yes No
Are equipment and utensils not in use clean?	Yes No	Yes No
Are all dishes, pots, pans and other utensils stored correctly to prevent contamination?	Yes No	Yes No
Is food stored in coolers and freezers covered and spaced correctly to allow air circulation?	Yes No	Yes No
Are cutting boards in good condition and used only for specific types of food preparation to avoid cross-contamination?	Yes No	Yes No
Are cutting boards cleaned and sanitized after each use?	Yes No	Yes No

DRY STORAGE

	MAIN KITCHEN	AUX KITCHEN
Is the food storage area enclosed, dry and free from dampness?	Yes No	Yes No
Are food supplies labeled, dated and stored to ensure "first in, first out" use?	Yes No	Yes No
Is food stored separately from non-food supplies?	Yes No	Yes No
Is there any evidence of insects or rodent droppings in the storage areas?	Yes No	Yes No
Is the food storage area clean and free of dust, empty food cartons and other debris (including shelves and floor)?	Yes No	Yes No
Are shelves at least 4 inches away from walls and floors?	Yes No	Yes No
Is the area underneath the shelves easily accessible for cleaning?	Yes No	Yes No

Notes or Concerns:

_____
_____
_____
_____
_____
_____
_____
_____
_____
_____
_____
_____
_____
_____
_____
_____
_____
_____
_____
_____
_____
_____
_____
_____
_____
_____
_____
_____
_____
_____

Comprehensive Sanitation Compliance Checklist

DATE: _____ TIME: _____ EMPLOYEE(S): _____

WALK-IN FREEZERS
Temperature

	MAIN KITCHEN _____ °F	AUX KITCHEN _____ °F
Are shelves and floor clean and free of empty cartons or debris?	Yes No	Yes No
Are all foods properly stored and covered?	Yes No	Yes No
Are food supplies labeled, dated and stored to ensure "first in, first out" use?	Yes No	Yes No
Can air circulate freely around stored food?	Yes No	Yes No
Does freezer need defrosting?	Yes No	Yes No

Notes or Concerns:
_____
_____
_____
_____
_____
_____
_____
_____
_____
_____

WALK-IN REFRIGERATORS
Temperature

	MEAT _____ °F	DAIRY _____ °F	VEGE _____ °F	AUX KITCHEN _____ °F
Are refrigerators clean, with no mold or offensive odors?	Yes No	Yes No	Yes No	Yes No
Can air circulate freely around stored food?	Yes No	Yes No	Yes No	Yes No
Is food stored on the the floor of the refrigerators?	Yes No	Yes No	Yes No	Yes No
Are foods labeled, dated and stored to ensure "first in, first out" use?	Yes No	Yes No	Yes No	Yes No
Are large-quantity containers used for storing cooked foods (ground meat, dressing or gravy)?	Yes No	Yes No	Yes No	Yes No
Are all containers clearly labeled with date and food item?	Yes No	Yes No	Yes No	Yes No
Is spoiled or outdated food promptly discarded?	Yes No	Yes No	Yes No	Yes No
Are proper storage techniques used, with cooked food on the top and raw meats or poultry on the bottom shelves?	Yes No	Yes No	Yes No	Yes No
Are shelves at least 6 inches from the floor to allow cleaning underneath?	Yes No	Yes No	Yes No	Yes No
Are cooked foods stored in clean, sanitized, covered containers (not their original cartons)?	Yes No	Yes No	Yes No	Yes No

Individual Sanitation Checklists

Cold Food Production

Date: **Employee:**

❏ YES   ❏ NO   1.   Before food preparation, are all equipment and utensils cleaned and sanitized (including work surfaces)?

❏ YES   ❏ NO   2.   Are all utensils and containers cleaned and sanitized prior to use?

❏ YES   ❏ NO   3.   Are potentially hazardous ingredients (including tuna fish and mayonnaise) refrigerated at least 24 hours before use?

❏ YES   ❏ NO   4.   Are all fruits and vegetables properly washed prior to use?

❏ YES   ❏ NO   5.   Before handling food, do employees wash hands properly with soap and water?

❏ YES   ❏ NO   6.   Is prepared food properly covered, labeled and refrigerated, and taken directly to the serving line?

❏ YES   ❏ NO   7.   Do all workstations have ready access to sanitizer solution?

❏ YES   ❏ NO   8.   After each use, are work areas cleaned and sanitized?

❏ YES   ❏ NO   9.   While preparing food, are employees wearing disposable gloves?

❏ YES   ❏ NO   10. Are all sinks in the food preparation area sanitized after each use?

❏ YES   ❏ NO   11. Are handwashing sinks easily accessible and stocked with handsoap from a proper dispenser and single-use paper towels?

❏ YES   ❏ NO   12. At the end of each day, is all food production equipment cleaned and sanitized?

Action Plan: **Completed By:**   **Comments:**

Supervisor:

Individual Sanitation Checklists

Vending Locations

Date: **Employee:**

❏ YES   ❏ NO   1.   Is the vending area cleaned and uncluttered, with no trash or other debris?

❏ YES   ❏ NO   2.   Is the vending machine area clean, in good condition and protected from overhead water, waste or sewer piping leakage and condensation?

❏ YES   ❏ NO   3.   Does the vending area have adequate lighting and proper ventilation?

❏ YES   ❏ NO   4.   Is the vending area free of insects and rodents?

❏ YES   ❏ NO   5.   Are cold, potentially hazardous foods held at the proper temperatures (41°F or less) at all times?

❏ YES   ❏ NO   6.   Are hot, potentially hazardous foods held at the proper temperatures (140°F or higher) at all times?

❏ YES   ❏ NO   7.   Do the vending machines have thermometers that are checked daily to ensure machines are maintaining safe, accurate temperatures?

❏ YES   ❏ NO   8.   Is food sold in the vending machines properly packaged and protected from contamination?

❏ YES   ❏ NO   9.   Are all vending machines cleaned on a regular basis?

❏ YES   ❏ NO   10. Is a trash receptacle located near vending machines to properly dispose of food cartons and other debris?

Action Plan: **Completed By:**   **Comments:**

Supervisor:

Individual Sanitation Checklists

Vending/Catering Food Transport Vehicles

Date: **Employee:**

❑ YES   ❑ NO   1.   During transport, are cold, potentially hazardous foods held at the proper temperatures (41°F or less) at all times?

❑ YES   ❑ NO   2.   During transport, are hot, potentially hazardous foods held at the proper temperatures (140°F or higher) at all times?

❑ YES   ❑ NO   3.   Are insulated containers used for food transport?

❑ YES   ❑ NO   4.   If warming cabinets are used, is the temperature 140°F or higher when handling or transporting hot foods?

❑ YES   ❑ NO   5.   Are foods and beverages protected from contaminations such as dirt, dust and insects?

❑ YES   ❑ NO   6.   Are vehicles cleaned and sanitized after each use?

Action Plan: **Completed By:**   **Comments:**

Supervisor:

Individual Sanitation Checklists

Hot Food Production

Date: **Employee:**

❑ YES   ❑ NO   1. Before and after food preparation, are all equipment and utensils cleaned and sanitized (including work surfaces)?

❑ YES   ❑ NO   2. Are frozen foods thawed correctly, either in the refrigerator, under cold, running water or thawed during the cooking process?

❑ YES   ❑ NO   3. Are potentially hazardous foods cooked thoroughly with proper internal temperatures: poultry, 165°F; beef, 155°F; pork, 155°F; and eggs, 145°F?

❑ YES   ❑ NO   4. Are hot, potentially hazardous foods cooled quickly by one of the following methods: with a rapid, cool stirring device, stirring while in an ice bath, in a blast chiller, by adding ice to the food, in shallow, iced pans or by separating food into smaller portions?

❑ YES   ❑ NO   5. Are leftovers heated to 165°F?

❑ YES   ❑ NO   6. Are sinks used for food preparation cleaned and sanitized between each use?

❑ YES   ❑ NO   7. Are handwashing sinks accessible and properly stocked with single-use towels and soap dispensers so employees can wash hands before food preparation?

❑ YES   ❑ NO   8. Are spills wiped up immediately?

❑ YES   ❑ NO   9. Are floors kept clean with regular sweeping and mopping?

❑ YES   ❑ NO   10. Does every workstation have easy access to sanitizing solution?

Action Plan:	Completed By:	Comments:
	Supervisor:	

Individual Sanitation Checklists

Line Serving Areas

| Date: | | Employee: |

❑ YES ❑ NO   1. Do all refrigerators have properly calibrated thermometers and maintain a temperature of 41°F or below?

❑ YES ❑ NO   2. Are all deli or line items items refrigerated until placement on the deli bar?

❑ YES ❑ NO   3. Are all items held at 45°F while on the deli bar?

❑ YES ❑ NO   4. Are properly calibrated thermometers used regularly to check product temperatures?

❑ YES ❑ NO   5. Are floors kept clean with regular sweeping and mopping?

❑ YES ❑ NO   6. At the end of each day, is all the deli bar equipment cleaned and sanitized?

❑ YES ❑ NO   7. Does every workstation have easy access to sanitizing solution?

Action Plan:	Completed By:	Comments:
	Supervisor:	

Individual Sanitation Checklists

Line Service/Hot Foods

Date:		Employee:

❑ YES ❑ NO 1. Do all refrigerators have properly calibrated thermometers and maintain a temperature of 41°F or below?

❑ YES ❑ NO 2. Are refrigerated items stored properly, with cooked or ready-to-eat items above raw products?

❑ YES ❑ NO 3. Are all refrigerated products stored in properly covered containers and labeled?

❑ YES ❑ NO 4. Is raw meat refrigerated prior to cooking?

❑ YES ❑ NO 5. Is the grill clean, in good working order and properly maintained?

❑ YES ❑ NO 6. Is the steam table clean and in good working condition?

❑ YES ❑ NO 7. Are all hot, cooked foods held at 140°F or higher?

❑ YES ❑ NO 8. Do soup kettles have a temperature of 140°F or higher?

❑ YES ❑ NO 9. Are properly calibrated thermometers used to take frequent temperature checks?

❑ YES ❑ NO 10. Are spills wiped up immediately?

❑ YES ❑ NO 11. Are floors mopped and swept on a regular basis?

Action Plan:	Completed By:	Comments:
	Supervisor:	

Individual Sanitation Checklists

Restrooms

Date:	Employee:

- ☐ YES ☐ NO   1.   Are restrooms clean and odor-free?
- ☐ YES ☐ NO   2.   Are restrooms well-ventilated?
- ☐ YES ☐ NO   3.   Do toilet stalls have self-closing, locking doors?
- ☐ YES ☐ NO   4.   Are soap and towel dispensers well-stocked and working properly?
- ☐ YES ☐ NO   5.   Does the sink(s) and have faucets with pressurized hot and cold water?
- ☐ YES ☐ NO   6.   Are the trash containers cleaned and emptied on a regular basis?
- ☐ YES ☐ NO   7.   Is the restroom used for storage of food, utensils, equipment or supplies?

Action Plan:	Completed By:	Comments:
	Supervisor:	

Individual Sanitation Checklists

Dry Storage

Date: **Employee:**

❑ YES   ❑ NO   1. Are all food goods stacked neatly, labeled and in proper containers?

❑ YES   ❑ NO   2. Are all storage shelves or racks at least 6 inches off the floor?

❑ YES   ❑ NO   3. Are shelves and storage area clean, free of dust, empty cartons and other debris?

❑ YES   ❑ NO   4. Is storage area swept daily?

❑ YES   ❑ NO   5. Are food items rotated properly using the "first in, first out" system?

❑ YES   ❑ NO   6. Is temperature of the the dry storage area regulated (between 60°F and 70°F) and ventilated to avoid dampness?

❑ YES   ❑ NO   7. Is the storage area large enough for ease of use?

❑ YES   ❑ NO   8. Is the storage area inspected for evidence of rodents and insects on a regular basis?

❑ YES   ❑ NO   9. Are food supplies stored separately from chemicals, cleaners and pesticides?

❑ YES   ❑ NO   10. Are water or sewer lines located in a separate area away from food storage?

❑ YES   ❑ NO   11. Is contaminated or spoiled food promptly discarded?

❑ YES   ❑ NO   12. Is the storage area well-lit?

Action Plan: **Completed By:**   **Comments:**

Supervisor:

Individual Sanitation Checklists

Dishroom/Pot & Pan Areas

Date: **Employee:**

❑ YES   ❑ NO   1.   Are the dishroom floors cleaned and sanitized on a regular basis?

❑ YES   ❑ NO   2.   Are sinks cleaned and sanitized before use?

❑ YES   ❑ NO   3.   Are sanitizing chemicals used according to specifications and at the proper strength?

❑ YES   ❑ NO   4.   Is a three-compartment sink utilized for dishwashing?

❑ YES   ❑ NO   5.   Before washing, all are dishware, utensils, pots and pans scraped and flushed?

❑ YES   ❑ NO   6.   Are dishes and utensils immersed for at least 30 seconds in hot water that is at or above 170°F?

❑ YES   ❑ NO   7.   Are sanitizer concentrations checked using test strips?

❑ YES   ❑ NO   8.   Is a sanitation log book kept of test results?

❑ YES   ❑ NO   9.   Are all dishware, pots and pans air-dried?

❑ YES   ❑ NO   10. Are all dishware, pots and pans stored in the proper manner, free from splashes and contamination?

❑ YES   ❑ NO   11. If used, is the dish machine in good working order?

❑ YES   ❑ NO   12. Is the final rinse temperature of the dish machine at or greater than 180°F?

❑ YES   ❑ NO   13. Is the dish machine cleaned daily at the end of its use?

❑ YES   ❑ NO   14. Are the detergent levels of the dish machine checked regularly?

Action Plan: **Completed By:**   **Comments:**

Supervisor:

Individual Sanitation Checklists

Refrigerator & Freezer Storage

Date: **Employee:**

❑ YES   ❑ NO   1.   Is the interior temperature of the refrigerators 41°F or lower?

❑ YES   ❑ NO   2.   Are all refrigerators and freezers equipped with interior and exterior thermometers?

❑ YES   ❑ NO   3.   Are the interior and exterior thermometers of the refrigerators and freezers calibrated regularly?

❑ YES   ❑ NO   4.   Are refrigerators cleaned on a regular basis (including coils, grills and compressor area) and free of mold and odors?

❑ YES   ❑ NO   5.   Is shelving at least 6 inches from the floor and free from dust or other debris?

❑ YES   ❑ NO   6.   Are foods and products covered, dated and properly spaced to provide adequate air circulation?

❑ YES   ❑ NO   7.   Are foods stored to allow "first in, first out" usage?

❑ YES   ❑ NO   8.   Are raw meats stored on the bottom shelves, away from cooked or prepared food?

❑ YES   ❑ NO   9.   Are all spills cleaned up immediately?

❑ YES   ❑ NO   10.   Are cooked foods labeled and stored in clean, sanitized, covered containers?

❑ YES   ❑ NO   11.   Is the temperature of freezer units 0°F or lower?

❑ YES   ❑ NO   12.   Are products in the freezer stored above floor level?

❑ YES   ❑ NO   13.   Are all frozen foods wrapped and covered to avoid freezer burn?

❑ YES   ❑ NO   14.   Are freezers clean, in good working condition and defrosted on a regular basis?

Action Plan:	Completed By:	Comments:
	Supervisor:	

Individual Sanitation Checklists

Garbage/Refuse Storage & Disposal Areas

Date: **Employee:**

❏ YES ❏ NO 1. Is the garbage area clean and well-maintained with no spilled liquids, food materials or debris?

❏ YES ❏ NO 2. Are garbage and refuse containers durable and easily cleaned?

❏ YES ❏ NO 3. Is garbage area cleaned regularly and are containers washed?

❏ YES ❏ NO 4. Are garbage and refuse containers insect- and rodent-proof with tight-fitting lids?

❏ YES ❏ NO 5. Are garbage and refuse materials disposed of on a regular basis, so there is no overflow or odors?

❏ YES ❏ NO 6. Are there any visible rodents or rodent droppings?

❏ YES ❏ NO 7. Is there any evidence of insect infestation?

❏ YES ❏ NO 8. Are dumpsters maintained and in good working condition?

❏ YES ❏ NO 9. Are hot water and detergents available to properly wash garbage containers?

❏ YES ❏ NO 10. Are refrigerated garbage rooms or boxes clean and in proper condition?

Action Plan: **Completed By:** **Comments:**

Supervisor:

Individual Sanitation Checklists

Cold Beverage Areas

Date:	Employee:

❏ YES ❏ NO   1. Are reach-in refrigerators used for storing cold beverages at a temperature of 41°F or lower?

❏ YES ❏ NO   2. Are all beverage hoses and nozzles maintained in a sanitary manner and cleaned regularly?

❏ YES ❏ NO   3. Are beverage dispensers maintained in a sanitary manner and cleaned regularly?

❏ YES ❏ NO   4. Are drinking cups, lids and straws easily accessible and stored in an orderly and sanitary manner?

❏ YES ❏ NO   5. Are ice machines cleaned and sanitized regularly?

❏ YES ❏ NO   6. Is the top of the ice machine free of obstructions and not being used as a storage area?

❏ YES ❏ NO   7. Are ice scoops being used in a sanitary manner and placed on a clean surface when not in use?

❏ YES ❏ NO   8. Are the storage cabinets under cold beverage dispensers clean, organized and inspected regularly?

Action Plan:	Completed By:	Comments:
	Supervisor:	

Individual Sanitation Checklists

Salad Bar

Date:	Employee:

❑ YES   ❑ NO   1.   Are salad bar utensils and dishes properly cleaned, sanitized and stored?

❑ YES   ❑ NO   2.   Is the area underneath the counter clean?

❑ YES   ❑ NO   3.   Are all salad bar crockery or containers in good condition, without chips or cracks?

❑ YES   ❑ NO   4.   Is the salad bar area cleaned and sanitized daily?

❑ YES   ❑ NO   5.   Are all spills cleaned up immediately?

❑ YES   ❑ NO   6.   Are all salad bar items kept at a temperature of 41°F?

❑ YES   ❑ NO   7.   Is the floor around the salad bar regularly swept and mopped?

❑ YES   ❑ NO   8.   Are ingredients on the salad bar refrigerated for at least 24 hours before use?

❑ YES   ❑ NO   9.   If ingredients need to be refilled, are the refill items from refrigerated materials?

❑ YES   ❑ NO   10. Are all vegetables and fruits properly washed before placement on the salad bar?

❑ YES   ❑ NO   11. Is the temperature of salad bar items maintained and checked on a regular basis?

❑ YES   ❑ NO   12. Do all food-handling employees wear gloves during salad preparation?

Action Plan:	Completed By:	Comments:
	Supervisor:	

Individual Sanitation Checklists

Employee Personal Hygiene

Date: **Employee:**

❑ YES   ❑ NO   1.   Are employees wearing clean uniforms or approved garments?

❑ YES   ❑ NO   2.   Is all jewelry removed (except plain wedding band) during working hours?

❑ YES   ❑ NO   3.   Are employees' fingernails clean and short, with no false fingernails or nail polish?

❑ YES   ❑ NO   4.   Do employees refrain from touching hair or scratching head and face while on duty?

❑ YES   ❑ NO   5.   Do employees practice proper handwashing techniques using soap or sanitizer?

❑ YES   ❑ NO   6.   Do employees wash hands after any activity that may cause contamination including when working between raw food and ready-to-eat foods, after coughing or sneezing, after touching soiled equipment or utensils and after using restrooms?

❑ YES   ❑ NO   7.   Do employees wear hats or hair coverings in the food preparation and serving areas?

❑ YES   ❑ NO   8.   Do employees refrain from eating, smoking, chewing gum and using toothpicks while on duty?

❑ YES   ❑ NO   9.   Do employees use tobacco products only in designated areas, away from food preparation, storage and service areas?

❑ YES   ❑ NO   10. Do employees show any sign of illness such as coughing or sneezing?

❑ YES   ❑ NO   11. Have employees been trained in safe food handling procedures

Action Plan: **Completed By:**   **Comments:**

Supervisor:

Individual Sanitation Checklists

Receiving

Date: **Employee:**

❑ YES   ❑ NO   1.   Is the receiving area clean, uncluttered and easily accessible?

❑ YES   ❑ NO   2.   Is food accepted only from previously approved vendors?

❑ YES   ❑ NO   3.   Does a designated employee inspect all incoming food shipments for any infestations, spoilage and/or unacceptable conditions (such as food not at the proper temperature, dented cans or open products)?

❑ YES   ❑ NO   4.   Does a designated employee inspect non-food supplies for infestations and foreign materials?

❑ YES   ❑ NO   5.   Upon arrival, are all food and non-food supplies properly labeled and dated?

❑ YES   ❑ NO   6.   Are potentially hazardous foods delivered at a temperature of 41°F?

❑ YES   ❑ NO   7.   Are frozen foods delivered frozen, with no evidence of thawing or refreezing?

❑ YES   ❑ NO   8.   Are deliveries rejected if the food is not at the proper temperature or in unacceptable condition?

❑ YES   ❑ NO   9.   Is food placed in proper storage locations promptly, with refrigerated and frozen foods stored immediately.

❑ YES   ❑ NO   10.   Are all empty shipping and packing materials promptly and properly discarded?

Action Plan: **Completed By:**   **Comments:**

Supervisor:

Food Safety Temperatures

212°F — Boiling Point
Most, but not all, bacteria are killed at this temperature.

165°F — Minimum Reheating Temperature

140°F — Minimum Hot Holding Temperature

DANGER ZONE
Rapid bacterial growth occurs
between 42°F and 140°F.

41°F
32°F
FREEZING
— Cold Storage Temperature Range

0°F

Frozen Food Storage

-10°F

Timed HACCP Checklist

DATE: _____ 9:00 a.m. **EMPLOYEE:** _____

3:00 p.m. **EMPLOYEE:** _____

10:00 p.m. **EMPLOYEE:** _____

Receiving & Storage — Cold Storage	9:00 a.m.	3:00 p.m.	10:00 p.m.
Walk-in refrigerator temperature	_____ °F	_____ °F	_____ °F
Walk-in freezer temperature	_____ °F	_____ °F	_____ °F
Other storage temperature (list area) _____	_____ °F	_____ °F	_____ °F
Raw meats stored in separate location or below any fruits, vegetables or cooked/prepared foods	❏ Y ❏ N	❏ Y ❏ N	❏ Y ❏ N

Back-of-House Preparation Area	9:00 a.m.	3:00 p.m.	10:00 p.m.
Temperature of concentrate(s), list:			
_____	_____ °F	_____ °F	_____ °F
_____	_____ °F	_____ °F	_____ °F
_____	_____ °F	_____ °F	_____ °F
Temperature of soup(s), list:			
_____	_____ °F	_____ °F	_____ °F
_____	_____ °F	_____ °F	_____ °F
_____	_____ °F	_____ °F	_____ °F
_____	_____ °F	_____ °F	_____ °F
Temperature of water in steam table	_____ °F	_____ °F	_____ °F
Effective sanitizing solution available	❏ Y ❏ N	❏ Y ❏ N	❏ Y ❏ N
Handwashing sink stocked with soap and disposable, single-use towels	❏ Y ❏ N	❏ Y ❏ N	❏ Y ❏ N

Grill Area	9:00 a.m.	3:00 p.m.	10:00 p.m.
Temperature inside service refrigerator	_____ °F	_____ °F	_____ °F
Sandwich boards and cutting boards cleaned and sanitized	❏ Y ❏ N	❏ Y ❏ N	❏ Y ❏ N
Forks and spatulas on hot grill	❏ Y ❏ N	❏ Y ❏ N	❏ Y ❏ N

Timed HACCP Checklist

Sandwich Preparation Area	9:00 a.m.	3:00 p.m.	10:00 p.m.
Temperature inside service refrigerator	_____ °F	_____ °F	_____ °F
Temperature of mayonnaise or dressings	_____ °F	_____ °F	_____ °F
Temperature inside reach-in freezer	_____ °F	_____ °F	_____ °F
Cold table above refrigerator covered	❑ Y ❑ N	❑ Y ❑ N	❑ Y ❑ N
Cutting boards clean and sanitized	❑ Y ❑ N	❑ Y ❑ N	❑ Y ❑ N
Microwaved products cooking times clearly marked	❑ Y ❑ N	❑ Y ❑ N	❑ Y ❑ N

Cold Food Preparation Area	9:00 a.m.	3:00 p.m.	10:00 p.m.
Temperature inside pie/salad refrigerator	_____ °F	_____ °F	_____ °F
Temperature inside service refrigerator	_____ °F	_____ °F	_____ °F
Temperature of mayonnaise or dressings	_____ °F	_____ °F	_____ °F
Temperature of side items (list):	_____ °F	_____ °F	_____ °F
_____	_____ °F	_____ °F	_____ °F
_____	_____ °F	_____ °F	_____ °F
_____	_____ °F	_____ °F	_____ °F
Microwaved products cooking times clearly marked	❑ Y ❑ N	❑ Y ❑ N	❑ Y ❑ N
Sanitizing solutions available and accessible	❑ Y ❑ N	❑ Y ❑ N	❑ Y ❑ N

NOTES:

_____

_____

_____

_____

_____

_____

_____

_____

_____

_____

Receiving Checklist

SUPPLIER: **TIME OF DELIVERY:**   a.m./p.m.

- ☐ Y ☐ N   Frozen products arrive frozen solid
- ☐ Y ☐ N   Refrigerated products arrive at a temperature below 41°F
- ☐ Y ☐ N   Frozen products put away within 15 minutes of delivery

- ☐ Y ☐ N   Refrigerated products put away within 30 minutes of delivery
- ☐ Y ☐ N   Refrigerated and frozen products dated and stored for FIFO usage
- ☐ Y ☐ N   Damaged products rejected

EMPLOYEE CHECKING IN PRODUCTS: **DATE:**

SUPPLIER: **TIME OF DELIVERY:**   a.m./p.m.

- ☐ Y ☐ N   Frozen products arrive frozen solid
- ☐ Y ☐ N   Refrigerated products arrive at a temperature below 41°F
- ☐ Y ☐ N   Frozen products put away within 15 minutes of delivery

- ☐ Y ☐ N   Refrigerated products put away within 30 minutes of delivery
- ☐ Y ☐ N   Refrigerated and frozen products dated and stored for FIFO usage
- ☐ Y ☐ N   Damaged products rejected

EMPLOYEE CHECKING IN PRODUCTS: **DATE:**

SUPPLIER: **TIME OF DELIVERY:**   a.m./p.m.

- ☐ Y ☐ N   Frozen products arrive frozen solid
- ☐ Y ☐ N   Refrigerated products arrive at a temperature below 41°F
- ☐ Y ☐ N   Frozen products put away within 15 minutes of delivery

- ☐ Y ☐ N   Refrigerated products put away within 30 minutes of delivery
- ☐ Y ☐ N   Refrigerated and frozen products dated and stored for FIFO usage
- ☐ Y ☐ N   Damaged products rejected

EMPLOYEE CHECKING IN PRODUCTS: **DATE:**

NOTES/CONCERNS:

Kitchen Sanitation Schedule Daily Tasks

DATE: _____

BATHROOM MIRRORS

WHEN: Once per shift   **HOW:** As needed   **CLEANSER:** Glass cleaner

PERSON RESPONSIBLE: _____   **INITIAL UPON COMPLETION:** _____

BATHROOM SUPPLIES

WHEN: Once per shift   **HOW:** Hand soap, paper towels, toilet paper

PERSON RESPONSIBLE: _____   **INITIAL UPON COMPLETION:** _____

BATHROOM FIXTURES AND SURFACES (other than floor, tiles and mirror)

WHEN: Daily   **HOW:** Spray, rinse and wipe with disposable towel   **CLEANSER:** Bathroom cleaner

PERSON RESPONSIBLE: _____   **INITIAL UPON COMPLETION:** _____

CONDIMENT CONTAINERS

WHEN: Daily   **HOW:** Wash, rinse, sanitize   **CLEANSER:** Dish machine

PERSON RESPONSIBLE: _____   **INITIAL UPON COMPLETION:** _____

COOLING RACKS

WHEN: Daily   **HOW:** Wipe clean of food debris with in-use wiping cloth   **CLEANSER:** Water and sanitizer 200ppm

PERSON RESPONSIBLE: _____   **INITIAL UPON COMPLETION:** _____

COUNTERS/SHELVES (FRONT)

WHEN: End of shift   **HOW:** Wash, rinse, sanitize   **CLEANSER:** Cleanser, fresh water and sanitizer 200ppm

PERSON RESPONSIBLE: _____   **INITIAL UPON COMPLETION:** _____

COUNTERS/SHELVES (COOLER)

WHEN: End of shift   **HOW:** Wash, rinse, sanitize   **CLEANSER:** Cleanser, fresh water and sanitizer 200ppm

PERSON RESPONSIBLE: _____   **INITIAL UPON COMPLETION:** _____

COUNTERS (DELIVERY)

WHEN: End of shift   **HOW:** Wash, rinse, sanitize   **CLEANSER:** Cleanser, fresh water and sanitizer 200ppm

PERSON RESPONSIBLE: _____   **INITIAL UPON COMPLETION:** _____

Kitchen Sanitation Schedule Daily Tasks

COUNTERS (PREP)

WHEN: Between uses/ every 4 hours

HOW: Wash, rinse, sanitize

CLEANSER: Cleanser, fresh water and sanitizer 200ppm

PERSON RESPONSIBLE: _____

INITIAL UPON COMPLETION: _____

DISH RACKS

WHEN: Daily

HOW: Wash, rinse, sanitize

CLEANSER: Cleanser, fresh water and sanitizer 200ppm

PERSON RESPONSIBLE: _____

INITIAL UPON COMPLETION: _____

DOORS (FRONT ENTRY)

WHEN: As needed

HOW: Spot clean glass; wipe clean other surfaces

CLEANSER: Glass cleaner

PERSON RESPONSIBLE: _____

INITIAL UPON COMPLETION: _____

DRAIN COVERS

WHEN: Daily

HOW: Clear debris; wash, rinse, sanitize

CLEANSER: Dish machine

PERSON RESPONSIBLE: _____

INITIAL UPON COMPLETION: _____

DRY STORAGE AREAS

WHEN: Daily

HOW: Sweep/mop

CLEANSER: Approved sanitizer

PERSON RESPONSIBLE: _____

INITIAL UPON COMPLETION: _____

FLOORS

WHEN: Daily/as needed

HOW: Sweep/mop

CLEANSER: Approved sanitizer

PERSON RESPONSIBLE: _____

INITIAL UPON COMPLETION: _____

FREEZERS

WHEN: Daily

HOW: Sweep/mop if walk-in; wipe exterior

CLEANSER: Approved sanitizer

PERSON RESPONSIBLE: _____

INITIAL UPON COMPLETION: _____

HANDWASHING SINK

WHEN: Every 4 hours

HOW: Wash, rinse, sanitize

CLEANSER: Cleanser, fresh water and sanitizer 200ppm

PERSON RESPONSIBLE: _____

INITIAL UPON COMPLETION: _____

Kitchen Sanitation Schedule Daily Tasks

HOOD FILTERS

WHEN: Every other p.m., end of shift

HOW: Soak in degreaser, spray clean with fresh water, air dry

CLEANSER: Non-caustic degreaser

PERSON RESPONSIBLE: _____

INITIAL UPON COMPLETION: _____

HOOD GREASE PANS

WHEN: Bi-weekly

HOW: Empty into grease bin; run through dishwasher; replace

CLEANSER: Dish machine:

PERSON RESPONSIBLE: _____

INITIAL UPON COMPLETION: _____

ICE CARRIERS

WHEN: Every 4 hours

HOW: Wash, rinse, sanitize; run through dishwasher; replace

CLEANSER: Dish machine

PERSON RESPONSIBLE: _____

INITIAL UPON COMPLETION: _____

ICE CREAM DIPPER WELL

WHEN: Daily

HOW: Wash, rinse, sanitize

CLEANSER: Cleanser, fresh water and sanitizer 200ppm

PERSON RESPONSIBLE: _____

INITIAL UPON COMPLETION: _____

KNIFE HOLDERS

WHEN: Every 4 hours

HOW: Wash, rinse, sanitize

CLEANSER: Cleanser, fresh water and sanitizer 200ppm

PERSON RESPONSIBLE: _____

INITIAL UPON COMPLETION: _____

MIXER BASE/EXTERIOR

WHEN: Daily

HOW: Wash, rinse, sanitize

CLEANSER: Cleanser, fresh water and sanitizer 200ppm

PERSON RESPONSIBLE: _____

INITIAL UPON COMPLETION: _____

MOPS/BRUSHES

WHEN: Daily

HOW: Wash, rinse and sanitize in mop sink; hang upside down to drip dry over sink

CLEANSER: Cleanser, fresh water and sanitizer 200ppm

PERSON RESPONSIBLE: _____

INITIAL UPON COMPLETION: _____

PIZZA OVEN

WHEN: Throughout shift

HOW: Wipe interior with clean, moist towel

CLEANSER: Water only

PERSON RESPONSIBLE: _____

INITIAL UPON COMPLETION: _____

Kitchen Sanitation Schedule Daily Tasks

PREMISES EXTERIOR

WHEN: Daily

HOW: Sweep entire areas of debris/trash

CLEANSER: Water spray if needed

PERSON RESPONSIBLE: _____

INITIAL UPON COMPLETION: _____

PREPARATION AREAS

WHEN: Each use

HOW: Wash, rinse, sanitize

CLEANSER: Cleanser, fresh water and sanitizer 200ppm

PERSON RESPONSIBLE: _____

INITIAL UPON COMPLETION: _____

REACH-IN HANDLES

WHEN: Daily

HOW: Wipe exterior with moist cloth

CLEANSER: Sanitizer bucket at 200ppm

PERSON RESPONSIBLE: _____

INITIAL UPON COMPLETION: _____

REACH-INS AND WELLS

WHEN: Daily

HOW: Wash, rinse, sanitize

CLEANSER: Cleanser, fresh water and sanitizer 200ppm

PERSON RESPONSIBLE: _____

INITIAL UPON COMPLETION: _____

ROTISSERIE SKEWERS/TINES

WHEN: End of use and end of day

HOW: Degrease and sanitize

CLEANSER: Non-caustic degreaser

PERSON RESPONSIBLE: _____

INITIAL UPON COMPLETION: _____

ROTISSERIE: HOLDING DRAWERS, EXTERIOR

WHEN: Daily

HOW: Wash, rinse, sanitize; buff exterior

CLEANSER: Cleanser, fresh water and sanitizer 200ppm

PERSON RESPONSIBLE: _____

INITIAL UPON COMPLETION: _____

SCALES

WHEN: Between each use, and every 4 hours

HOW: Wash, rinse, sanitize

CLEANSER: Cleanser, fresh water and sanitizer 200ppm

PERSON RESPONSIBLE: _____

INITIAL UPON COMPLETION: _____

SLICERS AND STAND

WHEN: Between each use (Stand: Daily)

HOW: Wash, rinse, sanitize

CLEANSER: Cleanser, fresh water and sanitizer 200ppm

PERSON RESPONSIBLE: _____

INITIAL UPON COMPLETION: _____

Kitchen Sanitation Schedule Daily Tasks

STORAGE BINS

WHEN: Daily   **HOW:** Wipe exterior with moist cloth   **CLEANSER:** Sanitizer at 200ppm

PERSON RESPONSIBLE: _____   **INITIAL UPON COMPLETION:** _____

THREE-COMPARTMENT SINK

WHEN: Daily or between use   **HOW:** Wash, rinse, sanitize   **CLEANSER:** Cleanser, fresh water and sanitizer 200ppm

PERSON RESPONSIBLE: _____   **INITIAL UPON COMPLETION:** _____

TRASH RECEPTACLES

WHEN: Daily   **HOW:** Wipe exterior with disposable cloth   **CLEANSER:** Water and sanitizer 200ppm

PERSON RESPONSIBLE: _____   **INITIAL UPON COMPLETION:** _____

UTENSILS (IN-USE)

WHEN: Every 4 hours or between products   **HOW:** Wash, rinse, sanitize   **CLEANSER:** Dish machine

PERSON RESPONSIBLE: _____   **INITIAL UPON COMPLETION:** _____

WALK-IN

WHEN: Daily   **HOW:** Sweep and clean floor   **CLEANSER:** Tile cleaner

PERSON RESPONSIBLE: _____   **INITIAL UPON COMPLETION:** _____

WIPING CLOTHS (IN-USE)

WHEN: Every 4 hours   **HOW:** Put in designated container to launder

PERSON RESPONSIBLE: _____   **INITIAL UPON COMPLETION:** _____

Hazard Analysis & Critical Control Point (HACCP) Chart

EMPLOYEE: _____ **DATE:** _____

WALK-IN COOLERS

A.M.	MIDDAY	P.M.	CORRECTIVE ACTION TAKEN:

COLD HOLDING STANDARDS: Foods should be held at a temperature of 41°F or below.

CORRECTIVE ACTION: Discard or if food has not been at the correct temperature for less than 4 hours, rapidly cool to 41°F or less.

COOKLINE COOLERS

A.M.	MIDDAY	P.M.	CORRECTIVE ACTION TAKEN:

COOKING

A.M.	MIDDAY	P.M.	CORRECTIVE ACTION TAKEN:

COOKING STANDARDS:
Poultry products: 165°F/15 seconds
Ground beef: 155°F/15 seconds
Eggs, fish, pork, beef: 145°F/15 seconds
All other foods: 145°F/15 seconds

CORRECTIVE ACTION: Continue cooking.

Hazard Analysis & Critical Control Point (HACCP) Chart

REHEATING

A.M.	MIDDAY	P.M.	CORRECTIVE ACTION TAKEN:

REHEATING STANDARDS: Reheat foods to 165°F within 2 hours.

CORRECTIVE ACTION: Discard if not reheated within 2 hours.

HOT HOLDING

A.M.	MIDDAY	P.M.	CORRECTIVE ACTION TAKEN:

HOT HOLDING STANDARDS: All foods should be held at 140°F or above.

CORRECTIVE ACTION: Discard or if food has been out of temperature for less than 4 hours, rapidly reheat to 165°F or hotter.

COOLING

2 HOURS	6 HOURS	CORRECTIVE ACTION TAKEN:

COOLING STANDARDS: Cool cooked foods from 140°F to 70°F in 2 hours. Continue to cool from 70°F to 41°F in 4 hours. Food made from room-temperature ingredients cooled to 41°F in 4 hours.

CORRECTIVE ACTION: Discard or reheat to 165°F, cool properly and serve.

RECEIVING

TEMPERATURE AT RECEIPT	CORRECTIVE ACTION TAKEN:

RECEIVING STANDARDS: All potentially hazardous foods must be at 41°F or less.

CORRECTIVE ACTION: Reject and discard food if not at proper temperature.

C1

Weekly Thermometer Calibration Chart

ICE WATER METHOD

Thermometers should be calibrated at least once a week. New thermometers should be calibrated before initial use. To calibrate a thermometer, fill a small container with ice and add water to form slush. Insert the stem of the thermometer into the slush. Temperature should read 32°F. If necessary, use a wrench to hold the nut at the base of the thermometer in place while turning the dial of the thermometer while it is still immersed until it reads the correct temperature. Boiling water (212°F) may also be used in the same manner.

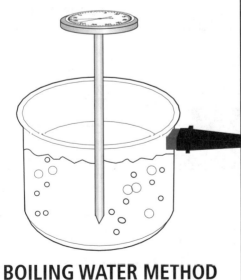

BOILING WATER METHOD

WEEK 1   DATE: _____

CALIBRATED BY: _____   INITIALS: _____

WEEK 2   DATE: _____

CALIBRATED BY: _____   INITIALS: _____

WEEK 3   DATE: _____

CALIBRATED BY: _____   INITIALS: _____

WEEK 4   DATE: _____

CALIBRATED BY: _____   INITIALS: _____

WEEK 5   DATE: _____

CALIBRATED BY: _____   INITIALS: _____

WEEK 6   DATE: _____

CALIBRATED BY: _____   INITIALS: _____

WEEK 7   DATE: _____

CALIBRATED BY: _____   INITIALS: _____

WEEK 8   DATE: _____

CALIBRATED BY: _____   INITIALS: _____

WEEK 9   DATE: _____

CALIBRATED BY: _____   INITIALS: _____

WEEK 10   DATE: _____

CALIBRATED BY: _____   INITIALS: _____

Hot/Cold Holding Chart

STANDARDS/CRITICAL LIMITS
Hot holding 140°F or above.
Cold holding 41°F or below.

CORRECTIVE ACTION
Rapidly reheat to 165°F or rapidly chill to 41°F and place back in the hot or cold holding unit. Discard if out of temperature more than 4 hours.

AREA	TIME & TEMPERATURE					
	a.m./p.m.	a.m./p.m.	a.m./p.m.	a.m./p.m.	a.m./p.m.	a.m./p.m.
STEAM TABLE						
FOOD ITEMS						
COOKLINE COOLER						
FOOD ITEMS						
WALK-IN						
FOOD ITEMS						
FREEZER						
FOOD ITEMS						

CORRECTIVE ACTION TAKEN:

CCP Decision Tree

CONSIDERATIONS WHEN USING THE DECISION TREE:

- After hazard analysis, use the decision tree.

- At a the step where a significant hazard has been identified, the decision tree is used.

- A subsequent step in the process may be more effective for controlling a hazard and may be the preferred CCP.

- To control a hazard, more than one step in the process may be involved.

- A specific control measure may take care of more than one hazard.

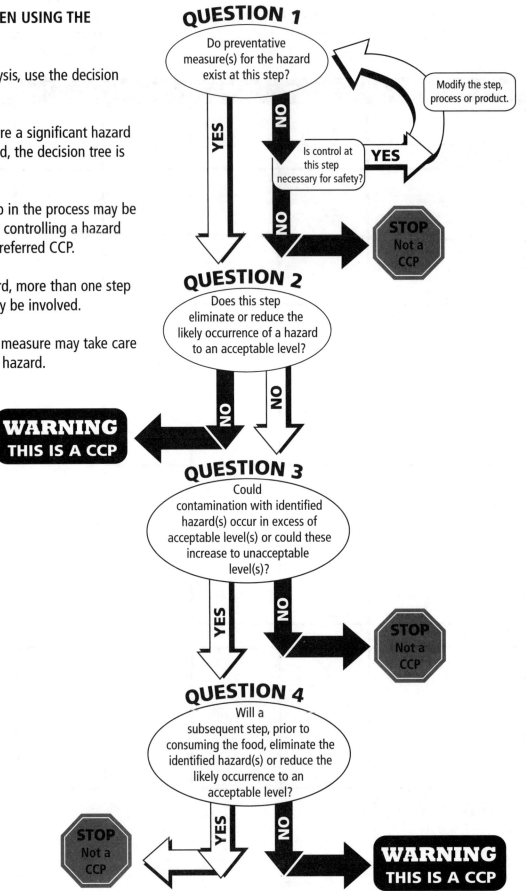

QUESTION 1
Do preventative measure(s) for the hazard exist at this step?

Modify the step, process or product.

YES

NO

Is control at this step necessary for safety? — YES

NO

STOP Not a CCP

QUESTION 2
Does this step eliminate or reduce the likely occurrence of a hazard to an acceptable level?

NO

NO

WARNING THIS IS A CCP

QUESTION 3
Could contamination with identified hazard(s) occur in excess of acceptable level(s) or could these increase to unacceptable level(s)?

YES

NO

STOP Not a CCP

QUESTION 4
Will a subsequent step, prior to consuming the food, eliminate the identified hazard(s) or reduce the likely occurrence to an acceptable level?

YES

NO

STOP Not a CCP

WARNING THIS IS A CCP

Hazard Analysis — CCP Decision Tree Form

DATE:	PRODUCT:

Process Step	Potential hazard introduced, controlled or enhanced at this step B = Biological C = Chemical P = Physical	Should the hazard be addressed in the HACCP plan?	Justification for decision	What control measures can be applied to prevent the significant hazards?

CCP Decision Tree Table

PRODUCT: **DATE:**

A critical control point is defined as a point, step or procedure at which control can be applied and a food-safety hazard can be prevented, eliminated or reduced. Steps presenting a significant potential food-safety risk (Q1, Hazard Analysis) are listed.

Process Step	Hazard B = Biological C = Chemical P = Physical	Q1. Do preventative measure(s) for the hazard exist at this step?	Q2. Does this step eliminate or reduce the likely occurrence of a hazard to an acceptable level?	If Q2 is NO Q3. Could contamination with identified hazard(s) occur in excess of acceptable level(s) or could these increase to unacceptable level(s)?	Q4. Will a subsequent step, prior to consuming the food, eliminate the identified hazard(s) or reduce the likely occurrence to an acceptable level?	CCP#

Establishing Critical Limits, Monitoring & Corrective Actions

PRODUCT:		DATE:	

Process Step/CCP	Critical Limits	Monitoring Procedures (Who/What/When/How)	Corrective Actions
		Who: What: When: How:	1. 2. 3. 4.
		Who: What: When: How:	1. 2. 3. 4.
		Who: What: When: How:	1. 2. 3. 4.

Recordkeeping & Verification

PRODUCT:		DATE:

Process Step/CCP	Records	Verification Procedures
		1. 2. 3. 4.
		1. 2. 3. 4.
		1. 2. 3. 4.

HACCP Plan Summary

PRODUCT:	DATE:

Process Step	
Hazard Description	
CCP Description	
Monitoring Procedures/ Frequency/ Person Responsible	Who: What: When: How:
Corrective Actions	
HACCP Records	
Verification Procedures/ Person Responsible	

HACCP Monitoring — Equipment Inspection Form

Equipment Inspected: _____

Inspected By: _____ **Inspection Date:** _____

Condition: _____

Improvements Needed: _____

Equipment Inspected: _____

Inspected By: _____ **Inspection Date:** _____

Condition: _____

Improvements Needed: _____

Equipment Inspected: _____

Inspected By: _____ **Inspection Date:** _____

Condition: _____

Improvements Needed: _____

Equipment Inspected: _____

Inspected By: _____ **Inspection Date:** _____

Condition: _____

Improvements Needed: _____

Equipment Inspected: _____

Inspected By: _____ **Inspection Date:** _____

Condition: _____

Improvements Needed: _____

Equipment Inspected: _____

Inspected By: _____ **Inspection Date:** _____

Condition: _____

Improvements Needed: _____

HACCP Monitoring — Temperature/Food Safety Chart

FOOD ITEM: **DATE:**

RECEIVING/STORING

CONTROL CRITERIA

- ☐ Approved source
- ☐ Item(s) inspected
- ☐ Shellfish tags
- ☐ Raw/cooked/separated in storage
- ☐ Refrigerated at 45°F or less
- ☐ Product condition (dents, open products, torn bags)

MONITORING

- ☐ Shellfish tags available and complete
- ☐ Food temperature checked
- ☐ Raw foods stored below cooked or ready-to-eat foods

ACTION

- ☐ Discard food
- ☐ Return food
- ☐ Separate raw and cooked food
- ☐ Discard cooked food contaminated by raw food
- ☐ Discard if food temperature is more than 45°F for 2 hours, or more than 70°F

COOKING

CONTROL CRITERIA

- ☐ Temperature to kill pathogens: Food temperature at thickest part at least _____°F

MONITORING

- ☐ Measure food temperature at thickest part

ACTION

- ☐ Continue cooking until food temperature at thickest part is at least _____°F

THAWING

CONTROL CRITERIA

- ☐ Refrigeration
- ☐ Under running water less than 70°F
- ☐ Microwave
- ☐ Cooked in frozen state (less than 3 lbs. only)

MONITORING

- ☐ Select thawing method, check food temperature

ACTION

- ☐ Discard if food temperature is more than 45°F for 2 hours, or more than 70°F

HOT HOLDING

CONTROL CRITERIA

- ☐ Food temperature at thickest part at least _____°F

MONITORING

- ☐ Measure food temperature at thickest part during hot holding every _____ minutes

ACTION

- ☐ Food Temperature: 140°F–120°F More than or equal to 2 hours, discard; less than 2 hours, reheat to 165°F and hold at 140°F
  120°F–45°F More than or equal to 2 hours, discard; less than 2 hours, reheat to 165°F and hold at 140°F

PRE-COOKING

CONTROL CRITERIA

- ☐ Food temperature no more than 45°F

MONITORING

- ☐ Observe quantity of food at room temperature
- ☐ Observe time food held at room temperature

ACTION

- ☐ Discard if food temperature is more than 45°F for 2 hours, or more than 70°F

REHEATING

CONTROL CRITERIA

- ☐ Food temperature at thickest part more than or equal to 165°F

MONITORING

- ☐ Measure food temperature at thickest part during reheating

ACTION

- ☐ Food temperature at thickest part less than 165°F, continue reheating

HACCP Monitoring — Temperature/Food Safety Chart

FOOD ITEM: **DATE:**

PROCESSING

CONTROL CRITERIA

Prevent contamination by:

- ☐ Employees' hands not touching ready-to-eat food
- ☐ Employees wash hands correctly and frequently
- ☐ No ill employees
- ☐ All utensils clean and sanitized
- ☐ Cold, potentially hazardous food at a temperature less than or equal to 45°F
- ☐ Hot, potentially hazardous food at a temperature more than or equal to 140°F

MONITORING

- ☐ Use of gloves and utensils
- ☐ Handwashing techniques and frequency
- ☐ Observe employees' health
- ☐ Use prechilled ingredients for cold foods
- ☐ Minimize quantity of food at room temperature

ACTION

Discard food if any of the following is observed:

- ☐ Cold, potentially hazardous food: More than 45°F more than or equal to 2 hours, discard; more than 70°F, discard
- ☐ Hot, potentially hazardous food: 140°F–120°F More than or equal to 2 hours, discard; less than 2 hours, reheat to 154°F and hold at 140°F 120°F–45°F More than or equal to 2 hours, discard; less than 2 hours, reheat to 154°F and hold at 140°F
- ☐ If raw food has contaminated other food or equipment/utensils, discard food in question or reheat to 165°F
- ☐ Ill worker handling food

COOLING

CONTROL CRITERIA

- ☐ Food 120°F to 70°F in 2 hours; 70°F to 45°F in 4 additional hours by the following methods:
- ☐ Product depth 4 inches or less
- ☐ Ice water bath, stirring
- ☐ Rapid-chill refrigeration
- ☐ Do not cover until cold

MONITORING

- ☐ Measure food temperature every _____ minutes
- ☐ Food depth
- ☐ Food iced
- ☐ Food stirred
- ☐ Food size
- ☐ Food placed in rapid-chill refrigeration unit
- ☐ Food uncovered

ACTION

- ☐ Food Temperature: 120°F–70°F More than 2 hours, discard food

  70°F–45°F More than 4 hours, discard food

  45°F or less But cooled too slowly, discard food

TRANSPORTING

CONTROL CRITERIA

- ☐ Hot Food: Temperature at thickest part at least 140°F
- ☐ Cold Food: Temperature at thickest part at least 45°F

MONITORING

- ☐ Measure food temperature at thickest part during hot holding every _____ minutes

ACTION

- ☐ Cold holding, potentially hazardous food: More than 45°F more than or equal to 2 hours, discard; more than 70°F, discard
- ☐ Hot holding, potentially hazardous food: 140°F–120°F More or equal to 2 hours, discard; less than 2 hours, reheat to 154°F and hold at 140°F

  120°F–45°F More or equal to 2 hours, discard; less than 2 hours, reheat to 165°F and hold at 140°F

NOTES

HACCP Monitoring — Cooking/Cooling Log

GUIDELINES

1. **Time & Temperature** – Always record the time when the temperature is taken.

2. **Final Cooking** – The foods' internal temperature must reach a minimum of 170°F.

3. **Initial Cooling** – Initial cooling begins at 140°F. Meet all cooling requirements:
   - Cool foods from 140°F to 70°F within 2 hours; and from 70°F to below 41°F within 4 hours, for a total of 6 hours. If food item goes directly into hot holding after cooking, cooling is not required.

4. **2-Hour Requirement** – Internal temperature must reach 70°F within 2 hours of initial temperature.

5. **4-Hour Requirement** – Internal temperature must reach below 41°F within 4 hours from the time the food is 70°F.

6. **Total Cooling Time 6 hours** – The final column should be initialed by the employee to certify the food has been cooled properly and checked at each increment.

7. **Reheating** – Reheat to proper internal temperature within 2 hours and serve. Reheat only once to 170°F and repeat chill process or discard food item.

8. **Corrective Action** – Continue to cook to required HACCP temperature for each food. Corrective actions should be listed below:

_____

_____

_____

EMPLOYEE: **DATE:**

PRODUCT	FINAL COOKING		INITIAL TEMP		2 HOURS		4 MORE HOURS		INITIALS
	TIME	TEMP	TIME	TEMP	TIME	TEMP	TIME	TEMP	

Daily Equipment Cleaning Chart

ITEM	CLEANING TASK	WHEN
Beverage dispensers	Wipe spills and splashes Take apart, clean and sanitize dispenser spouts Clean drain tray	Upon each occurance Daily Once per shift
Breath guards	Wipe spills and splashes Clean and sanitize all surfaces	Upon each occurance Once per shift
Can openers	Clean and sanitize	After every use, and once per shift
Carts, food transport equipment	Wipe spills and splashes Clean and sanitize shelves and racks	Upon each occurance Daily, after use
Coffee and tea machines	Wipe spills and splashes Rinse baskets, urns and pots Take apart, clean and sanitize spray heads and spouts	Upon each occurance After each use Daily
Deep fryer	Clean outside surfaces Clean and filter grease	Once per shift Once per shift
Dishwashing machines	Take apart and clean Clean doors, gaskets and surfaces	On a regular basis to remove build-up and ensure clean water Daily
Floors	Wipe spills Sweep Damp mop Sanitize and scrub	Upon each occurance As needed After each shift Daily
Frozen dessert machines	Wipe spills and splashes Clean drain tray Take apart, clean and sanitize parts, interior surfaces and dispenser spouts	Upon each occurance Once per shift Daily
Grill, griddle, broiler	Clean and brush grill surfaces Clean surrounding surfaces and grease tray Clean cooking surfaces and backsplash	As needed, or once per shift Once per shift Daily
Hot holding	Wipe spills Clean interior surfaces and racks Clean exterior surfaces	Upon each occurance Daily Daily

Daily Equipment Cleaning Chart

ITEM	CLEANING TASK	WHEN
Ice machine	Clean doors, gaskets and exterior surfaces	Daily
Microwave	Wipe spills Clean and sanitize interior surfaces Clean and sanitize fan shield and tray Clean outside surfaces	Upon each occurance Once per shift Daily Daily
Mixers, slicers and food processors	Take apart, clean and sanitize parts, surfaces and work tables	After each use, or between each food item change
Ovens	Wipe spills	Upon each occurance
Range	Wipe spills Clean and sanitize work surfaces	Upon each occurance Once per shift
Reach-in refrigerators and freezers	Wipe spills Clean outside, doors and gaskets	Upon each occurance Daily
Scales	Clean and sanitize weighing tray Clean and sanitize exposed surfaces	After each use Daily
Sinks	Clean and sanitize sink interior Clean exterior surfaces and backsplash	After each use Daily, at closing
Steam tables	Drain water and clean wells Clean outside and surrounding surfaces	Once per shift Once per shift
Steamer	Wipe spills Clean and sanitize interior surfaces and racks Clean exterior surfaces	Upon each occurance Daily Daily
Walk-in refrigerators and freezers	Wipe spills Sweep and damp mop (freezer, sweep only) Clean door surfaces and gaskets Scrub floors	Upon each occurance Once per shift Daily Daily (except freezer)
Walls	Splashes Wash walls in prep and cooking areas	Upon each occurance Daily, at closing
Work tables	Clean and sanitize tops and shelves	After each use and after each shift

Weekly & Monthly Equipment Cleaning Chart

Weekly Cleaning

ITEM	CLEANING TASK
Carts and transport equipment	Thoroughly clean and sanitize supports and exterior
Coffee and tea machines	Clean and brush urn, pots and baskets using cleaner specified by manufacturer
Deep fryer	Boil out fryers
Ovens	Clean interior surfaces and racks
Range	Take apart burners, and empty and sanitize catch trays
Reach-in refrigerators	Empty, clean and sanitize
Sinks	Clean legs and supports
Steam tables	De-lime
Walk-in refrigeration and freezer units	Wipe clean and sanitize walls
Work tables	Clean legs and supports; empty, clean and sanitize drawers

Monthly Cleaning

ITEM	CLEANING TASK
Dishwashing machines	De-lime machine
Ice machine	Drain ice, clean and sanitize interior surfaces Flush ice-making unit Defrost and clean
Reach-in freezers	Empty, clean and sanitize
Reach-in refrigeration and freezer units	Defrost
Steamer	De-lime
Walk-in refrigeration and freezer units	Clean fans Empty, clean racks, walls, floors and corners Defrost freezer

Daily Facilities Cleaning Chart

ITEM	CLEANING TASK	WHEN
Carpets	Vacuum	Daily
Chairs	Clean and sanitize seat	After each use
Dining tables	Clean and sanitize	After each use
Display cabinets	Clean and sanitize surfaces	Once per shift
Drains	Scrub covers	Daily
Dry storage areas	Sweep and mop floors	Daily
Employee areas	Clean and sanitize tables used for eating Sweep and mop, if applicable	After each use Once per shift
Floors	Wipe spills Sweep Damp mop Scrub	Upon each occurance As needed, or between meals Once per shift Daily
Garbage cans	Scrub clean and sanitize cans with hot water or steam and detergent	After emptying, or at closing
Hoods	Clean walls and exposed surfaces of hoods Clean removable filters	Daily Daily
Office areas	Sweep and mop, if applicable Clean work surfaces	Daily Daily
Self-service beverage areas	Wipe spills and splashes Clean and sanitize surfaces	Upon each occurance Once per shift
Self-service condiment areas	Wipe spills and splashes Clean and sanitize surfaces Take apart, clean and sanitize dispensers	Upon each occurance Once per shift Daily
Upholstery	Vacuum or brush clean	Daily
Walls	Splashes Wash	As soon as possible Daily (in kitchen and cooking areas)

Weekly & Monthly Facilities Cleaning Chart

Weekly Cleaning

ITEM	CLEANING TASK
Chairs	Clean chair backs, rails and legs
Dining tables	Clean table bases
Display cabinets	Clean cabinet interior
Drains	Flush drains with disinfectant
Dry storage areas	Clean shelves, scrub floors, baseboards and corners
Employee areas	Clean employee lockers and storage areas
Fans	Clean fan guards
Floors	Scrub baseboards and corners
HVAC system	Clean air intake and output ducts
Walls	Wash all walls

Monthly Cleaning

ITEM	CLEANING TASK
Carpets	Steam clean and shampoo, bi-monthly
Ceilings	Wash
Floors	Strip and reseal twice per year
Grease traps	Remove grease and clean
Hoods	Clean and degrease hood system, bi-monthly
HVAC system	Check filters
Light fixtures	Clean shields and fixtures
Upholstery	Steam clean or shampoo, bi-monthly
Walls	Wash all walls

To Prevent Bacterial Growth, Cool Food Rapidly

**140°F–70°F
First 2 Hours**

**70°F–40°F
Next 4 Hours**

TOTAL COOLING = 6 HOURS

COOL FOOD PROPERLY
To Prevent Contamination & Bacterial Growth

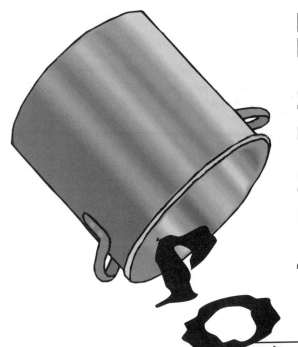

1. **Pour food into shallow pan (large pots should not be used to cool food).**

2. **Food in pan should not be more than 2 inches in depth.**

3. **Surround with another large container filled with ice.**

4. **Stir frequently.**

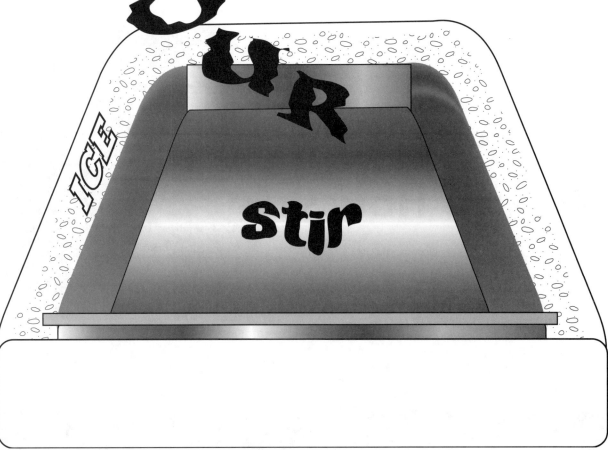

Food-borne Illness Complaint Form

RESTAURANT INFORMATION

Restaurant Name: _____ Date complaint reported:____/____/____

Address: _____

City: _____ State:_____ Zip Code: _____

Phone Number:_____

COMPLAINANT INFORMATION

Name: _____ Date of visit: _____

Address: _____

City: _____ State:_____ Zip Code: _____

Phone Number:_____

Do you have any food allergies? Yes or No List: _____

Number of people dining in your party? 1 2 3 4 5 6 7 8 9 10+

Check items eaten (and write in specific details):   Time meal was eaten: _____ a.m./p.m.

- ☐ Bread/Butter Appetizer _____
- ☐ Side Orders _____
- ☐ Beverage _____
- ☐ Entrée _____
- ☐ Dessert _____
- ☐ Other _____

ILLNESS INFORMATION

Time illness occurred: _____ a.m./p.m.   Length of illness: 1 2 3 4 5 6 7 8 9 10 hours days weeks

Type of illness (Mark a ✓ next to any the complainant mentions. Do not read off possible symptoms.):

- ☐ Nausea
- ☐ Lethargy
- ☐ Dizziness
- ☐ Difficulty Breathing/Swallowing
- ☐ Vomiting
- ☐ Backache
- ☐ Headache
- ☐ Abdominal Pain
- ☐ Rash on _____
- ☐ Chills
- ☐ Other_____
- ☐ Diarrhea
- ☐ Flushed
- ☐ Fever

How was the illness treated? _____

Medical center where treated: _____ Physician: _____

Medical center address and phone:_____

Was an official diagnosis given? Yes or No Explain: _____

Did any other members of your party become ill? Yes or No Explain: _____

Name: _____

Did you eat any of the same items? Yes or No List: _____

Other items eaten (circle and write in):

- ☐ Bread/Butter Appetizer _____
- ☐ Side Orders _____
- ☐ Beverage _____
- ☐ Entrée _____
- ☐ Dessert _____
- ☐ Other _____

Check with your local Health Department for follow-up procedures regarding handling food-borne illness complaints. For future reference, attach to this report a list of all food items sold the day of illness.

Title/Name of Person Taking Information: _____

Signature: _____

Allergen-Control Program Worksheet

Name: _____ Inspection Date: _____

Address: _____

Inspector: _____ Firm License #: _____

❑ Y ❑ N   Is an allergen-control program in place at this establishment?

❑ Y ❑ N   Are employees trained in and understand the allergen-control program?

❑ Y ❑ N   To prevent cross-contamination, are all raw ingredients transported and stored properly?

❑ Y ❑ N   If raw materials contain an allergen, are they properly labeled with allergen specifics?

❑ Y ❑ N   Are equipment lockouts, batch sequencing and correct wash procedures used to isolate allergen ingredients?

❑ Y ❑ N   Does food production take place only on dedicated lines using dedicated rooms and equipment?

❑ Y ❑ N   Are single-service items discarded in a sanitary manner after only one use?

❑ Y ❑ N   Are all ingredients clearly listed on the final product label?

❑ Y ❑ N   Are labels checked frequently for accuracy and any obsolete labels discarded?

❑ Y ❑ N   In the event of a recall, is there a complete recordkeeping system or log book to trace back all products?

❑ Y ❑ N   Are standardized procedures for sanitation operations used?

❑ Y ❑ N   Is sanitation effectiveness tested by procedures such as bioluminescence or ELISA testing?

Daily Sanitation Inspection Form

EMPLOYEES

❏ Yes   ❏ No   Employees are wearing clean uniforms or clothing.

❏ Yes   ❏ No   Employees use hair restraints and remove all jewelry.

❏ Yes   ❏ No   Employees are presentable and practice good personal hygiene.

❏ Yes   ❏ No   Eating or drinking is not allowed in food preparation area.

❏ Yes   ❏ No   Ill or infectious employees are not allowed to work.

FOOD HANDLING PRACTICES

❏ Yes   ❏ No   Fresh foods are in good condition, and properly labeled and stored.

❏ Yes   ❏ No   Canned goods are sealed and have no dents, bulges, swelling or leaks and rust.

❏ Yes   ❏ No   Cereals, sugar, dried fruits, flour and other dry bulk items are labeled and stored in proper containers and free from insect infestation.

❏ Yes   ❏ No   Refrigeration and freezer units are clean and free of excess ice buildup.

❏ Yes   ❏ No   Refrigerator temperature _____ °F.

❏ Yes   ❏ No   Freezer temperature _____ °F.

❏ Yes   ❏ No   Refrigeration (or other approved method) is used for thawing.

❏ Yes   ❏ No   Milk and milk products are inspected upon delivery, stored in unopened individual containers, and have a temperature of 41°F or lower.

❏ Yes   ❏ No   Cold foods are maintained at 41°F or lower and temperature checked every 2 hours.

❏ Yes   ❏ No   Hot foods are maintained at 140°F or higher and temperature checked every 2 hours.

❏ Yes   ❏ No   Leftovers are properly labeled with time, date and use-by date.

❏ Yes   ❏ No   All foods are properly cooked and/or reheated (165°F).

❏ Yes   ❏ No   All foods are properly cooled (140°F to 70°F within 2 hours; 70°F to 41°F in 4 hours).

Daily Sanitation Inspection Form

FOOD EQUIPMENT AND UTENSILS...

❑ Yes   ❑ No   Food contact and work surfaces are constructed of proper materials, installed correctly and in good, workable condition.

❑ Yes   ❑ No   Proper dishwashing facilities are available (a three-compartment sink or dish machine) and used correctly.

❑ Yes   ❑ No   Signs with correct dishwashing procedures (pre-flush, scrape, wash, rinse, sanitize and air-dry) are posted and visible in area.

❑ Yes   ❑ No   Dishwashing machine clean, free of food particles or residue, uses proper levels of sanitizer and maintains correct water temperature.

❑ Yes   ❑ No   All food service equipment and utensils are cleaned, sanitized and stored correctly to prevent contamination.

❑ Yes   ❑ No   Clean in-place equipment is adequately cleaned and sanitized, with no leftover food residue.

FACILITY/STRUCTURE...

❑ Yes   ❑ No   Floors, walls, ceilings and fixtures are clean and properly constructed.

❑ Yes   ❑ No   Lighting is adequate and well-shielded.

❑ Yes   ❑ No   Water sources are safe, with adequate supplies of pressurized hot and cold water.

❑ Yes   ❑ No   All handwashing sinks have hot and cold water and are stocked with soap, single-use paper towels and covered waste receptacles.

❑ Yes   ❑ No   Sewage and wastewater is correctly piped for proper disposal.

❑ Yes   ❑ No   Plumbing is installed professionally and maintained with back-flow and back-siphonage devices.

❑ Yes   ❑ No   Ventilation systems are in place and working properly.

Daily Sanitation Inspection Form

GARBAGE/INSECT CONTROL ....

❑ Yes   ❑ No   All garbage containers have tight-fitting covers to prevent insect and rodent infestation.

❑ Yes   ❑ No   There are adequate garbage containers available and they are not overfilled.

❑ Yes   ❑ No   Garbage containers are cleaned often and no offensive odors exist.

❑ Yes   ❑ No   Outside refuse storage area is clean and enclosed.

❑ Yes   ❑ No   Outer openings are protected from insects and rodents, with functional, self-closing doors.

NOTE VIOLATIONS AND CORRECTIVE ACTIONS BELOW:

Safety Policy

Safety For All Employees

Employee safety is our first priority. Our goal is to have no employees injured while on the job. Accidents affect everyone involved; they reduce your earnings and cause physical discomfort. We are concerned about your overall health and need your skills on the job!

Management Obligations

- Provide a safe workplace

- Provide training on all equipment prior to employee use

- Provide proper training for any potentially dangerous activities such as cutting or lifting

- Be aware of safety record and make any changes needed for zero injuries

If An Injury Occurs

- Immediately inform your supervisor

- Fill out an employee accident form

- No matter how small—report all cuts and injuries

- Seek medical attention if needed

- Report unsafe conditions to a supervisor immediately

Employee Responsibilities

- Practice safety at all times

- Notify your supervisor if you see other employees acting in a manner which could lead to injury

PROPER FOOD STORAGE

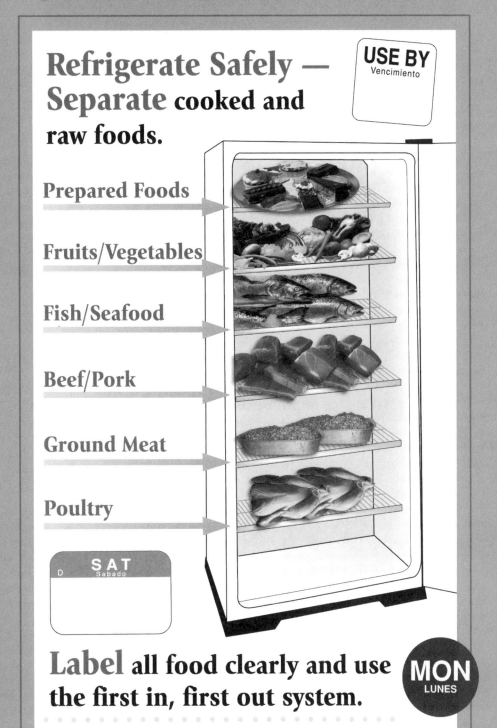

Refrigerate Safely — Separate cooked and raw foods.

USE BY
Vencimiento

Prepared Foods

Fruits/Vegetables

Fish/Seafood

Beef/Pork

Ground Meat

Poultry

D **S A T** Sabado

Label all food clearly and use the first in, first out system.

MON
LUNES

ALMACENE ALIMENTO APROPIADAMENTE

COOKING TEMPERATURES

Hold at specified temperature for 15 seconds to kill bacteria.

Poultry 165°F

- Includes chicken, turkey, duck, goose—whole, parts or ground
- Soups, stews, stuffing, casseroles
- Stuffed meat, poultry, fish and pasta
- Leftovers (to reheat)

Ground Beef 155°F

- Hamburger, meatloaf and other ground meats; ground fish
- Fresh shell eggs—cooked and held for service (such as scrambled)

Pork & Fish 145°F

- Pork, ham, beef, corned beef, roasts (hold 4 minutes)
- Beef, lamb, veal, pork (steaks or chops)
- Fish, shellfish
- Fresh shell eggs—broken, cooked and served immediately

Wash and sanitize your thermometer after each use.

Las TEMPERATURAS que COCINAN

DISHWASHING

The correct procedure for manual dishwashing. Use a 3-compartment sink:

1 **Sort and Scrape** dishes.

2 **Wash** with detergent in hot water at least 110°F.

3 **Rinse** in clean water to remove detergent.

4 **Sanitize** in hot water 171°F for at least 30 seconds or chemical sanitizer 75°F.

5 **Air Dry.** Do not towel dry.

LAVAR de PLATO

DON'T CONTAMINATE

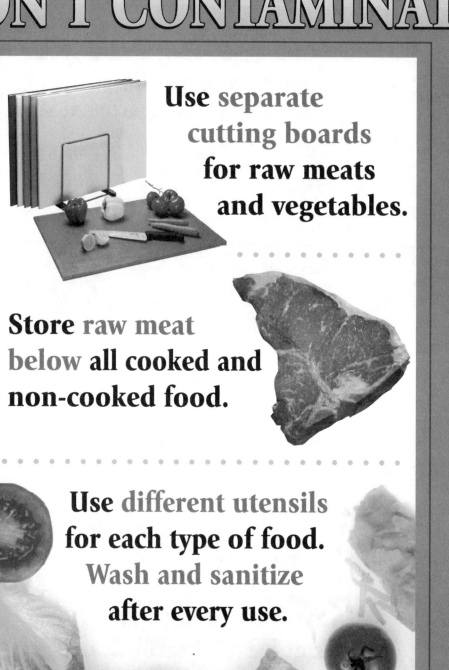

Use separate cutting boards for raw meats and vegetables.

Store raw meat below all cooked and non-cooked food.

Use different utensils for each type of food. Wash and sanitize after every use.

NO CONTAMINE

CALIBRATE THERMOMETERS

Fill glass with finely crushed ice. Add clean tap water to top and stir well.

· · · · · · · · · · · · · · · ·

Immerse stem into glass, without touching sides or glass bottom.

· · · · · · · · · · · · · · · ·

Wait a minimum of 30 seconds. Check temp.

· · · · · · · · · · · · · · · ·

Thermometer should read 32°F. If not, it needs to be adjusted.

· · · · · · · · · · · · · · · ·

To adjust, hold the nut under the head of the thermometer with a suitable tool and turn the head so the pointer reads 32°F.

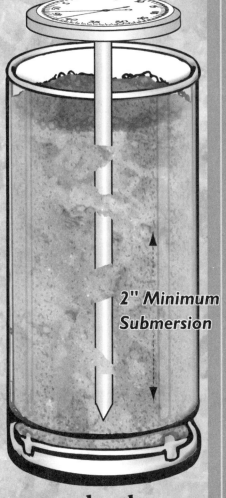

2" Minimum Submersion

CALIBRE TERMÓMETROS

FIRST IN, FIRST OUT

Rotate food to prevent food-borne illness and reduce spoilage.

Label the day food was received and when it should be used.

USE BY
Vencimiento

MON
LUNES

Store foods so labels are clearly visible and use products expiring first.

D SAT
Sabado

Check food expiration dates and throw away at or before expiration.

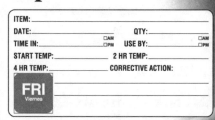

ITEM: _____

DATE: _____ QTY: _____

TIME IN: _____ ☐AM ☐PM   USE BY: _____ ☐AM ☐PM

START TEMP: _____   2 HR TEMP: _____

4 HR TEMP: _____   CORRECTIVE ACTION: _____

FRI
Viernes

Call DayMark Food Safety Systems at 1-800-847-0101 for all your food-safety label needs or visit their Web site at www.dissolveaway.com

PRIMERO EN, PRIMERO FUERA

1 Analyze Hazards.
Analice los Peligros.

2 Identify Critical Control Points.
Identifique los Puntos Críticos del Control.

3 Establish Critical Limits.
Establezca los Límites Críticos.

4 Monitor CCPs.
Controle CCPs.

5 Establish Corrective Action.
Establezca la Accione Correctiva.

6 Keep Records.
Lleve Registros.

7 Verify HACCP System.
Verifique HACCP Sistema.

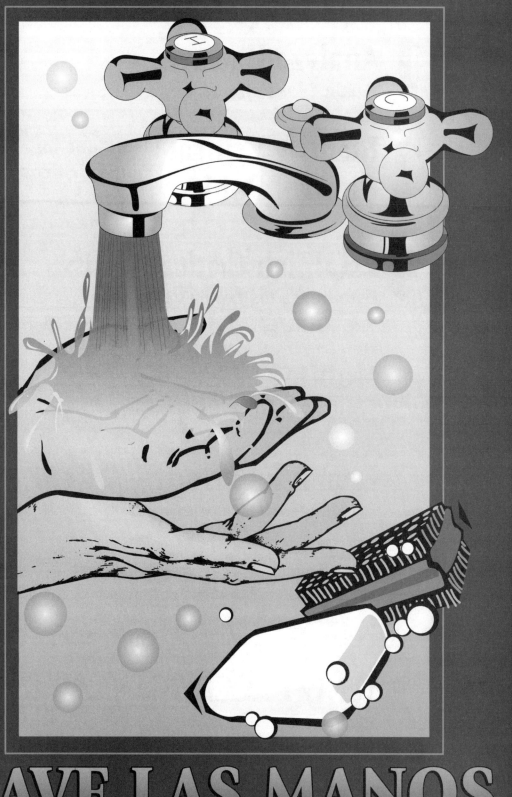

STEP-BY-STEP HANDWASHING

1  Use soap and warm, running water.

2 Rub hands together, under water, for at least 20 seconds.

3 Wash backs of hands, wrists, between fingers and under fingernails. Rinse.

4 Turn off water with a paper towel, not your bare hands.

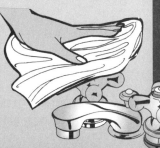

5  Dry hands with an air dryer or paper towel.

El PASO POR PASO MANO LAVANDO

PERSONAL HYGIENE

Wear hair restraints at all times.

Remove all jewelry including rings, watches, necklaces and earrings.

Uniforms must be neat and clean.

La HIGIENE PERSONAL

KEEP IT CLEAN

1 Rough Clean.
Aspero Limpio.

2 Soap.
El jabón.

3 Sanitize.
Desinfecte.

DISINFECTANT

MANTÉNGALO LIMPIA

CLEAN UP SPILLS

LIMPIE ROCIE

WASH YOUR HANDS AFTER

LAVE las MANOS DESPUÉS

WEAR FOOD-SAFETY EQUIPMENT PROVIDED

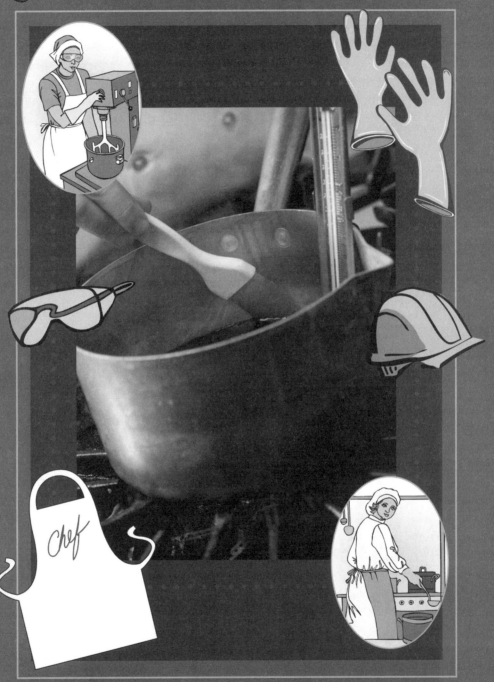

Chef

LLEVE el EQUIPO de la SEGURIDAD de ALIMENTO PROPORCIONADO

KEEP DOORS &
WINDOWS CLOSED

MANTENGA PUERTAS &
VENTANAS CERRARON

© 2003 Atlantic Publishing Group, Inc.   Item #FSP12-PS to re-order please call 1-800-541-1336

CHAPTER 2

Proper kitchen management is essential for a successful restaurant. This section will enable the restaurant manager, through the use of the sample forms and simple procedures, to know exactly where every food item and every cent the restaurant business spent went. The last few pages of this section consolidate all the personnel, procedures and sample forms into a sequence of daily events. This illustrates how every food item is controlled, from the initial purchasing stage to when the cashier rings up the sale.

Kitchen Management

Kitchen Management

Common Equivalents

6 ounce	➡	$^3/_4$ cup
8 ounce	➡	1 cup
12-ounce (vacuum)	➡	$1^1/_2$ cups
#300	➡	$1^3/_4$ cups (14 to 16 ounces)
#303	➡	2 cups (16 to 17 ounces)
#2	➡	$2^1/_2$ cups (20 ounces)
#$2^1/_2$	➡	$3^1/_2$ cups (29 ounces)
#3 cylinder	➡	$5^3/_4$ cups (46 fluid ounces)
#5	➡	$1^1/_2$ quarts
#10	➡	12 - 13 cups (6 lbs 8 oz - 7 lbs 5 oz)

BASIC MEASURES

3 teaspoons	➡	1 tablespoon	➡	
8 tablespoons	➡	$^1/_2$ cup	➡	4 oz
16 tablespoons	➡	1 cup	➡	8 oz
1 cup	➡		➡	8 oz
1 pint	➡	2 cups	➡	16 oz
1 quart	➡	4 cups	➡	32 oz
$^1/_2$ gallon	➡	8 cups	➡	64 oz
1 gallon	➡	16 cups	➡	128 oz
1 pound	➡			16 oz

Metric Equivalents

¼ teaspoon	➡	1.23 milliliters
½ teaspoon	➡	2.46 milliliters
1 teaspoon	➡	4.93 milliliters
1¼ teaspoons	➡	6.16 milliliters
1½ teaspoons	➡	7.39 milliliters
1¾ teaspoons	➡	8.63 milliliters
2 teaspoons	➡	9.86 milliliters
1 tablespoon	➡	14.79 milliliters
1 fluid ounce	➡	29.57 milliliters
2 tablespoons	➡	29.57 milliliters
¼ cup	➡	59.15 milliliters
½ cup	➡	118.3 milliliters
1 cup	➡	236.59 milliliters
2 cups, or 1 pint	➡	473.18 milliliters
3 cups	➡	709.77 milliliters
4 cups, or 1 quart	➡	946.36 milliliters
4 quarts, or 1 gallon	➡	3.785 liters

WEIGHT

1 ounce	➡	28.35 grams
8 ounces, or ½ pound	➡	226.8 grams
16 ounces, or 1 pound	➡	453.6 grams
2 pounds	➡	907.2 grams
2 pounds + 3 ounces	➡	1 kilogram, or 1,000 grams

Weights & Measures

LADLES

1 ounce	➡	2 tablespoons
2 ounces	➡	1/4 cup
4 ounces	➡	1/2 cup
6 ounces	➡	3/4 cup
8 ounces	➡	1 cup
10 ounces	➡	1 1/4 cups
12 ounces	➡	1 1/2 cups

COMMON U.S. MEASUREMENTS

1/8 teaspoon	➡	dash
1 teaspoon	➡	1/3 tablespoon
3 teaspoons	➡	1 tablespoon (1/2 fl oz)
1/2 tablespoon	➡	1 1/2 teaspoons
1 tablespoon	➡	3 teaspoons (1/2 fl oz)
2 tablespoons	➡	1 fluid ounce
3 tablespoons	➡	1 1/2 fl oz (1 jigger)
4 tablespoons	➡	1/4 cup (2 fl oz)
8 tablespoons	➡	1/2 cup (4 fl oz)
12 tablespoons	➡	3/4 cup (6 fl oz)
16 tablespoons	➡	1 cup (8 fl oz)
1/8 cup	➡	2 tablespoons (1 fl oz)
1/4 cup	➡	4 tablespoons (2 fl oz)
1/3 cup	➡	5 tablespoons + 1 teaspoon
1/2 cup	➡	8 tablespoons (4 fl oz)
3/4 cup	➡	12 tablespoons (6 fl oz)
1 cup	➡	16 tablespoons (1/2 pint, or 8 fl oz)
2 cups	➡	1 pint (16 fl oz)
1 pint	➡	2 cups (16 fl oz)
1 quart	➡	2 pt (4 cups, or 32 fl oz)
1 gallon	➡	4 qt (8 pt, or 16 cups, or 128 fl oz)
2 gallons	➡	1 peck
4 pecks	➡	1 bushel

Ingredient Substitutions

Ingredient	Recipe Substitutions
1 tsp allspice	$^1/_2$ tsp cinnamon + $^1/_2$ tsp ground cloves
1 tsp baking powder	$^1/_4$ tsp baking soda + $^1/_2$ tsp cream of tartar + $^1/_4$ tsp cornstarch, or $^1/_3$ tsp baking soda + $^1/_2$ tsp cream of tartar
1 cup bread crumbs	$^2/_3$ cup all-purpose flour
1 cup butter	1 cup margarine, or 1 cup shortening + $^1/_2$ tsp salt, or $^7/_8$ cup cooking oil + $^1/_2$ tsp salt
1 cup buttermilk	1 Tbsp vinegar or lemon juice + enough milk (or plain yogurt) to make 1 cup; let stand 5 minutes
1 cup catsup	1 cup tomato sauce + $^1/_2$ cup sugar + 2 tbsp vinegar
1 oz chocolate, unsweetened	3 Tbsp unsweetened cocoa + 1 Tbsp oil
$^1/_4$ cup cocoa	1 ounce (square) chocolate (decrease fat called for in recipe by $^1/_2$ tbsp)
1 cup cornmeal (self-rising)	$^7/_8$ cup plain cornmeal + $1^1/_2$ tbsp baking powder + $^1/_2$ tsp salt
1 Tbsp cornstarch	2 Tbsp all-purpose flour, or 2 Tbsp granulated tapioca
1 cup corn syrup	$^3/_4$ cup sugar + $^1/_4$ cup water or 1 cup honey
1 cup cream, half and half	$^7/_8$ cup milk + $1^1/_2$ Tbsp melted butter
1 cup cream, heavy	$^3/_4$ cup milk + $2^1/_2$ Tbsp fat
$^1/_2$ tsp cream of tartar	$1^1/_2$ tsp lemon juice or vinegar
1 large egg, whole	4 Tbsp beaten egg, or 2 yolks + 1 Tbsp water
1 egg yolk	2 Tbsp sifted, dry egg yolk powder + 2 tsp water, or $1^1/_3$ Tbsp thawed frozen egg yolk
1 cup flour, all-purpose	1 cup + 2 Tbsp cake flour, or $^1/_2$ cup all-purpose flour + $^1/_2$ cup whole-wheat flour, or 1 cup rolled oats, $^1/_2$ cup all-purpose flour + $^1/_2$ cup bran, or $^5/_8$ cup potato flour, or $^7/_8$ cup cornmeal, or $1^1/_4$ cups rye flour
1 Tbsp flour, all-purpose (as thickener)	$^1/_2$ Tbsp cornstarch, potato starch or arrowroot, or 2 tsp quick-cooking tapioca
1 cup flour, self-rising	1 cup all-purpose flour + $1^1/_4$ tsp baking powder + $^1/_4$ tsp salt
Flour, whole wheat (any amount)	Substitute whole wheat flour for $^1/_4$ to $^1/_2$ of the white flour called for

Ingredient Substitutions

Ingredient

Recipe Substitutions

1 medium clove garlic .... $\frac{1}{8}$ tsp garlic powder or instant minced garlic, or $\frac{1}{2}$ to 1 tsp garlic salt (reduce amount of salt called for in recipe)

3-ounce package gelatin, flavored .... 1 Tbsp plain gelatin and 2 cups fruit juice

1 Tbsp ginger, fresh, minced .... $\frac{1}{4}$ tsp ground ginger

1 Tbsp herbs, fresh .... 1 tsp whole dried, or $\frac{1}{4}$ tsp ground

1 cup honey .... $1\frac{1}{4}$ cups granulated sugar + $\frac{1}{4}$ cup liquid

1 Tbsp horseradish, fresh, grated .... 2 Tbsp prepared horseradish

1 tsp lemon juice .... $\frac{1}{2}$ tsp vinegar

2 cups maple syrup .... 2 cups sugar and 1 cup water, bring to clear boil; take off heat; add $\frac{1}{2}$ tsp maple flavoring

1 cup milk, skim .... $\frac{1}{3}$ cup instant nonfat dry milk + water to make 1 cup, or $\frac{1}{2}$ cup evaporated skim milk + $\frac{1}{2}$ cup water

1 cup milk, whole .... 2 tsp melted butter + enough skim milk to make 1 cup, or $\frac{1}{2}$ cup evaporated milk + $\frac{1}{2}$ cup water, or 1 cup soy milk, or $\frac{1}{3}$ cup nonfat dry milk + water to make 1 cup + 1 Tbsp fat

1 can milk, sweetened condensed .... Heat the following ingredients until sugar and butter are dissolved: $\frac{1}{3}$ cup and 2 Tbsp evaporated milk + 1 cup sugar + 3 Tbsp butter or margarine

1 small onion .... 1 tsp onion powder, or 1 Tbsp instant minced onion

1 tsp pumpkin pie spice .... $\frac{1}{2}$ tsp cinnamon, $\frac{1}{4}$ tsp ginger, $\frac{1}{8}$ tsp allspice, and $\frac{1}{8}$ tsp nutmeg

1 cup sour cream .... 1 cup yogurt or $\frac{1}{3}$ cup butter + $\frac{3}{4}$ cup buttermilk

4 Tbsp soy sauce .... 3 Tbsp Worcestershire sauce + 1 Tbsp water

1 cup sugar, granulated .... 1 cup packed brown sugar, or $1\frac{3}{4}$ cups powdered sugar (do not substitute in baking), or $1\frac{1}{2}$ cups corn syrup (reduce liquid in recipe by $\frac{1}{2}$ cup), or 1 cup honey (reduce liquid in recipe by $\frac{1}{4}$ to $\frac{1}{3}$ cup)

1 cup tomato juice .... $\frac{1}{2}$ cup tomato sauce + $\frac{1}{2}$ cup water + 1 dash salt

1 cup tomato puree .... $\frac{1}{2}$ cup tomato paste + $\frac{1}{2}$ cup water

1 Tbsp yeast, dry active .... 1 package ($\frac{1}{4}$ oz) active dry yeast, or 1 cake compressed yeast

1 cup yogurt, plain .... 1 cup buttermilk, or 1 cup sour milk

Tablespoons Per Ounce

Allspice, ground	5		Margarine	2
Baking Powder	3		Marjoram	10
Basil	8		Milk, dry	4
Celery Seed	6		Milk, whole liquid	2
Chili Powder	4		Mustard, dry	5
Cinnamon, ground	6		Mustard, prepared	4
Cloves, ground	5		Nutmeg, ground	6
Cloves, whole	6		Oil, salad	2
Cocoa Powder	4		Onion Salt	3
Coconut, grated	6		Oregano, ground	6
Coffee, ground	5		Paprika, ground	6
Corn Meal	3		Pepper, black, ground	5
Cornstarch	3		Pepper, white, ground	6
Corn Syrup	1½		Pickling Spice	8
Cream of Tartar	3		Poppy Seeds	6
Cumin	4		Poultry Seasoning	10
Curry Powder	8		Rosemary	10
Flour, all-purpose	4		Sage, ground	8
Garlic Powder	4		Salt	2
Garlic Salt	3		Shortening	2
Ginger, ground	8		Soda, baking	3
Honey	1		Thyme	12
Mace	6		Vanilla Extract	2

Standard Portion Sizes

VEGETABLES

Beans-Green or Wax
Buttered.............3 oz
Creamed ....$3^1/2$ oz

Beans-Lima
Buttered ....3 oz
Succotash........$3^1/2$ oz

Beets
Buttered.............3 oz
Harvard ....3 oz

Broccoli
Au Gratin........$3^1/2$ oz
Buttered.............3 oz

Cabbage
Buttered.............3 oz

Carrots
Buttered..........$3^1/2$ oz
With Peas........$3^1/2$ oz

Cauliflower
Au Gratin............3 oz
Buttered ....3 oz

Corn
Buttered..........$2^1/2$ oz
Creamed ....3 oz
Escalloped ......$3^1/2$ oz

Onions
Creamed ....$3^1/2$ oz
Fried....................3 oz

Parsnips
Baked ....3 oz
Buttered ....3 oz

Peas
Buttered ....3 oz
Creamed ....3 oz

Potatoes
Au Gratin............5 oz
Boiled..............$4^1/2$ oz
French Fried ....2 oz
Mashed ....$4^1/2$ oz

Tomatoes
Stewed ....4 oz

MEATS

Beef
Braised ....5 oz
Corned..............4 oz
Ground ....5 oz
Liver ....3 oz
Pot Roast............4 oz
Prime Rib............4 oz
Stew ....6 oz

Lamb
Roast ....3 oz
Shoulder Chop....4 oz
Stew ....7 oz

Pork
Baked Ham ....3 oz
Chops ....4 oz
Fresh Ham ....3 oz
Roast Loin ....3 oz

Veal
Heart ....$3^1/2$ oz
Roast..................3 oz

FRUITS/OTHER

Fruits
Apple Sauce ......3 oz
Baked
 Apple Rings ......4 oz
Rhubarb Sauce ..3 oz

Meat Substitutes
Baked Beans ......6 oz
Chili ....6 oz
Macaroni &
 Cheese..............6 oz
Spanish Rice ......8 oz

FISH & POULTRY

Fish
Fillets (raw) ....5 oz
Haddock (baked)..4 oz
Salmon Loaf........4 oz
Scallops ....5 oz

Poultry
Chicken a
 la King..............5 oz
Creamed Chicken &
 Sweetbreads ....6 oz
Roast Turkey ......3 oz
Turkey
 Sandwich..........3 oz

Kitchen Employee Training Schedule

DATE _____   EMPLOYEE(S) _____

☐ **Kitchen sanitation & cleanliness**

☐ **Kitchen organization**

☐ **Productivity**

☐ **Prep sheets**

☐ **Line set-up**

☐ **Ordering food**

☐ **Receiving deliveries**

☐ **Line quality**

☐ **Thawing procedures**

☐ **Cook procedures**

☐ **Recipe cards & specifications**

☐ **HACCP & health standards**

☐ **Sanitation**

☐ **Food-cost control**

☐ **Security**

☐ **Food-waste tracking**

☐ **Meat count**

☐ **Closing procedures**

☐ **Quality standards**

Notes or Concerns:

_____

Employee Signature

_____

Manager Signature

Standard Recipe Card A

Recipe No.   Name:

Portion Size: Yields:

Cost Per Portion:

Ingredients   **Weight/Measure Cost**

Directions:

Service:

Standard Recipe Card B

RECIPE NAME: _____

RECIPE NUMBER: _____ QUANTITY: _____

INGREDIENTS: PREPARATION:

_____   _____

_____   _____

_____   _____

_____   _____

_____   _____

_____   _____

_____   _____

_____   _____

_____   _____

RECIPE NAME: _____

RECIPE NUMBER: _____ QUANTITY: _____

INGREDIENTS: PREPARATION:

_____   _____

_____   _____

_____   _____

_____   _____

_____   _____

_____   _____

_____   _____

_____   _____

_____   _____

Standard Recipe Card C

ITEM:

FORECASTED YIELD: _____   PORTION SIZE: _____

INGREDIENTS:	ACTUAL:		PREPARED YIELD:	
	Weight	Measure	Weight	Measure

DIRECTIONS:

ORDERING/NOTES:

Cooking Yield Chart

ITEM:

PREPARED BY: DATE:

ITEM DESCRIPTION:

PREPARATION PROCEDURES:

GROSS WEIGHT OR VOLUME: _____

COOKING OR PREPARATION LOSS: _____

YIELD AFTER COOKING: _____

ALLOWANCE FOR SERVICE LOSS: _____

TRIMMING, SLICING AND TASTING: _____

NET YIELD:_____

Storage Life of Meat Products

MAXIMUM storage time recommendations for fresh, cooked and processed meat.
For best quality, fresh meats should be used within 2 or 3 days, ground meat should be used within 24 hours.

ITEM	REFRIGERATOR (36° to 40°F)	FREEZER (0°F or lower)
Ground beef, veal & lamb	1 to 2 days	3 to 4 months
Beef (fresh)	2 to 4 days	6 to 12 months
Corned Beef	7 days	2 weeks
Veal (fresh)	2 to 4 days	6 to 9 months
Lamb (fresh)	2 to 4 days	6 to 9 months
Ground pork	1 to 2 days	1 to 3 months
Pork (fresh)	2 to 4 days	3 to 6 months
Sausage, fresh pork	7 days	2 months
Sausage, smoked	3 to 7 days	should not freeze
Sausage, dry & semi-dry	2 to 3 weeks	should not freeze
Variety meats	1 to 2 days	3 to 4 months
Bacon	5 to 7 days	1 month
Smoked ham, whole	7 days	2 months
Ham slices	3 to 4 days	2 months
Leftover cooked meat	4 to 5 days	2 to 3 months
Luncheon meats	7 days	should not freeze
Hot Dogs/Frankfurters	4 to 5 days	1 month
Meat pies (cooked)	-----	3 months
Swiss steak (cooked)	-----	3 months
Stews (cooked)	-----	3 months
Prepared meat dinner	-----	2 to 6 months

Cooking Temperature Guide

MEAT THERMOMETER READINGS

BEEF

Rare (cold, red center) ———140°F

Medium Rare ———150°F
(warm, red center)

Medium ———160°F
(warm, pink center)

Medium Well———165°F
(hot, pink center)

Well-done———170°F
(brown center, no pink)

VEAL ———170°F

LAMB

Rare ———140°F

Medium ———160°F

Well-done ———170°-180°F

FRESH PORK ———170°F

SMOKED PORK

Fully cooked ———140°F

Cooked before eating ——160°F

OVEN TEMPERATURE GUIDE

Very slow oven ———250°-275°F

Slow oven ———300°-325°F

Moderate oven ———350°-375°F

Hot oven ———400°-475°F

Extremely hot oven ———500°-525°F

CANDY & FROSTING SYRUP TEMPERATURES

Thread———230°-234°F

Soft Ball———234°-240°F

Firm Ball ———244°-248°F

Hard Ball ———250°-266°F

Soft Crack ———270°-290°F

Hard Crack———300°-310°F

Meat Count Form

DATE: SUN   M   T   W   TH   F   SAT (circle one)   MANAGER:

OPENING COUNTS

Item	Beginning Count	+ / - Purchases	Total Start

CLOSING COUNTS

Ending Counts	Total End	Use	Actual Use	Variance + / -

Thaw Pull Chart

Be sure to thaw food correctly in one of the following ways:

UNDER COLD RUNNING WATER

IN THE REFRIGERATOR

DURING THE COOKING PROCESS

IN THE MICROWAVE

All thaw items should be pulled far enough in advance so they are THAWED COMPLETELY at the time of use. All thaw items must be labeled, dated and rotated.

ITEM	THAW TIME	SHELF LIFE	ON HAND	PULL	NOTES

Prep Chart

ITEM	SHELF	MON			TUES			WED			THURS			FRI			SAT			SUN		
		1	P	Y	1	P	Y	1	P	Y	1	P	Y	1	P	Y	1	P	Y	1	P	Y

Prep Sheet

DATE: SUN   M   T   W   TH   F   SAT (circle one)   EMPLOYEE:

ITEM	LIFE	ON HAND	PREP	YIELD	NOTES

Prep Sheet II

DATE: SUN   M   T   W   TH   F   SAT (circle one)   EMPLOYEE:

ITEM	SHELF LIFE	ON HAND	PREP	NOTES

Product Mix Tracking

ITEM	MON		TUES		WED		THURS		FRI		SAT		SUN	
	L	D	L	D	L	D	L	D	L	D	L	D	L	D

C2

22

The Encyclopedia of Restaurant Forms

Waste Report

ITEM:_____

_____

POUNDS
RECEIVED:_____

POUNDS OF TRIM REMOVED PRIOR
TO USE:_____

USABLE WEIGHT: _____

ITEM:_____

_____

POUNDS
RECEIVED:_____

POUNDS OF TRIM REMOVED PRIOR
TO USE:_____

USABLE WEIGHT: _____

ITEM:_____

_____

POUNDS
RECEIVED:_____

POUNDS OF TRIM REMOVED PRIOR
TO USE:_____

USABLE WEIGHT: _____

ITEM:_____

_____

POUNDS
RECEIVED:_____

POUNDS OF TRIM REMOVED PRIOR
TO USE:_____

USABLE WEIGHT: _____

Spoilage Report

DATE:_____ EMPLOYEE:_____

ITEM:_____ PRICE:_____

_____

_____

REASON FOR SPOILAGE: _____

_____

_____

_____

ITEM:_____ PRICE:_____

_____

_____

REASON FOR SPOILAGE: _____

_____

_____

_____

ITEM:_____ PRICE:_____

_____

_____

REASON FOR SPOILAGE: _____

_____

_____

_____

TOTAL POUNDS SPOILED: _____ TOTAL COST: _____

Weekly Food Mishap Report

ITEM:_____

MISHAP: _____

_____

EMPLOYEE: _____ DAY: _____ DATE: _____ TIME: _____

ITEM:_____

MISHAP: _____

_____

EMPLOYEE: _____ DAY: _____ DATE: _____ TIME: _____

ITEM:_____

MISHAP: _____

_____

EMPLOYEE: _____ DAY: _____ DATE: _____ TIME: _____

ITEM:_____

MISHAP: _____

_____

EMPLOYEE: _____ DAY: _____ DATE: _____ TIME: _____

ITEM:_____

MISHAP: _____

_____

EMPLOYEE: _____ DAY: _____ DATE: _____ TIME: _____

ITEM:_____

MISHAP: _____

_____

EMPLOYEE: _____ DAY: _____ DATE: _____ TIME: _____

ITEM:_____

MISHAP: _____

_____

EMPLOYEE: _____ DAY: _____ DATE: _____ TIME: _____

Cost of Food Consumed

UNIT NAME:

Accounting Period _____

Beginning Inventory $_____

    plus (+)

Purchases $_____

Goods Available $_____

    less (-)

Ending Inventory $_____

    less (-)

Employee Meals $_____

COST OF FOOD CONSUMED $_____

UNIT NAME:

Accounting Period _____

Beginning Inventory $_____

    plus (+)

Purchases $_____

Goods Available $_____

    less (-)

Ending Inventory $_____

    less (-)

Employee Meals $_____

COST OF FOOD CONSUMED $_____

Attainable Food Cost

DATE PREPARED:	PREPARED BY:	TIME PERIOD:

ITEM	# SOLD	PORTION COST	TOTAL COST	MENU PRICE	TOTAL SALES	ATTAINABLE FOOD COST
TOTAL						

Food Cost Report

PERIOD ENDING:	DATE PREPARED:	PREPARED BY:

DEBITS

Opening Inventory _____

Total Food Purchases _____

DEBIT TOTAL _____ ← **A**

CREDITS

Closing Inventory _____

Employee Meal Credit _____

Promotional/Free Meals _____

Steward Sales _____

CREDIT TOTAL _____ ← **B**

COST OF FOOD SOLD

Debit Total **A** less (-) **Credit Total** **B** equals (=)

COST OF FOOD SOLD _____ ← **C**

TOTAL FOOD SALES _____

FOOD COST PERCENTAGE

Cost of Food Sold divide (÷) **Total Food Sales** equals (=) _____

multiply (x) by 100

equals (=) **FOOD COST PERCENTAGE** _____

Department Food Cost Report

DEPARTMENT:	PERIOD ENDING:
DATE PREPARED:	PREPARED BY:

DEBITS

Opening Inventory _____

Total Food Requisitions:

      Storeroom _____

      Production Kitchen _____

      Transfers In _____

         DEBIT TOTAL _____ ◄— **A**

CREDITS

Closing Inventory _____

Employee Meal Credit _____

Promotional/ Free Meals _____

Steward Sales _____

         CREDIT TOTAL _____ ◄— **B**

COST OF FOOD SOLD

Debit Total **A** less (-) **Credit Total** **B** equals (=)

         COST OF FOOD SOLD _____ ◄— **C**

         TOTAL FOOD SALES _____

FOOD COST PERCENTAGE

Cost of Food Sold divide (÷) **Total Food Sales** equals (=) _____

         multiply (x) by 100

      equals (=) **FOOD COST PERCENTAGE** _____

Food Cost Calculator

MENU ITEM:	DATE PREPARED:	PREPARED BY:

INGREDIENT	QUANTITY	UNIT	UNIT COST	EXTENSION

Total Recipe Cost
Per Serving Cost

CALCULATE NUMBER OF SERVINGS
Enter Recipe Yield (in ounces) _____
Ounces Per Serving _____
Figure Servings Per Recipe _____

CALCULATE MENU PRICE

Cost Per Serving _____
MENU ITEM CALCULATION
   Portion Cost of Recipe _____
   Additional Side Item _____
   Additional Side Item _____
TOTAL PLATE COST _____

Number of Servings _____
   Target Food Cost   30%
   Target Menu Price _____
   Current Menu Price _____
   Current Food Cost _____

Product Request Log

DATE	ITEM	REQUESTED BY

Product Specification

Product Name: _____

Specification Number: _____ Pricing Unit: _____

Standard/Grade: _____

_____

_____

_____

_____

Weight: _____

_____

_____

_____

_____

Packaging: _____

_____

_____

_____

_____

_____

_____

Container Size: _____

_____

_____

Additional Information: _____

_____

_____

_____

_____

_____

_____

_____

_____

_____

_____

_____

_____

_____

_____

_____

_____

_____

_____

_____

_____

_____

_____

Event Food Production & Portion Control Form

Name of Event: _____   Date of Event: _____

Prepared By: _____   Day of Week of Event: _____

Guaranteed Guest Count: _____   Amount to Prepare Count: _____   Confirmed Count: _____

○ Full-Service   ○ Buffet   ○ Other _____   Food Service Time: _____

MENU ITEM	Quantity Prepared	Portion Size	Possible Number	Weight of Amount Left	Portions of Amount Left	Amount Used

Daily Production Report

DATE:	DEPARTMENT:			SHIFT:	

MENU ITEM	AMT. ORDERED	AMT. PRODUCED	# SOLD	% OF SALES	LEFTOVERS

Portion Control Chart

Department: _____ Day: _____

Final Amounts Recorded By: _____ Date: _____

Amounts Sold/Differences By: _____ Time: _____

Approved By: _____

MENU ITEM	Recipe No.	Quantity Prepared	Portion Size	Possible No.	Amount Sold	Difference	Amount Left	+ / - Diff.

Food Production Chart

Department: _____ Date: _____

Prepared By: _____ Week: _____

MENU ITEM	Recipe No.	MON	TUE	WED	THU	FRI	SAT	SUN

Transfer Form

Transfer From: _____   Transfer To: _____

Transfer Number: _____   Date: _____ Time: _____

Prepared By: _____   Priced By: _____

Delivered By: _____   Received By: _____

Approved By: _____   Extended By: _____

Item Description	Unit	Quantity	Price		Extension	

	Total

Cooked Yield Test Form

Item Name: _____

Date: _____ Prepared By: _____

Net Weight: _____

_____

_____

Net Cost Per Pound: _____

_____

_____

Net Cost: _____

_____

_____

Portion Size: _____

_____

_____

Portions Served: _____

_____

Total Weight as Served: _____

_____

Cooked Cost Per Pound: _____

_____

Shrinkage: _____

_____

Percent of Shrinkage: _____

_____

Total Percent of Increase: _____

_____

Additional Information: _____

_____

_____

_____

_____

_____

_____

_____

_____

_____

_____

_____

_____

Buffet or Salad Bar Product Usage Form

Name: _____

Date: _____ Prepared By: _____

ITEM	Category	Beginning Amount	Additions	Ending Amount	Total Usage	Unit Cost	Total Cost

Total Product Cost: _____ Guests Served: _____ Cost Per Guest: _____

Bid Sheet

Category: _____

Date Bid: _____ **Bids Reviewed By:** _____

Vendors: A. _____ **Bid Received By:** ○ phone ○ fax ○ mail

Vendors: B. _____ **Bid Received By:** ○ phone ○ fax ○ mail

Vendors: C. _____ **Bid Received By:** ○ phone ○ fax ○ mail

ITEM	Quantity	VENDOR A		VENDOR B		VENDOR C	
		Unit	Total	Unit	Total	Unit	Total
TOTAL							

Storeroom Requisition

Requisition #: _____ Date: _____

Approved By: _____ Filled By: _____

Requisition To : ○ kitchen ○ bar ○ other _____

Item Description	Storage Unit	Requested Amt.	Unit Cost	Total Cost
TOTAL				

Notes: _____

_____

_____

Butcher's Yield Test Results

Item: _____ Date Tested: _____ Time: _____

Specification: _____ Tested By: _____

AP Amount Tested: _____ Price Per Pound AP: _____

LOSS DETAIL	WEIGHT LOSS (Pounds)	% OF ORIGINAL
AP		
Fat Loss		
Bone Loss		
Cooking Loss		
Carving Loss		
TOTAL PRODUCT LOSS		

NET PRODUCT YIELD: _____ COST PER SERVABLE POUND: _____

Item: _____ Date Tested: _____ Time: _____

Specification: _____ Tested By: _____

AP Amount Tested: _____ Price Per Pound AP: _____

LOSS DETAIL	WEIGHT LOSS (Pounds)	% OF ORIGINAL
AP		
Fat Loss		
Bone Loss		
Cooking Loss		
Carving Loss		
TOTAL PRODUCT LOSS		

NET PRODUCT YIELD: _____ COST PER SERVABLE POUND: _____

Dishroom Equipment Layout

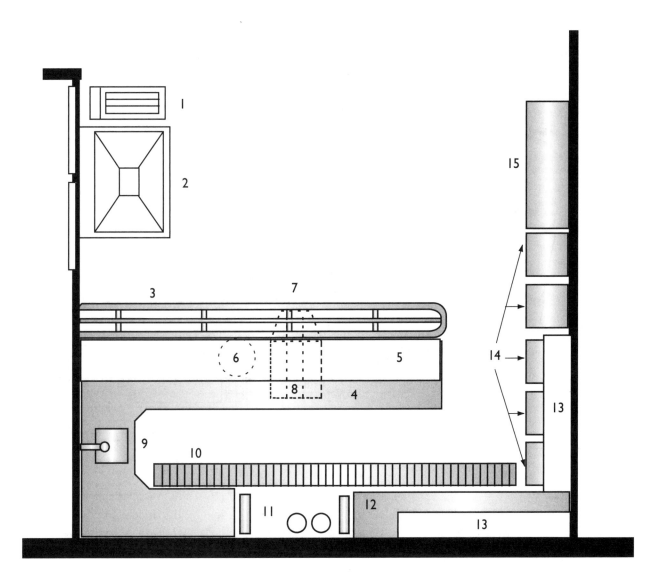

1. Silver burnisher	6. Disposal (3 h.p. hammermill type) and scrap chute	10. Dish-rack conveyor
2. Linen hamper	7. Silverware chute	11. Dish machine
3. Tray rail	8. Silverware soak tank	12. Clean-dish table
4. Soiled-dish table	9. Prerinse sink with flexible spray arm	13. Overshelves (two)
5. Glass rack overshelf		14. Dish-rack dollies (five)
		15. Storage cabinet

Detailed Layout of Kitchen Equipment

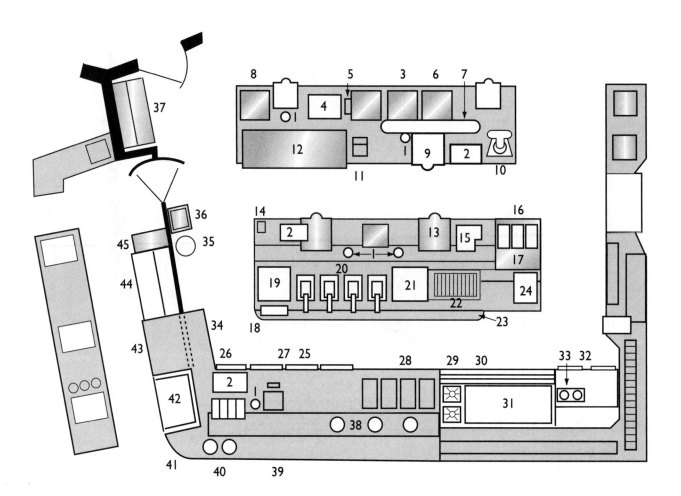

1. Knife wells (five)
2. Composition cutting boards (three)
3. Stainless-steel combination pot and pan washing table with three-compartment sink and meat and vegetable drawers (two)
4. Disposal (3 h.p. hammermill type)
5. Recirculating centrifugal pump
6. Flexible spray rinse arm
7. Overhead pot rack
8. Single-compartment sink
9. Stainless-steel salad preparation work table with undershelf
10. 12-quart mixer on mobile stand
11. Portion scale
12. Reach-in refrigerator
13. Stainless-steel meat and vegetable preparation worktable with angle-compartment sink, drawers (two), overshelf and undershelf

14. Can opener
15. Slicer
16. Closed-top range
17. Exhaust canopy
18. Wooden cutting board
19. Microwave oven
20. Deep fat fryers (four)
21. Griddle
22. Open-top broiler
23. Base cabinet refrigerator with overshelf
24. Steamer
25. Base cabinet refrigerator
26. Cold food wells (eight)
27. Sandwich grill
28. Hot food wells (four) and undercounter dish storage
29. Open-top burners (two)

30. Wooden cutting board
31. Griddle
32. Base cabinet refrigerator
33. Waffle grill
34. Pass-through window
35. Trash can
36. Wash basin
37. Ice machine
38. Heat lamps (two)
39. Waitstaff pickup counter
40. Soup wells (two)
41. Soup bowl lowerators
42. Reach-in refrigerator, sliding-door type
43. Customer takeout back counter
44. Fountain
45. Milkshake machine

Comprehensive Food Costing System

The following example enables you to envision precisely how the personnel procedures and controls combine to control the restaurant's food cost. The next ten forms (pages C2-46 through C2-55) follow a standard sequence of events. In the example you will trace 25 pounds of shrimp through a typical day's operation, from the initial purchasing to the final product. The first column in each of the example forms are filled out so you will be able to see how they are used and why each one is a critical part in the overall control system. The manager should put the following list in the form of a check-off sheet for his or her own organizational purposes.

Note: Blank versions of the ten forms on pages C2-46 through C2-55 are included on the CD-Rom which accompanies this book.

SEQUENCE OF EVENTS

____ 1. Determine the need to purchase shrimp.

____ 2. Purchase the amount needed. In example: 25 pounds.

____ 3. Shrimp is delivered. Follow the receiving and storing procedures.

____ 4. Enter on the Perpetual Inventory Form the amount delivered. In example:
5 boxes of 5 pounds each.

____ 5. Preparation cooks compute the opening counts. In example: 25 shrimp dinners is the beginning count.

____ 6. Determine the Minimum Amount Needed: 33. The preparation cooks need to prepare 8 more dinners for that night. They remove 5 pounds, or 1 box, of shrimp from the freezer.

____ 7. Sign out the 5 pounds of shrimp on the Sign-out Sheet.

____ 8. Place the amount, 5 pounds, in the "Amount Ordered or Defrosted" column on the Preparation Form.

____ 9. Prepare the shrimp as prescribed in the Recipe and Procedure Manual.

____ 10. The number of dinners prepared is 9; enter this figure in the "Amount Prepared" column. The starting total would be 34 (9 + 25). Enter these figures on the Preparation Form.

____ 11. The Preparation Form is completed and given to the kitchen director. All storage areas are locked before leaving. The invoices are brought to the manager's office.

____ 12. The kitchen director computes the yields.

____ 13. The cooks enter and count all the items for the Starting Total.

____ 14. The manager verifies that the Starting Total on the Preparation Form is the same as on the Cook's Report.

____ 15. The manager issues the tickets to the waitstaff. The manager issues the cash drawer to the cashier and verifies the starting amount.

____ 16. The manager checks the perpetual inventory.

____ 17. The waitstaff gives the order tickets to the expediter.

____ 18. The expediter reads off the items to the cooks who start the cooking of the menu items.

____ 19. When completed, the waiter/waitress takes the dinner to the customer.

____ 20. The bill is totaled and given to the customer.

____ 21. The cashier verifies the amount and collects the money or charge.

____ 22. The cooks count the Balance Ending. In example: Starting Total is 34, and the ending balance is 21, leaving 13 as sold.

____ 23. The expediter itemizes the carbon copies: 13 shrimp dinners sold.

____ 24. The manager cashes out with the cashier. Ticket itemization: 13 sold.

____ 25. All three figures verified: cooks to expediter to cashier.

____ 26. The following morning the manager verifies the ending balance of the Cook's Report (21) to the Beginning Amount of the Preparation Form.

____ 27. The bookkeeper rechecks and verifies all the transactions of the previous night.

Perpetual Inventory Form

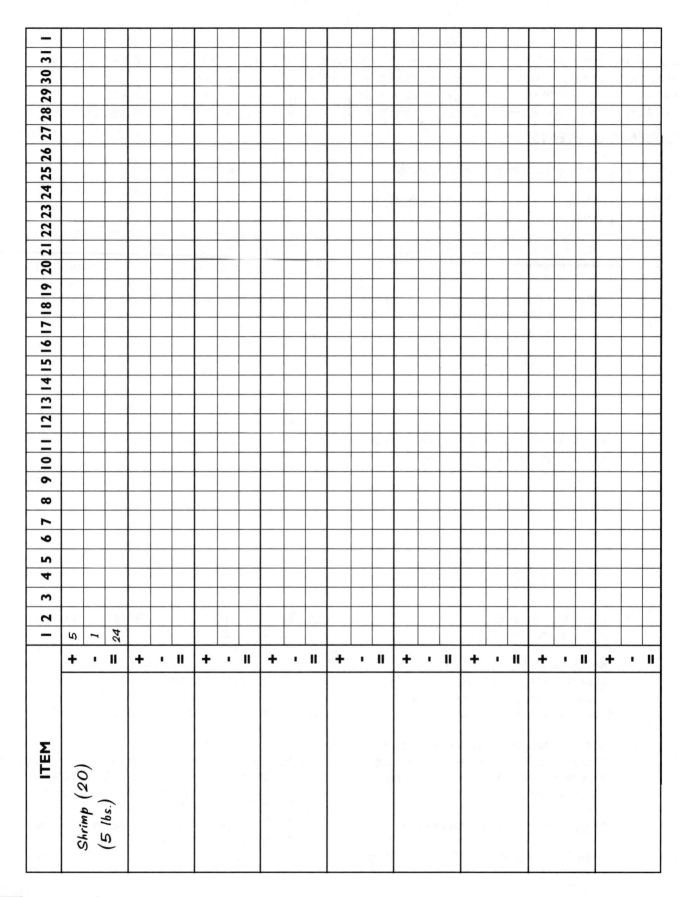

ITEM		1	2	3	4	5	6	7	8	9	10	11	12	13	14	15	16	17	18	19	20	21	22	23	24	25	26	27	28	29	30	31	
Shrimp (20) (5 lbs.)	+	5																															
	-	1																															
	=	24																															

Sign Out Sheet

ITEM	DATE	AMOUNT/WT.	EMPLOYEE
Shrimp-box	11-30	1-5lb. box	Joe B.

Preparation Form

ITEM	MINIMUM AMOUNT	AMOUNT DEF./ORD.	BEGINNING AMOUNT	AMOUNT PREPPED	STARTING TOTAL
Shrimp	33	5 lbs.	25	9	34

Minimum Amount Needed Form

ITEM	MON	TUE	WED	THU	FRI	SAT	SUN
Shrimp dinners						33	

Yield Sheet

ITEM	STARTING WEIGHT (OZ.)	# OF PORTIONS	TOTAL PORTION WEIGHT (OZ.)	YIELD %	PREP. COOK
Shrimp dinner	80.0	9	9 x 8.0oz = 72 oz.	90%	Bob S.

Cashier's Report Form

Prepared By: _____

Date: _____ **Day:** _____ **Shift:** _____

		BAR REGISTER		SERVICE REGISTER		TOTAL
		Day	Night	Day	Night	All Shifts
1	**BANK DEPOSIT** Part 1					
2	Currency					
3	Silver					
4	Checks					
5	**SUB TOTAL**					
6	**CREDIT CARDS:**					
7	MasterCard/Visa					
8	American Express					
9	Diners Club					
10	Other					
11	**OTHER RECEIPTS:**					
12	**TOTAL BANK DEPOSIT**					
13	**CASH SUMMARY** Part II					
14	Sales per Register					
15	Sales Tax per Register					
16	**ADJUSTMENTS:**					
17	Over/Under Rings					
18	Other: Complimentaries					
19	Other					
20	**TOTAL ADJUSTMENTS**					
21	Sales to Be Accounted For					
22	Sales Tax to Be Acctd. For					
23	Accounts Collected					
24	Other Receipts:					
25						
26						
27	**TIPS CHARGED:**					
28	MasterCard/Visa					
29	American Express					
30	Diners Club					
31	Other					
32	House Accounts-Tips					
33	**TOTAL RECEIPTS**					
34	**DEDUCT: PAID OUTS**					
35	Tips Paid Out					
36	House Charges					
37	Total Deductions					
38	**NET CASH RECEIPTS**					
39	**BANK DEPOSIT** (Line 12)					
40	**OVER or SHORT**					

Ticket Issuance Form

WAITPERSON	TOT #	#THRU	INITIALS	RETURN # VERIFIED
			TOTAL	

Cook's Report

ITEM	START	ADDITIONS	STARTING BALANCE	BALANCE ENDING	# SOLD
Shrimp dinners	25	9	34	21	13
				TOTAL	

Ticket Itemization Form

ITEM	USE A ✔ MARK TO DESIGNATE ONE SOLD	TOTAL SOLD
Shrimp dinner	✓ ✓ ✓ ✓ ✓ ✓ ✓ ✓ ✓ ✓ ✓ ✓	13
	TOTAL	

Want Sheet

ITEM	EMPLOYEE	APPROVED	ORDERED ON	RECEIVED

Kitchen Personnel & Job Descriptions

THE KITCHEN DIRECTOR

The primary objective of the kitchen director, or head chef, is to establish the maximum operational efficiency and food quality of the kitchen. The director is responsible for all the kitchen personnel and their training.

KITCHEN DIRECTOR'S MAIN RESPONSIBILITIES

1. Overseeing and training kitchen personnel.
2. Food quality.
3. Controlling waste and food cost.
4. Ordering, receiving, storing and issuing all food products.
5. Morale of the kitchen staff.
6. Health and safety regulation enforcement.
7. Communicating possible problem areas to the manager.
8. Scheduling all kitchen personnel.
9. Scheduling his/her own time.
10. Maintaining a clean and safe kitchen.
11. Holding kitchen staff meetings.
12. Filling out all forms for kitchen controls.

PREPARATION COOK

The preparation ("prep") cook generally is part of a team of other preparation cooks. Their primary responsibility is to prepare all the food items in the restaurant. Preparation cooks must follow the Recipe and Procedure Manual exactly as it is printed in order to ensure consistent products and food costs.

PREPARATION COOKS' RESPONSIBILITIES

1. Prepare all food products according to the prescribed methods.
2. Maintain the highest level of food quality obtainable.
3. Receive and store all products.
4. Maintain a clean and safe kitchen.
5. Follow all health and safety regulations.
6. Follow all restaurant regulations.
7. Control waste.
8. Communicate all problems and ideas for improvement to management.
9. Communicate and work together with co-workers as a team.
10. Arrive on time and ready to work.

---

11. Attend all meetings.
12. Maintain all equipment and utensils.
13. Organize all areas of the kitchen.
14. Follow proper rotation procedures.
15. Label and date all products prepared.
16. Follow management's instructions and suggestions.

COOKING STAFF

The cooking staff arrives one to two hours before the restaurant opens for business. Their primary responsibility is to cook the prepared food items. They must ensure that all food products have been prepared correctly before cooking. They are the last quality-control check before the food is presented to the waitstaff and the public.

COOKING STAFF RESPONSIBILITIES

1. Arrive on time and ready to work.
2. Ensure that proper preparation procedures have been completed.
3. Prepare the cooking areas for the shift.
4. Maintain high level of food quality.
5. Communicate with co-workers, waitstaff and management.
6. Be aware of what is happening in the dining room (e.g., arrival of a large group).
7. Account for every food item used.
8. Maintain a clean and safe kitchen.
9. Follow all health and safety regulations.
10. Follow all the restaurant regulations.
11. Control and limit waste.
12. Communicate problems and ideas to management.
13. Attend all meetings.
14. Fill out all forms required.
15. Maintain all kitchen equipment and utensils.
16. Keep kitchen clean and organized.
17. Follow the proper rotation procedures.
18. Label and date all products used.
19. Follow management's instructions and suggestions.

THE EXPEDITER

The expediter sets the pace and flow in the kitchen. He or she receives the order ticket from a server or from a printer in the kitchen and communicates which menu items need to be cooked to the cooking staff. The expediter lays out and garnishes all plates. He or she makes certain that the waitstaff receives the correct plates with the correct items. The expediter ensures that every food item leaving the kitchen has an order ticket.

EXPEDITER'S RESPONSIBILITIES

1. Communicate with everyone in the kitchen.
2. Always get an order ticket from a waiter/waitress or kitchen printer.
3. Ensure all food leaving the kitchen is of the level of quality prescribed.
4. Make certain all plates are hot and garnished correctly.
5. Make certain that every food item is accounted for.
6. Store all food order tickets for reference.
7. Fill out all required forms appropriately.
8. Maintain all equipment and utensils.
9. Keep own work area of the kitchen organized.
10. Follow all rotation procedures.
11. Follow management's instructions and suggestions.

DISHWASHER

A dishwasher must supply spotless, sanitized dishes to the dining room and clean kitchen utensils to the cooks. A slowdown in the dishwashing process will send repercussions throughout the restaurant. Improperly cleaned china, glassware or flatware can ruin an otherwise enjoyable dining experience.

DISHWASHER'S RESPONSIBILITIES

1. Know all glassware, china, flatware and kitchen utensils washing requirements.
2. Know the correct chemical usage.
3. Operate and maintain dish machines.
4. Keep dish area clean and organized.
5. Store all dishware properly to avoid contamination.
6. Follow management's instructions and suggestions.

CHAPTER 3

Liquor ordering is not as involved as purchasing food items. Liquor has a long shelf life and will rarely turn bad, which enables it to be ordered in large quantities on a less-frequent basis. Moreover, the quality is always consistent among distributors; they all carry the same products. Thus, it is far simpler to compare prices and terms knowing that each supplier has the same item. However, it is vital to be familiar with your state's laws and regulations regarding the sale and distribution of alcoholic beverages.

Bar & Beverage Management

Layout of a Typical Bar

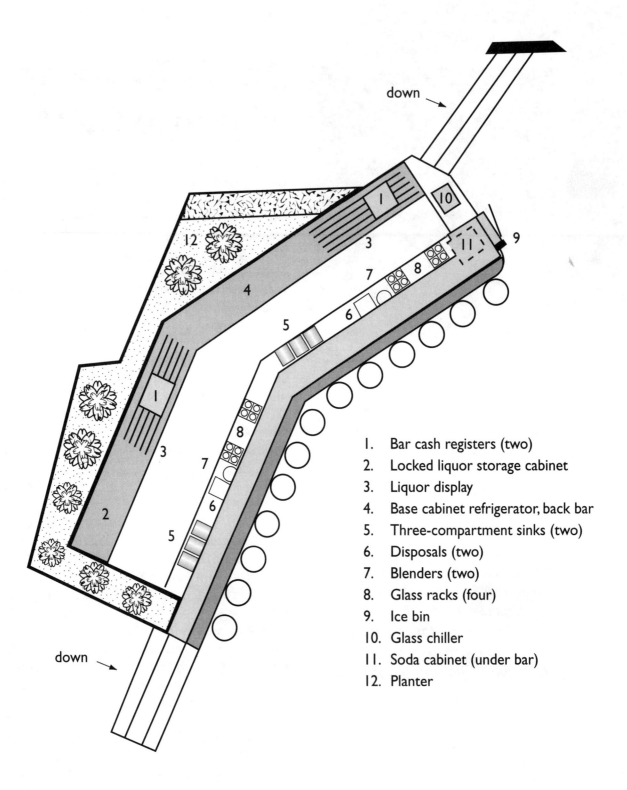

1. Bar cash registers (two)
2. Locked liquor storage cabinet
3. Liquor display
4. Base cabinet refrigerator, back bar
5. Three-compartment sinks (two)
6. Disposals (two)
7. Blenders (two)
8. Glass racks (four)
9. Ice bin
10. Glass chiller
11. Soda cabinet (under bar)
12. Planter

Bar Terminology

APERITIF A drink taken before a meal designed to stimulate the taste buds and appetite. It can be a liqueur, wine or cocktail. Sherry is an example of a popular aperitif.

BACK The companion drink, or a second cocktail, served in a second glass. "Bloody Mary with beer back" would be served in two glasses; one with the Bloody Mary and the other with the beer. Also referred to as a chaser.

BITTERS A very concentrated flavoring made from roots, barks, herbs and berries; used in an Old Fashioned cocktail.

CALL LIQUOR Any liquor other than well liquor. The term refers to "calling" the liquor brand by name, such as "Captain Morgan® and Coke" rather than "rum and coke."

CORDIAL A liquor (or liqueur) made by mixing or redistilling neutral spirits. Fruits, flowers, herbs, seeds, roots, plants or juices are used and a sweetening is added. Most cordials are sweet, colorful and highly concentrated. Many are made from secret recipes and processes.

CREME A cordial, such as Creme de Menthe, with a very high sugar content. Its cream-like consistency gives it its prefix.

DASH One-sixth of a teaspoon.

DRY "Dry" typically means "not sweet." A dry Manhattan means use dry vermouth instead of sweet vermouth. A dry martini refers to the use of dry vermouth.

DOUBLE Combining two drinks in one large glass. Double drinks may be stronger as there is less room for the mixer.

FLAG An orange slice and a cherry garnish held together by a fruit pick.

---

25 OF THE MOST COMMONLY ORDERED COCKTAILS:

- Screwdriver
- Sombrero
- Mai-Tai
- Piña Colada
- Old Fashioned
- Tequila Sunrise
- Gimlet
- Margarita
- Martini
- Cosmopolitan
- Manhattan
- Gibson
- Bloody Mary
- Stingers
- Coffee
- Collins Drinks
- Fizzes
- Daiquiri
- Sours
- White Russian
- Black Russian
- Alabama Slammer
- Gin and Tonic
- Juice/Punch Drinks
- Long Island Iced Tea

FRAPPES Several liqueurs combined and poured over shaved or crushed ice.

HIGHBALL A liquor served with ice, soda, plain water, ginger ale or other carbonated liquids.

JIGGER A jigger, or shot, is a small drinking glass-shaped container used to measure liquor.

LIQUEUR A sweet alcoholic beverage made from an infusion of flavoring ingredients and a spirit.

LIQUOR A distilled, alcoholic beverage made from a fermented mash of various ingredients.

MIST Crushed ice rather than cubed.

NEAT Liquor that is drank undiluted by ice, water or mixers.

ON THE ROCKS A beverage served over ice without adding water or other mixers.

PROOF The measure of the strength of the alcohol. One (degree) proof equals one-half of one percent of alcohol. For example, 100 proof equals 50% alcohol.

STRAIGHT UP Cocktails that are served up without ice.

TOP SHELF Expensive, high-quality brands such as Courvoisier®.

TWIST A lemon peel garnish. The peel is twisted over the drink, run around the rim and dropped in the drink.

VIRGIN A cocktail without alcohol.

WELL The standard "house" brand of liquors. Also the area where the drinks are made.

Liquid Measure Conversion Chart & Bar Supplies

CONVERSION CHART FOR LIQUID MEASURES

METRIC SIZE	FLUID OUNCES	U.S. MEASURE	FLUID OUNCES
50 ml	1.7	Miniature	1.6
200 ml	6.8	½ Pint	8.0
500 ml	16.9	1 Pint	16.0
750 ml	25.4	⅘ Quart	25.6
1 Liter	33.8	1 Quart	32.0
1.75 Liters	59.2	½ Gallon	64.0

SOME COMMONLY USED BAR MIXERS, JUICES & GARNISHES

JUICES

Orange juice

Cranberry juice

Pineapple juice

Grapefruit juice

Tomato juice

Lime juice

Lemon juice

FRESH FRUIT

Oranges

Limes

Bananas

Cherries

Strawberries

Lemon peels

Lemons

Pineapple

SODA & WATER

Coke or Pepsi

Diet Coke or Diet Pepsi

Sprite or 7-Up

Ginger ale

Tonic water

Soda water

Sparkling or mineral water

Purified water

GARNISHES

Cherries

Stuffed olives

Cocktail onions

Kosher salt

Celery salt

Super-fine bar sugar

MIXERS, MISC.

Sweet-and-sour bar mix

Coconut cream concentrate

Grenadine

Bitters

Orgeat syrup

Worcestershire sauce

Tabasco sauce

Sugar-saturated water

Beverage-Specific Garnishes & Drink Recipe Card

GARNISH GUIDELINES

- For alcoholic beverages, one straw for every drink with ice.

- Kiddie Cocktails – an orange flag or two cherries.

- Three cocktail onions per sword – in drink.

- Two olives per sword – in drink.

- Cherries – no sword.

- Twist – lemon peel used to flavor rim of glass, then dropped in drink.

DRINK GARNISHES

Manhattans: cherry

Gibson: cocktail onions

Martini: olives or a twist (ask customer's preference)

Collins and Sours: orange speared with a cherry

Tonic Drinks: lime wedge

Rob Roy: cherry

Old Fashioned: cherry

Drinks with Bloody Mary Mix: lime wedge or wheel and celery or pickle

Coffee Drinks: whipped cream, cherry

All Coolers: lime wheel or wedge

Pineapple Juice Drinks: pineapple wedge speared with a cherry

Orange Juice Drinks: orange speared with a cherry

Margaritas/Daiquiri: lime wheel or wedge

ITEM _____

INGREDIENTS:

_____

_____

_____

_____

_____

_____

_____

_____

_____

PROCEDURE:

_____

_____

_____

_____

_____

_____

_____

_____

_____

GLASS:

_____

_____

_____

GARNISH:

_____

_____

_____

Bar Abbreviations

MOST COMMONLY USED ABBREVIATIONS

And ...../	Straight Up ......↑	Coke ....../C	Grapefruit Juice ..../Grp
Vodka V	On The Rocks X	7-Up...../7	Tomato Juice ..../Tm
Gin .....G	Perfect.....Perf	Soda Water...../s	Pineapple Juice ../Pine
Rum .....R	Dry.....Dry	Tonic .....T	Cranberry Juice...../Crn
Tequila.....Teq	Extra Dry .....xDry	Splash .....Spl	Twist.....~
Bourbon .....B	Double .....Dbl	Ginger Ale ..../Gngr	Onion .....On
Scotch .....S	Tall.....Tall	Cream...../Cr	Olive .....Olv
Brandy .....Br	Water.....W	Orange Juice ..../OJ	Frozen .....Fr

POURING INSTRUCTIONS

Back.....Bk
Blended .....Blnd
Double .....Dbl
Dry .....Dry
Extra Dry.....xDry
Mist .....Mist
Neat.....Nt
Perfect .....Perf
Rocks.....X
Shot .....Sht
Splash .....Spl
Tall .....Tall
Virgin.....Vgn
With.....w/

WELL LIQUOR ABBREVIATIONS

Bourbon.....B
Brandy .....Br
Gin .....G
Rum .....R
Scotch .....S
Tequila .....Teq
Vodka V

MIXER ABBREVIATIONS

Coffee.....Cof
Coke ...../C
Cranberry juice ...../Crn
Diet Coke ...../Diet or /DC
Ginger ale ...../Gngr
Grapefruit juice ...../Grp
Half & Half ...../Cr
Orange juice ...../OJ
Pineapple juice...../Pine
Soda water or seltzer ...../s
7-Up ...../7
Sweet and Sour...../SS
Tomato juice ...../Tm
Water.....W

DRINK NAME ABBREVIATIONS

Black Russian.....Bl Rs
Bloody Maria.....B Maria
Bloody Mary.....B Mary
Brandy Alexander .....B Alex
Brandy Manhattan .....Br–Man
Cosmopolitan .....Cosmo
Daiquiri .....Daq
Dry Manhattan .....Dry–Man
Dry Martini .....Dry–Mar
Fuzzy Navel.....Fuzzy
Golden Cadillac .....G Cad
Grasshopper .....Grass
Greyhound.....Grey or V–Grape
Harvey Wallbanger .....Harv
Irish Coffee .....Irish C
John Collins.....John C
Kamikaze .....Kami
Lemon Drop .....Lem D
Long Island Iced Tea .....Tea
Manhattan .....Man
Margarita .....Marg
Martini .....Marti
Old Fashioned .....OF
Piña Colada.....Piña
Pink Lady.....P Lady
Pink Squirrel .....Sqrl
Presbyterian .....Press
Rob Roy .....R Rob
Rusty Nail.....Nail
Screwdriver .....V–OJ
Seabreeze .....Breeze

Bar Abbreviations

Singapore Sling ....Sling

Sombrero ....Kah–Cr

Stinger ....Sting

Tequila Sunrise ....T Sun

Toasted Almond ....TA

Tom Collins ....Tom C

Vodka Gimlet ....V–Gim

Vodka Martini ....V–Marti

White Russian ....W–Russ

NAME BRAND LIQUOR & LIQUEURS

Absolut 80° ....Absol

Absolut Citron ....Ab Citron

Absolut Mandarin .... Ab Mand

Absolut Peppar ....Ab Peppar

Bacardi Light Rum ....Bac

Bacardi Limon ....Bac Limon

Bacardi Select ....Bac Select

Bailey's Irish Cream ....Baileys

Beefeater ....Beef

Belvedere Vodka ....Belved

Benedictine & Brandy ....B&B

Benedictine ....Bene

Bombay Sapphire........Bom Sapph

Bombay .... Bom

Booker Noe Bourbon ....Booker

Bushmill's Irish ....Bush

Canadian Club........................CC

Chivas Regal ....Chivas

Chivas Royal Salute ....Salute

Chopin Vodka ....Chopin

Cointreau ....Coin

Courvoisier VS ....Cour VS

Courvoisier VSOP ....Cour VSOP

Crown Royal ....Crown

Cuervo 1800 1800

Cuervo Esp. Tequila ....Gold

Cutty Sark ....Cutty

Dewar's White ....Dewars

Di Saranno Amaretto ....Amo

Drambuie ....Dram

E & J Brandy ....E&J

Frangelico ....Fran

Galliano ....Gall

Gentleman Jack ....Gentleman

Glenfiddich ....Fiddich

Glenlivet................................Livet

Glenmorangie ....Moran

Godiva Chocolate ....Godiva

Goldschlager ....Schlager

Grand Marnier..................Marnier

Herradura Tequila..........Herradura

Irish Mist...............................Mist

J & B...JB

J. Walker Black Label ....Black

J. Walker Blue Label .... Blue

J. Walker Gold Label ....Gold Label

J. Walker Red Label ....Red

Jack Daniel's ....Jack

Jägermeister ....Jäger

Jameson Irish ....Jameson

Jim Beam Bourbon ....Beam

Kahlúa ....Kahlua

Leyden Gin ....Leyden

Maker's Mark ....Makers

Midori ....Midori

Myers's Jamaican ....Myers

Ouzo ....Ouzo

Patrón Tequila ....Patron

Peppermint Schnapps ......Pep Snp

Pinch 12-Year Scotch ....Pinch

Rumple Minze ....Rumple

Sauza Hornitos.....................Horn

Sauza Triada ....Triada

Seagram's Seven s7

Seagram's V.O..........................VO

Smirnoff ....Smirnoff

Smirnoff Black.............Smir Black

Southern Comfort ....Comfort

Stolichnaya ....Stoli

Stolichnaya Gold ....Stoli Gold

Stolichnaya Ohranj ....Ohranj

Stolichnaya Pertsovka....Pertsovka

Tanqueray Gin ....Tanq

Tanqueray Malacca..........Malacca

Tanqueray Ten ....Tanq 10

Tia Maria................................Tia

Van Gogh Gin ....Van Gogh

Wild Turkey 101 ....Turk 101

Wild Turkey 80 ....Turk 80

Wild Turkey Rare Breed ....Rare

Yukon Jack ....Yukon

Wine Terminology

ACIDITY   Refers to the wine's degree of sharpness or tartness to the taste. Acidity is an essential element that applies to the citric, malic, tartaric and lactic acids in wine. Acidic components give wine its longevity, but they need to be present in balance with other components of the wine.

AFTERTASTE   Aftertaste is the the taste that lingers in the back of your mouth. Also known as "finish."

AROMA   The scent of the grape rather than the wine-making process.

ASTRINGENCY   The quality that creates the dry, puckering sensation in the mouth, typically a result of the tannin content. Moderate astringency is considered desirable in most red table wines.

AUSTERE   Tannin or acid can make a wine hard or uninteresting.

BALANCE   A pleasing proportion of fruit, sugar, acidity, tannins, alcohol and other constituents of wine.

BODY   A wine's density and viscosity with reference to the impression of fullness or weight on the palate, such as light-bodied, medium-bodied, full-bodied.

BOUQUET   The part of a wine's fragrance which originates from fermentation and aging; as distinguished from aroma.

BREATHING   Leaving wine at room temperature for approximately 30 minutes upon opening to let the air mix with the wine to enhance flavor and aromas.

BRUT   Very dry champagne.

CELLAR   Storage place for wine, typically temperature-controlled.

CLEAR   A brilliant wine with no suspended solids or cloudiness.

COMPLEX   A variety and range of aromas and bouquets and multiple layers of flavor.

CORKING   The process of removing the cork from a bottle of wine.

DECANT   To pour wine from an old vintage bottle in which sediment has deposited.

DRY   The absence of sweetness. A wine in which most of the original grape sugar has been converted into alcohol.

FERMENTATION   The process of transforming sugar into alcohol (the juice of grapes into wine).

FORTIFIED   Increasing the alcohol content of wine by adding brandy. Fortified wines, such as Sherry and port, are about 50% stronger than table wines.

SEDIMENT   Material that settles to the bottom of a wine, common in old vintage red wines. The bottle should be stored upright before serving, so particles settle to the bottom.

SOFT   Low in acid and/or tannin; wines with a pleasant finish.

SOMMELIER   A wine steward or expert who offers guidance on choosing wine and serves wine.

SOUND   A wine with overall pleasing qualities: pleasant to look at, good-smelling and tasting.

SOUR   Wine that is too high in acid.

SPLIT   A 6-ounce bottle of wine.

SWEET WINE   Rich in natural sugar, the fermentation in sweet wine has been stopped before all the grape sugar has been turned into alcohol.

TANNIN   The organic compounds more often found in red wines than white. Tannins influence the flavor and taste on the palate. In red wines, they convey a fullness of body, giving a zing-like experience to the mouth. In sweet wines, tannin helps balance the sugar.

TART   Lots of acidity resulting in a wine agreeably flavored by fruit acids.

TAWNY   Rich, brownish hue and color.

THIN   Watery-tasting with little body or depth.

VARIETAL WINE   For a wine to be labeled a varietal, it must contain at least 75% of the named grape variety. Some examples are Cabernet Sauvignon, Chardonnay, Riesling, Zinfandel, etc.

VINTAGE WINE   If a vintage date is used on a label (1980), it means that at least 95% of the wine must be from grapes grown in that year.

WINERY   The building where the grapes are fermented into wine.

Wine Definitions & Stocking Guidelines

DEFINITIONS OF WINE CLASSIFICATIONS

LIGHT	Refers to the wine's body and/or alcohol content.
BODY	Refers to the fullness of the wine—its substantiality—which is described as light, medium or full.
DRY	Refers to the lack of sweetness in the wine.
SEMI-SWEET	Refers to the underlying sweetness of a wine.

RED WINE	NUMBER TO STOCK
Light-bodied—RED MEATS	4
Full-bodied—ALL RED MEATS, DUCK	4
Semi-sweet—DESSERT. Never before dinner, as the sweetness will spoil the customer's appetite.	4

WHITE WINE	NUMBER TO STOCK
Dry light-bodied—SHELLFISH, SOME SEAFOOD	2
Full-bodied—WHITE MEATS, SEAFOOD	4
Semi-sweet—SEAFOOD	4

ROSÉ	NUMBER TO STOCK
Dry light-bodied—Can be served in place of either dry white or red wines.	1

SPARKLING WINES	NUMBER TO STOCK
Dry—May be served in place of dry white wines.	1
Semi-sweet—May be served in place of semi-sweet whites.	1

CHAMPAGNE	NUMBER TO STOCK
Dry—WITH ANY ITEM	1
Extra-dry (Brut)—WITH ANY ITEM	1

Wine Pronunciation & Food Accompaniment

WINE PRONUNCIATION

Cabernet Sauvignon
Cah-bear-nay So-veen-yohn

Chardonnay
Shar-done-nay

Chenin Blanc
Chen-nahn Blohn

Fume Blanc
Foo-may Blohn

Johannisberg Riesling
Yo-han-iss-bairg Reez-ling

Merlot
Mare-low

Pinot Noir
Pea-no Nwar

Sauvignon Blanc
So-veen-yohn Blohn

FOOD ACCOMPANIMENT

To achieve the best match of food and wine, it is necessary to analyze the basic components in both the wine and the food. Neither the food nor the wine should overpower the other. The main elements to consider are:

- Flavor Intensity and Characteristic
- Weight
- Acidity
- Salt
- Sweetness

White Wines
Serve with: Seafood, Fish, Poultry, Creamed Soups, Cream Sauces

- Chardonnay
- Semillon
- Sauvignon Blanc
- Riesling
- Chenin Blanc

Blush Wines
Serve with: Desserts, Fruit, Ham, Pork, Salads

- White Zinfandel

Red Wines
Serve with: Steak, Roasts, Game, Pasta, Cheese, Ham, Veal, Pork

- Cabernet Sauvignon
- Merlot
- Pinot Noir
- Zinfandel

Proper Wine Opening

1. To ensure a correct order, always repeat the name of the wine once the guest has made a wine selection.

2. Upon serving, always place a napkin behind the bottle.

3. Display the bottle to the person who ordered it (usually the host). Give the guest plenty of time to examine the label: the guest will want to make sure it is the wine and vintage desired.

4. The wine opener used should be the waitperson's folding pocketknife, with the open spiral corkscrew and smooth edges.

5. With the knife blade, remove the capsule and foil.

6. Clean the neck and bottle with the napkin.

7. Hold the bottle firmly, and slowly insert the corkscrew into the center of the cork. Stop about two-thirds of the way through the cork. Don't go all the way, as this may result in dropping a few pieces of the cork into the wine.

8. With the bottle on the table, pull straight up, steadily. Do not jerk out the cork.

9. After opening, check the cork for dryness, and place it end up on the table so that the host may examine it.

10. When the host is satisfied, pour about an ounce into his glass. He must approve of the wine before the other people in the party are served.

11. The customer has the prerogative to reject a bottle of wine at any stage of the service. However, once the bottle is opened, his reasoning for rejection must be due to there being something wrong with the wine itself, not because he doesn't like it. If a bottle is rejected, it should be removed from the table and brought to the kitchen where the manager may examine it and act accordingly. Some distributors may issue a credit for damaged bottles, however, there is usually no obligation to do so, particularly with older, more expensive bottles.

12. It is customary to pour all the women's glasses first and the host's last. When you are finished pouring a glass, give the bottle a slight twist: this will prevent any dripping. Always pour wine with the label facing you. Serve fresh glasses with each new bottle.

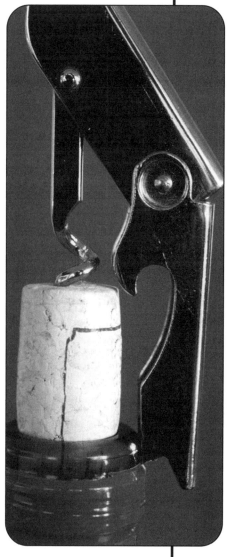

Alcohol Awareness

BLOOD ALCOHOL LEVELS

Alcohol is is a mood-altering drug. It may appear to be a stimulant, but it is actually a depressant, limiting bodily functions. As it is absorbed into the bloodstream, behavioral changes can occur. As the the liver oxidizes the alcohol and removes it from the body, the person's behavior returns to normal. This is often called "sobering up."

Only the passage of time rids the body of the effects of alcohol. Unfortunately, remedies such as black coffee, cold showers and exercise are not effective.

When you consume more alcohol than your liver can oxidize, the amount of alcohol in your blood increases. Blood Alcohol Concentration (BAC) is the amount of alcohol in the bloodstream. It is measured in percentages. For instance, having a BAC of 0.10 percent means that a person has 1 part alcohol per 1,000 parts blood in the body. BAC is the legal standard frequently used to indicate when a person is "driving under the influence" (DUI) or "driving while intoxicated" (DWI). BAC can be measured by breath, blood or urine tests.

Visible changes occur as a person's BAC increases. Their behavior changes visibly. Responsible servers are aware of the the progressive affects of alcohol and alert to the signs of over-indulgence. Although any one particular behavior may not indicate intoxication, a combination of several behaviors is a definite warning signal.

INTOXICATION VS. IMPAIRMENT

Impairment and intoxication are not the same thing. Impairment starts at the first drink. Impairment is the point where a person's intake of alcohol affects their ability to perform appropriately. Judgement, coordination and reaction time may be affected. Intoxication is a **legal** term defining the level of alcohol in the blood where impairment is so severe that criminal actions may be taken for driving or other activities. The level of legal intoxication is .08 in most states. Several states have additional definitions for people under age 21 (.00-.02). Some states also have mandatory jail time for drinking and driving while intoxicated.

CHECKING IDS

Serving alcohol to a minor can have very serious consequences. In fact, it is advisable to check the ID of any patron under who appears to be under 30, unless you are certain of a guest's age. In some cases, you could even be held accountable for serving someone with a fake ID. So be careful.

- Look for state seals or holograms.

- Look for any alterations, such as a cut around year of birth, or typesets that don't match.

- Make sure it's not someone else's ID. Carefully examine the picture/description to make sure it matches the person using it.

- Look for groups that 'pool' cash to an older person in the party.

In most states an acceptable ID is:
- A valid state driver's license, or a valid state identification for non-drivers.

- A valid passport.

- A valid United States Uniformed Service Identification (your employer should provide you with an example).

All IDs should have a picture, signature, birth date and description. Expired IDs are not acceptable.

Alcohol Awareness

GUIDELINES TO DETERMINE THE SYMPTOMS OF INTOXICATION

Service Guidelines

- Before serving a guest, determine his or her condition.

- If you think a customer is already intoxicated, offer snacks and get them a menu quickly.

- Keep track of drinks served. The service order is a ready reference of how many drinks each person consumed.

- Watch for changes in the customer's behavior. Don't hesitate to decline further service, if you think the customer is becoming intoxicated.

- Don't serve. If you have any doubts about a customer's condition, refuse service.

Intoxication Indicators

- Ordering more than one drink at a time.

- Buying drinks for others.

- Concentration problems, losing train of thought (especially when ordering).

- Drinking very fast.

- Careless with money on the bar, or can't pick up change.

- Complaining about drink strength, preparation or prices.

- Overly friendly with customers or employees.

- Loud behavior: talking or laughing and annoying other patrons or making too many comments about others in the establishment.

- Brooding, remaining very quiet, detached from others, continually drinking.

- Mood swings: happy to sad, or vice versa.

- Use of foul language.

- Lighting the wrong end of a cigarette.

DEALING WITH INTOXICATED PATRONS

If you notice someone appears to be intoxicated:

- Do not offer alcohol. Refill water, nonalcoholic beverages and bread. Offer dessert.

- Alert your supervisor immediately. He or she may arrange for a safe ride home for the guest or refuse service.

Employer Responsibilities

- Employers should record incidences of refusal of sales in your manager's log. It serves as a legal record of your responsible alcohol practices in the event of a liability claim.

- Signs should be posted within guests' view with policies on alcohol consumption and responsible hospitality.

- All employees are trained in alcohol awareness and attendance has been documented.

Alcohol Awareness Test

1. Drinking and driving is the number two killer of Americans between the ages of 17–24, second only to cancer.
   a. True
   b. False

2. Statistically, in the United States, one person is killed in drunk driving accidents every:
   a. 24 hours
   b. 72 hours
   c. 90 minutes
   d. 22 minutes

3. A bartender sells a pitcher of beer with four glasses to a customer who is over 21 years of age. The customer takes the beer and glasses to a table. Later, police officers determine two of the four at the table are only 18. The bartender is not at fault.
   a. True
   b. False

4. The legal drinking age in your area is:
   a. 18
   b. 20
   c. 21

5. If a customer appears to be over the legal drinking age, you do not have to request an ID in order to serve them an alcoholic beverage.
   a. True
   b. False

6. Due to their bodies' fat distribution and a decreased amount of alcohol-metabolizing enzymes, women may respond more quickly to alcohol:
   a. True
   b. False

7. Intoxication is a legal term that establishes a certain level of alcohol in the blood as the point of impairment severe enough that criminal sanctions may be enforced for driving and other actions. You can be impaired without being intoxicated.
   a. True
   b. False

9. To counter the effects of alcohol, people should drink coffee or take a cold shower to "sober up."
   a. True
   b. False

8. Which of the following are acceptable IDs to determine the age of a guest who is requesting an alcoholic beverage:
   a. A valid state driver's license, a valid state identification with a photograph and date of birth for those who don't drive, a valid passport, a valid United States Uniformed Service Identification.
   b. A valid state driver's license, a birth certificate and credit card with the same name listed in combination, a school ID from a valid university with a birth date listed next to the picture, a valid passport.
   c. A valid state driver's license, a school ID from a valid university with a birth date listed next to the picture, a valid passport, a valid United States Uniformed Service Identification.

10. One drink is the equivalent of a 12-oz. glass of beer, a 5-oz. pour of wine or a mixed drink with about 1 oz. of alcohol. Approximately how long does it take the liver to eliminate the alcohol in one drink from the body?
    a. 15 minutes
    b. 30 minutes
    c. One hour
    d. Two hours

11. Blood Alcohol Concentration charts are the only way of determining the amount of alcohol circulating in a person's bloodstream.
    a. True
    b. False

12. Everyone metabolizes alcohol at the same rate.
    a. True
    b. False

13. Beer and wine have less alcohol than tequila.
    a. True
    b. False

14. Offering low- or nonalcoholic beverages, appetizers, bread and water are good ways of promoting responsible alcohol consumption.
    a. True
    b. False

Alcohol Awareness Test

15. Which of the following behaviors are possible signs that a customer may be intoxicated? (Check all that apply.)
    - ❑ He or she is overly friendly and annoying other customers.
    - ❑ Eyes are glassy, the pupils are somewhat dilated, unfocused, sleepy-looking.
    - ❑ Trying to light a cigarette but is unable to do so upon the first try.
    - ❑ Purse is open and items are falling out but doesn't notice.
    - ❑ Spilling drinks.
    - ❑ Speech is slurred.
    - ❑ Loses his train of thought while trying to communicate order to you.
    - ❑ Sways and staggers a little and appears to lose balance only for a quick moment.

16. Once you have determined that a customer entering the establishment is intoxicated, what is the proper course of action?
    a. The customer should be served no more than one drink. Since he or she drank more elsewhere, if you serve them only one drink, you will not be liable and won't make him or her angry.
    b. The customer should be asked to leave.
    c. The customer should not be served any additional alcoholic beverages, and arrangements should be made so the customer is not driving.

17. Restaurant patrons' dining experience can be enhanced by enjoying wine and alcohol with their meal in a responsible manner.
    a. True
    b. False

18. As a special promotion for a certain brands of alcohol, it is legal to have "super cheap and super double shooter nights" if you count the number of "super cheap and super double shooters" each customer consumes.
    a. True
    b. False

19. The best way to inform someone that they have had their quota of drinks is by:
    a. Communicating with him or her in a friendly, caring and non-threatening manner and alerting a manager if necessary.
    b. Pretending not to hear his or her requests for additional drinks.
    c. Asking the patron to leave.

20. Food and water may slow the onset of alcohol into the bloodstream, so it's important that water and appetizers are offered, and bread is served right away. As long as a customer is eating, you can serve him or her as much alcohol as he or she would like.
    a. True
    b. False

21. If you serve alcohol to someone who is intoxicated, you may be personally liable for any damages that incur from their drunken behavior and may have to pay monetary damages.
    a. True
    b. False

22. Statistically, how many Americans do NOT drink alcohol?
    a. One in ten
    b. One in twenty
    c. One in three

23. Serving alcohol in a responsible manner protects you, your friends, your family and your employer's or your business.
    a. True
    b. False

24. Intoxication is the point where one's intake of alcohol affects their ability to perform appropriately.
    a. True
    b. False

25. Blood Alcohol Concentration, or BAC, measures the number of grams of alcohol in 100 milliliters of blood. The level of legal intoxication is .20 in most states.
    a. True
    b. False

Alcohol Awareness Test Answer Key

1. Drinking and driving is the number two killer of Americans between the ages of 17–24, second only to cancer.
    a. True
    (b.) **False–it is the number one killer.**

2. Statistically, in the United States, one person is killed in drunk driving accidents every:
    a. 24 hours
    b. 72 hours
    c. 90 minutes
    (d.) **22 minutes**

3. A bartender sells a pitcher of beer with four glasses to a customer who is over 21 years of age. The customer takes the beer and glasses to a table. Later, police officers determine two of the four at the table are only 18. The bartender is not at fault.
    a. True
    (b.) **False**

4. The legal drinking age in your area is:
    a. 18
    b 20
    (c.) **21–in most states**

5. If a customer appears to be over the legal drinking age, you do not have to request an ID in order to serve them an alcoholic beverage.
    a. True
    (b.) **False**

6. Due to their bodies' fat distribution and a decreased amount of alcohol-metabolizing enzymes, women may respond more quickly to alcohol:
    (a.) **True**
    b. False

7. Intoxication is a legal term that establishes a certain level of alcohol in the blood as the point of impairment severe enough that criminal sanctions may be enforced for driving and other actions. You can be impaired without being intoxicated.
    (a.) **True**
    b. False

9. To counter the effects of alcohol, people should drink coffee or take a cold shower to "sober up."
    a. True
    (b.) **False–Only removal of alcohol from the body via the liver sobers people**

8. Which of the following are acceptable IDs to determine the age of a guest who is requesting an alcoholic beverage:
    (a.) **A valid state driver's license, a valid state identification with a photograph and date of birth for those who don't drive, a valid passport, a valid United States Uniformed Service Identification.**
    b. A valid state driver's license, a birth certificate and credit card with the same name listed in combination, a school ID from a valid university with a birth date listed next to the picture, a valid passport.
    c. A valid state driver's license, a school ID from a valid university with a birth date listed next to the picture, a valid passport, a valid United States Uniformed Service Identification.

10. One drink is the equivalent of a 12-oz. glass of beer, a 5-oz. pour of wine or a mixed drink with about 1 oz. of alcohol. Approximately how long does it take the liver to eliminate the alcohol in one drink from the body?
    a. 15 minutes
    b. 30 minutes
    (c.) **One hour**
    d. Two hours

11. Blood Alcohol Concentration charts are the only way of determining the amount of alcohol circulating in a person's bloodstream.
    a. True
    (b.) **False**

12. Everyone metabolizes alcohol at the same rate.
    a. True
    (b.) **False**

13. Beer and wine have less alcohol than tequila.
    a. True
    (b.) **False**

14. Offering low- or nonalcoholic beverages, appetizers, bread and water are good ways of promoting responsible alcohol consumption.
    (a.) **True**
    b. False

Alcohol Awareness Test Answer Key

15. Which of the following behaviors are possible signs that a customer may be intoxicated? (Check all that apply.)
    - ☑ **He or she is overly friendly and annoying other customers.**
    - ☑ **Eyes are glassy, the pupils are somewhat dilated, unfocused, sleepy-looking.**
    - ☑ **Trying to light a cigarette but is unable to do so upon the first try.**
    - ☑ **Purse is open and items are falling out but doesn't notice.**
    - ☑ **Spilling drinks.**
    - ☑ **Speech is slurred.**
    - ☑ **Loses his train of thought while trying to communicate order to you.**
    - ☑ **Sways and staggers a little and appears to lose balance only for a quick moment.**

16. Once you have determined that a customer entering the establishment is intoxicated, what is the proper course of action?
    a. The customer should be served no more than one drink. Since he or she drank more elsewhere, if you serve them only one drink, you will not be liable and won't make him or her angry.
    b. The customer should be asked to leave.
    (c.) **The customer should not be served any additional alcoholic beverages, and arrangements should be made so the customer is not driving.**

17. Restaurant patrons' dining experience can be enhanced by enjoying wine and alcohol with their meal in a responsible manner.
    (a.) **True**
    b. False

18. As a special promotion for a certain brands of alcohol, it is legal to have "super cheap and super double shooter nights" if you count the number of "super cheap and super double shooters" each customer consumes.
    a. True
    (b.) **False**

19. The best way to inform someone that they have had their quota of drinks is by:
    (a.) **Communicating with him or her in a friendly, caring and non-threatening manner and alerting a manager if necessary.**
    b. Pretending not to hear his or her requests for additional drinks.
    c. Asking the patron to leave.

20. Food and water may slow the onset of alcohol into the bloodstream, so it's important that water and appetizers are offered, and bread is served right away. As long as a customer is eating, you can serve him or her as much alcohol as he or she would like.
    a. True
    (b.) **False**

21. If you serve alcohol to someone who is intoxicated, you may be personally liable for any damages that incur from their drunken behavior and may have to pay monetary damages.
    (a.) **True**
    b. False

22. Statistically, how many Americans do NOT drink alcohol?
    a. One in ten
    b. One in twenty
    (c.) **One in three**

23. Serving alcohol in a responsible manner protects you, your friends, your family and your employer's or your business.
    (a.) **True**
    b. False

24. Intoxication is the point where one's intake of alcohol affects their ability to perform appropriately.
    a. True
    (b.) **False–that is the definition of impairment.**

25. Blood Alcohol Concentration, or BAC, measures the number of grams of alcohol in 100 milliliters of blood. The level of legal intoxication is .20 in most states.
    a. True
    (b.) **False–the level of legal intoxication is between .08 and .10 in most states.**

Blood Alcohol Content Chart

ONE DRINK EQUALS

12 ounces of beer
(5% alcohol content)

=

3 ounces of wine
(12% alcohol content)

=

1 ounce of spirits
(80 proof)

BAC CHARTS ARE ONLY A GUIDELINE.
THERE ARE NUMEROUS VARIABLES THAT DETERMINE HOW ALCOHOL AFFECTS INDIVIDUALS

MALE

Percentage of alcohol in bloodstream based on weight and consumption.

Weight	NUMBER OF DRINKS CONSUMED IN ONE HOUR OF TIME								
	1	2	3	4	5	6	7	8	9
100	.04	.08	.11	.15	.19	.23	.26	.30	.34
120	.03	.06	.09	.12	.16	.19	.22	.25	.28
140	.03	.05	.08	.11	.13	.16	.19	.21	.24
160	.02	.05	.07	.09	.12	.14	.16	.19	.21
180	.02	.04	.06	.08	.11	.13	.15	.17	.19
200	.02	.04	.06	.08	.09	.11	.13	.15	.17
220	.02	.03	.05	.07	.09	.10	.12	.14	.15
240	.02	.03	.05	.06	.08	.09	.11	.13	.14

FEMALE

Percentage of alcohol in bloodstream based on weight and consumption.

Weight	NUMBER OF DRINKS CONSUMED IN ONE HOUR OF TIME								
	1	2	3	4	5	6	7	8	9
100	.05	.09	.14	.18	.23	.27	.32	.36	.41
120	.04	.08	.11	.15	.19	.23	.27	.30	.34
140	.03	.07	.10	.13	.16	.19	.23	.26	.29
160	.03	.06	.09	.11	.14	.17	.20	.23	.26
180	.03	.05	.08	.10	.13	.15	.18	.20	.23
200	.02	.05	.07	.09	.11	.14	.16	.18	.20
220	.02	.04	.06	.08	.10	.12	.14	.17	.19
240	.02	.04	.06	.08	.09	.11	.13	.15	.17

Alcohol's Effect on Driving Skills

ONE DRINK EQUALS

12 ounces of beer (5% alcohol content) =  **3 ounces of wine (12% alcohol content)** = **1 ounce of spirits (80 proof)**

 **Blood Alcohol Content .02%**
Tracking ability diminishing. The ability to focus on tasks and pay attention may suffer.

Blood Alcohol Content .05%
Vision is impaired. Judgment and restraint slacken. Steering errors increase.

3-4 drinks
Blood Alcohol Content .08% (legally drunk in most states)
Reaction times noticeably slower. You're 3 to 4 times more likely to have an accident than a sober driver.
 2-4 drinks

3-5 drinks
Blood Alcohol Content .10%
Reaction time slows even more. Movements are clumsy and uncoordinated. You are 6 times more likely to have an accident.
 2-5 drinks

4-7 drinks
Blood Alcohol Content .15%
Reaction time increasingly affected. Your field of vision narrows. You are 25 times more likely to have an accident.
 3-7 drinks

Employee Alcohol Policy Notification Agreement

Date: _____ Employee: _____

As a server of alcoholic beverages, I understand that I have a legal responsibility to refuse service to anyone under the legal drinking age or to anyone who is already intoxicated.

I will immediately stop serving alcoholic beverages to any person who exhibits signs of intoxication, such as the following:

- ❑ He or she is overly friendly and annoying other customers.
- ❑ His or her eyes are glassy, the pupils are somewhat dilated, unfocused and sleepy-looking.
- ❑ He or she is trying to light a cigarette but is unable to do so upon the first try.
- ❑ Her purse is open and items are falling out but she doesn't notice.
- ❑ He or she is spilling drinks.
- ❑ His or her speech is slurred.
- ❑ He or she loses train of thought while trying to communicate.
- ❑ He or she sways and staggers and appears to lose balance.

I agree to follow the policies established by management for the responsible service of alcoholic beverages.

_____
Signature

Service Refusal Form

If, at any time, you feel a patron is intoxicated and should not be served any more alcohol, notify your supervisor immediately. Then fill out the form below to the best of your ability.

Date: _____

Name of Employee Refusing Service:

_____

Please write a short description of why you felt the individual should not have been served alcohol or when the decision was made to discontinue further service.

_____

_____

_____

_____

_____

_____

_____

Did the patron exhibit signs of intoxication, such as the following? Check all that apply.

- ❑ Slurred speech
- ❑ Difficulty lighting a cigarette
- ❑ Arguing with or annoying other guests
- ❑ Tearfulness
- ❑ Drowsiness
- ❑ Difficulty focusing eyes
- ❑ Memory loss
- ❑ Spilling drinks
- ❑ Falling or stumbling
- ❑ Difficulty picking up change

Please provide specific information about the customer.

Customer's Name (if known): _____

Sex: ○ M ○ F   Height: _____ Weight: _____

Hair: _____   Eyes: _____   Age: _____

Approximately how long was the customer on the premises?

_____

Please list, if known, the time the customer entered, left and was denied service:

Arrival	_____	a.m./p.m
Departure	_____	a.m./p.m.
Time Service Denied	_____	a.m./p.m.

How many drinks did the customer have on the premises?
○ 1-2   ○ 3-4   ○ 5-6   ○ 7-10   ○ _____

What was the customer drinking?

_____

How much money did the patron spend?

_____

What was the customer's reaction to being refused service?

_____

_____

_____

Was a cab called for the customer? ○ Yes   ○ No

Was an alternate method of transportation offered?
○ Yes (please list) _____   ○ No

Were the police called? ○ Yes   ○ No

Did anyone witness the refusal of service? ○ Yes   ○ No
If so, please list their names.

_____

_____

_____

_____

_____

_____

Signature of Employee   **Print Name**   **Position**

_____

Signature of Manager on Duty   **Print Name**

WARNING
Drinking Alcoholic Beverages During Pregnancy Can Cause Birth Defects

Liquor Requisition

DATE:	SERVICE AREA:		SHIFT:	

ITEM	# EMPTIES	BOTTLE SIZE	BAR	MANAGEMENT

Beverage Requisition Form

DATE:	ISSUED FROM:		ISSUED TO:			

BRAND & KIND OF BEVERAGE	Size	Ordered	Delivered	Perpetual Marked	Cost	Extension

Beverage Perpetual Inventory

Product: _____   Distributor: _____

Size: _____   Case Cost: $_____   Bottle Cost: $ _____

Date	Requisitioned Inventory/Size	Purchases/ Size	On-Hand Inventory/Size	Manager's Initials

NOTES/COMMENTS:

Bar Inventory & Requisition

Date: _____ Inventory Taken By: _____

Issued By: _____ Received By: _____

Description	List #	Size	Par Stock	On Hand	REQUISITION					INVENTORY	
					Qty.	Unit Cost	Total Cost	Unit Sale Value	Total Sale Value	Unit Cost	Total Cost

Wine Cellar Issue

Date: _____

Product	Vintage	# of Bottles	Guest Check #	Removed By

NOTES/COMMENTS:

Wine Cellar Bin Card

BIN CARD _____

Date: _____ Product: _____

Balance Brought Forward: _____ Bottle Size: _____

DATE	IN	OUT	TOTAL ON HAND

BIN CARD _____

Date: _____ Product: _____

Balance Brought Forward: _____ Bottle Size: _____

DATE	IN	OUT	TOTAL ON HAND

Bottled Beer Count Form

Date: _____ Employee: _____

Brand	Begin Inventory	Bar Req.	Adjust. Inventory	End Inventory	Depletion	Sales Price	Est. Sales
	+	=	-	=	X	$	$
	+	=	-	=	X	$	$
	+	=	-	=	X	$	$
	+	=	-	=	X	$	$
	+	=	-	=	X	$	$
	+	=	-	=	X	$	$
	+	=	-	=	X	$	$
	+	=	-	=	X	$	$
	+	=	-	=	X	$	$
	+	=	-	=	X	$	$
	+	=	-	=	X	$	$
	+	=	-	=	X	$	$
	+	=	-	=	X	$	$
	+	=	-	=	X	$	$
	+	=	-	=	X	$	$
	+	=	-	=	X	$	$
	+	=	-	=	X	$	$

Total Estimated Sales	$
(subtract) Complimentary Sales @ Retail	$
(subtract) Waste & Spillage @ Retail	$
(EQUALS) Adjusted Estimated Sales	$
(subtract) Cash Register Sales	$
EXTENSION TOTAL	$

Bartender's Report

BARTENDER —————————————— BARTENDER ——————————————

MANAGER —————————————— MANAGER ——————————————

BOOKKEEPER —————————————— BOOKKEEPER ——————————————

CASH IN

$100.00 _____	$1.00 _____
$50.00 _____	$0.50 _____
$20.00 _____	$0.25 _____
$10.00 _____	$0.10 _____
$5.00 _____	$0.05 _____
$1.00 _____	$0.01 _____
TOTAL	TOTAL

CASH OUT

$100.00 _____	$1.00 _____
$50.00 _____	$0.50 _____
$20.00 _____	$0.25 _____
$10.00 _____	$0.10 _____
$5.00 _____	$0.05 _____
$1.00 _____	$0.01 _____
TOTAL	TOTAL

CHARGES

1. _____
2. _____
3. _____
4. _____
5. _____
6. _____

TOTAL

SALES SUMMARY

LIQUOR SALES _____

FOOD SALES _____

WINE SALES _____

MISC. SALES _____

TOTAL

SALES TAX _____

VOID SALES _____

Note: Itemize checks separately on back.
Enter figure in sale and sales breakdown.

ITEM	LIQUOR	WINE
Housed	_____	_____
Manager	_____	_____
Comp	_____	_____

EMPLOYEE _____
Total # _____   #__# _____   Initial ____
Return _____   Verify _____

EMPLOYEE _____
Total # _____   #__# _____   Initial ____
Return _____   Verify _____

EMPLOYEE _____
Total # _____   #__# _____   Initial ____
Return _____   Verify _____

Liquor Order Form

ITEM	BUILD TO AMT.	DATE									

Liquor/Wine Inventory Form

ITEM	SIZE	QUANTITY				TOTAL	COST	EXTENSION

Inventory Form

Date: _____   Total Liquor: _____

Inventory By: _____   Total Beer: _____

Extension By: _____   Total Wine: _____

Examined By: _____

Product	Size	Open Bottles	Full Bottles	Store-room	Total	Cost	Extension

EXTENSION [   ]

Liquor Used & Restocked Form

LIQUOR	USED	RESTOCKED	LIQUOR	USED	RESTOCKED

Bar & Inventory Control Report

Date: _____ Time: _____

Inventory By: _____ Approved By: _____

ITEM _____ Unit _____

Opening Inventory _____

+ Requisitions: _____

TOTAL Inventory: _____

Closing Inventory: _____

TOTAL OF AMOUNT SOLD: _____
(subtract Closing Inventory from Total Inventory)

TOTAL OF AMOUNT SOLD: _____

x Price _____

Cost of Goods Sold: _____
(multiply the Total of Amount Sold by the Price)

# of Drinks Sold: _____

x Sales Price _____

TOTAL RETAIL VALUE: _____
(multiply the Number of Drinks Sold by the Sales Price)

LIQUOR COST PERCENTAGE: _____
(divide the Cost of Goods Sold by the Total Retail Value)

ITEM _____ Unit _____

Opening Inventory _____

+ Requisitions: _____

TOTAL Inventory: _____

Closing Inventory: _____

TOTAL OF AMOUNT SOLD: _____
(subtract Closing Inventory from Total Inventory)

TOTAL OF AMOUNT SOLD: _____

x Price _____

Cost of Goods Sold: _____
(multiply the Total of Amount Sold by the Price)

# of Drinks Sold: _____

x Sales Price _____

TOTAL RETAIL VALUE: _____
(multiply the Number of Drinks Sold by the Sales Price)

LIQUOR COST PERCENTAGE: _____
(divide the Cost of Goods Sold by the Total Retail Value)

ITEM _____ Unit _____

Opening Inventory _____

+ Requisitions: _____

TOTAL Inventory: _____

Closing Inventory: _____

TOTAL OF AMOUNT SOLD: _____
(subtract Closing Inventory from Total Inventory)

TOTAL OF AMOUNT SOLD: _____

x Price _____

Cost of Goods Sold: _____
(multiply the Total of Amount Sold by the Price)

# of Drinks Sold: _____

x Sales Price _____

TOTAL RETAIL VALUE: _____
(multiply the Number of Drinks Sold by the Sales Price)

LIQUOR COST PERCENTAGE: _____
(divide the Cost of Goods Sold by the Total Retail Value)

Liquor Storeroom Inventory Report

Date: _____ Time: _____

Inventory By: _____ Approved By: _____

Item	Unit	Opening Invent.	Purchases	Totals (A)	Requisitions by day of period month:							Totals (B)	Balance (A less B)	Closing Invent.	+ / -	Price	Extension

Beverage Consumption Report

Date: _____   Event: _____

Beverage Type	Beginning Amount	Additions	Total Avail.	End Amount	Total Usage	Unit Cost	Total Cost
BEER							
1.							
2.							
3.							
4.							
LIQUOR							
1.							
2.							
3.							
4.							
5.							
6.							
WINE							
1.							
2.							
3							
OTHER							
1.							
2.							

TOTAL PRODUCT COST

Total Product Cost: _____   Cost Per Guest: _____   # Guests Served: _____

Liquor Waste Tracking Sheet

DATE	ITEM WASTED	AMOUNT	UNIT	REASON	COST
				TOTAL WASTE	

Drink Spill Sheet

DATE	SERVER NAME	DRINK	REASON	INITIALS

Cost of Beverage Consumed

Accounting Period

_____ to _____

Beginning Inventory $ _____

    (+)

Purchases $ _____

Goods Available $ _____

    (-)

Ending Inventory $ _____

    (-) $ _____

Transfers from Bar $ _____

    (+) $ _____

Transfers to Bar $ _____

Cost of Beverage Consumed $ _____

Beverage Cost Estimate

DATE	ISSUES		SALES		BEV. COST ESTIMATE	
	TODAY	TO DATE	TODAY	TO DATE	TODAY	TO DATE
Subtotal						
+ / -						
TOTAL						

Beverage Cost Report

Prepared By: _____   **Date:** _____

DATE	DAY		SALES
	SUNDAY	1st shift	
		2nd shift	
	MONDAY	1st shift	
		2nd shift	
	TUESDAY	1st shift	
		2nd shift	
	WEDNESDAY	1st shift	
		2nd shift	
	THURSDAY	1st shift	
		2nd shift	
	FRIDAY	1st shift	
		2nd shift	
	SATURDAY	1st shift	
		2nd shift	
		TOTAL	$

$$\frac{\text{Cost of Goods Sold (\$} \underline{\hspace{2cm}})}{\text{Total Beverage Sales (\$} \underline{\hspace{2cm}})} = \text{Beverage Cost Percentage (} \underline{\hspace{1cm}} \text{ x 100 = } \underline{\hspace{1cm}} \text{\%)}$$

Beverage Cost Report II

Prepared By: _____   Date: _____

	SUN	MON	TUE	WED	THUR	FRI	SAT	TOTAL
1st Shift Sales								
LIQUOR								
WINE								
BEER								
SHIFT TOTAL								
2nd Shift Sales								
LIQUOR								
WINE								
BEER								
SHIFT TOTAL								
DAILY TOTAL								

PERIOD BEVERAGE COST BREAKDOWN — SALES MANAGEMENT ANALYSIS

	Cost of Goods Sold	Sales (Shift Totals)	Beverage Cost %	Sales	Retail Value	Over (Short)
Item						
LIQUOR						
WINE						
BEER						
TOTAL						

Cost Per Ounce — 750ML

The table below shows the cost per ounce for 750ml bottles ranging in price between $1.02 and $25.65. To figure the cost per ounce for 750ml bottles that cost more than $25.65, divide the bottle cost by 25.4 oz.

750ml Cost	$/oz.	750ml Cost	$/oz.	750ml Cost	$/oz.	750ml Cost	$/oz.
$1.02 – $1.26	.04	$7.37 – $7.61	.29	$13.73 – $13.97	.54	$20.07 – $20.31	.79
$1.27 – $1.52	.05	$7.62 – $7.87	.30	$13.98 – $14.22	.55	$20.32 – $20.57	.80
$1.53 – $1.77	.06	$7.88 – $8.12	.31	$14.23 – $14.47	.56	$20.58 – $20.82	.81
$1.78 – $2.03	.07	$8.13 – $8.38	.32	$14.48 – $14.73	.57	$20.83 – $21.08	.82
$2.04 – $2.28	.08	$8.39 – $8.63	.33	$14.74 – $14.98	.58	$21.09 – $21.33	.83
$2.29 – $2.53	.09	$8.64 – $8.88	.34	$14.99 – $15.23	.59	$21.34 – $21.58	.84
$2.54 – $2.79	.10	$8.89 – $9.14	.35	$15.24 – $15.49	.60	$21.59 – $21.84	.85
$2.80 – $3.04	.11	$9.15 – $9.39	.36	$15.50 – $15.74	.61	$21.85 – $22.09	.86
$3.05 – $3.30	.12	$9.40 – $9.65	.37	$15.75 – $16.00	.62	$22.10 – $22.35	.87
$3.31 – $3.55	.13	$9.66 – $9.90	.38	$16.01 – $16.25	.63	$22.36 – $22.60	.88
$3.56 – $3.80	.14	$9.91 – $10.15	.39	$16.26 – $16.50	.64	$22.61 – $22.85	.89
$3.81 – $4.06	.15	$10.16 – $10.41	.40	$16.51 – $16.75	.65	$22.86 – $23.11	.90
$4.07 – $4.31	.16	$10.42 – $10.66	.41	$16.76 – $17.01	.66	$23.12 – $23.36	.91
$4.32 – $4.57	.17	$10.67 – $10.92	.42	$17.02 – $17.27	.67	$23.37 – $23.62	.92
$4.58 – $4.82	.18	$10.93 – $11.17	.43	$17.28 – $17.52	.68	$23.63 – $23.87	.93
$4.83 – $5.07	.19	$11.18 – $11.42	.44	$17.53 – $17.77	.69	$23.88 – $24.12	.94
$5.08 – $5.33	.20	$11.43 – $11.68	.45	$17.78 – $18.03	.70	$24.13 – $24.38	.95
$5.34 – $5.58	.21	$11.69 – $11.93	.46	$18.04 – $18.28	.71	$24.39 – $24.63	.96
$5.59 – $5.84	.22	$11.94 – $12.19	.47	$18.29 – $18.54	.72	$24.64 – $24.89	.97
$5.85 – $6.09	.23	$12.20 – $12.44	.48	$18.55 – $18.79	.73	$24.90 – $25.14	.98
$6.10 – $6.34	.24	$12.45 – $12.69	.49	$18.80 – $19.04	.74	$25.15 – $25.39	.99
$6.35 – $6.60	.25	$12.70 – $12.95	.50	$19.05 – $19.30	.75	$25.40 – $25.65	1.00
$6.61 – $6.85	.26	$12.96 – $13.20	.51	$19.31 – $19.55	.76		
$6.86 – $7.11	.27	$13.21 – $13.46	.52	$19.56 – $19.81	.77		
$7.12 – $7.36	.28	$13.47 – $13.72	.53	$19.82 – $20.06	.78		

Cost Per Ounce — Liters

The table below shows the cost per ounce for liter bottles ranging in price between $1.00 and $34.13. To figure the cost per ounce for liters that cost more than $34.13, divide the bottle cost by 33.8 oz.

Liter Cost	$/oz.	Liter Cost	$/oz.	Liter Cost	$/oz.	Liter Cost	$/oz.
$1.00 – $1.35	.03	$9.47 – $9.80	.28	$17.92 – $18.25	.53	$26.37 – $26.70	.78
$1.36 – $1.68	.04	$9.81 – $10.13	.29	$18.26 – $18.58	.54	$26.71 – $27.03	.79
$1.69 – $2.02	.05	$10.14 – $10.47	.30	$18.59 – $18.92	.55	$27.04 – $27.37	.80
$2.03 – $2.36	.06	$10.48 – $10.81	.31	$18.93 – $19.26	.56	$27.38 – $27.71	.81
$2.37 – $2.70	.07	$10.82 – $11.15	.32	$19.27 – $19.60	.57	$27.72 – $28.05	.82
$2.71 – $3.04	.08	$11.16 – $11.49	.33	$19.61 – $19.94	.58	$28.06 – $28.39	.83
$3.05 – $3.37	.09	$11.50 – $11.82	.34	$19.95 – $20.27	.59	$28.40 – $28.72	.84
$3.38 – $3.71	.10	$11.83 – $12.16	.35	$20.28 – $20.61	.60	$28.73 – $29.06	.85
$3.72 – $4.05	.11	$12.17 – $12.50	.36	$20.62 – $20.95	.61	$29.07 – $29.40	.86
$4.06 – $4.39	.12	$12.51 – $12.84	.37	$20.96 – $21.29	.62	$29.41 – $29.74	.87
$4.40 – $4.73	.13	$12.85 – $13.18	.38	$21.30 – $21.63	.63	$29.75 – $30.08	.88
$4.74 – $5.06	.14	$13.19 – $13.51	.39	$21.64 – $21.96	.64	$30.09 – $30.41	.89
$5.07 – $5.40	.15	$13.52 – $13.85	.40	$21.97 – $22.30	.65	$30.42 – $30.75	.90
$5.41 – $5.74	.16	$13.86 – $14.19	.41	$22.31 – $22.64	.66	$30.76 – $31.09	.91
$5.75 – $6.08	.17	$14.20 – $14.53	.42	$22.65 – $22.98	.67	$31.10 – $31.43	.92
$6.09 – $6.42	.18	$14.54 – $14.87	.43	$22.99 – $23.32	.68	$31.44 – $31.77	.93
$6.43 – $6.75	.19	$14.88 – $15.20	.44	$23.33 – $23.65	.69	$31.78 – $32.10	.94
$6.76 – $7.09	.20	$15.21 – $15.54	.45	$23.66 – $23.99	.70	$32.11 – $32.44	.95
$7.10 – $7.43	.21	$15.55 – $15.88	.46	$24.00 – $24.33	.71	$32.45 – $32.78	.96
$7.44 – $7.77	.22	$15.89 – $16.22	.47	$24.34 – $24.67	.72	$32.79 – $33.12	.97
$7.78 – $8.11	.23	$16.23 – $16.56	.48	$24.68 – $25.01	.73	$33.13 – $33.46	.98
$8.12 – $8.44	.24	$16.57 – $16.89	.49	$25.02 – $25.34	.74	$33.47 – $33.79	.99
$8.45 – $8.78	.25	$16.90 – $17.23	.50	$25.35 – $25.68	.75	$33.80 – 34.13	1.00
$8.79 – $9.12	.26	$17.24 – $17.57	.51	$25.69 – $26.02	.76		
$9.13 – $9.46	.27	$17.58 – $17.91	.52	$26.03 – $26.36	.77		

Pour Cost Chart

Drink: _____ Priced By: _____ Date: _____

UNIT	ITEM	PRICE/OZ	TOTAL
Subtotal			
Loss			
TOTAL			

CHAPTER 4

Restaurant management presents many unique challenges — from cooking to costing. Organization is the key to success and the forms in this chapter are specifically targeted towards general management topics, as there are many steps and costs involved in presenting food, liquor and wine products to the public.

General Management

Daily Planner

DATE: **DAY:**

DAILY SCHEDULE & APPOINTMENTS
7:00
7:30
8:00
8:30
9:00
9:30
10:00
10:30
11:00
11:30
12:00
12:30
1:00
1:30
2:00
2:30
3:00
3:30
4:00
4:30
5:00
5:30
6:00
6:30

DAILY TO-DO LIST:

❑ _____
❑ _____
❑ _____
❑ _____
❑ _____
❑ _____
❑ _____
❑ _____
❑ _____

EXPENSES: CONTACTS:

❑ _____   ❑ _____
❑ _____   ❑ _____
❑ _____   ❑ _____
❑ _____   ❑ _____
❑ _____   ❑ _____
❑ _____   ❑ _____

NOTES:

To-Do List

DATE: _____   DAY: _____

HIGH PRIORITY:

☐ _____

☐ _____

☐ _____

☐ _____

☐ _____

☐ _____

MEDIUM PRIORITY:

☐ _____

☐ _____

☐ _____

☐ _____

☐ _____

☐ _____

LOW PRIORITY:

☐ _____

☐ _____

☐ _____

☐ _____

☐ _____

☐ _____

ON HOLD:

☐ _____

☐ _____

☐ _____

☐ _____

NOTES:

Monthly Calendar

MONTH:	Sunday	Monday	Tuesday	Wednesday	Thursday	Friday	Saturday

Action Plan Worksheet

Date	Task to be Completed	Action Steps	Target Completion	Actual Completion	Completed By

Important Phone Numbers

UPDATED ON:

NAME	PHONE NUMBER	EXTENSION	PURPOSE/COMPANY

Emergency Contacts

AMBULANCE: _____

FIRE-RESCUE: _____

HOSPITAL: _____

PHYSICIAN: _____

POLICE: _____

POISON CONTROL: _____

LOCAL OSHA OFFICE: _____

Our address is:

_____

_____

Memo

MEMO

Date: _____

To: _____

From: _____

Subject: _____

Memo

To: _____   **From:** _____

Date: _____   **Subject:** _____

_____

_____

_____

_____

_____

_____

_____

_____

_____

_____

_____

_____

_____

_____

_____

_____

_____

_____

_____

_____

_____

_____

Purveyor Order Schedule

Prepared By: _____ **Date:** _____

PURVEYOR	SUN	MON	TUE	WED	THUR	FRI	SAT	PH #

The Encyclopedia of Restaurant Forms

Purveyor Information

Prepared By: _____ Date: _____

PURVEYOR	PHONE NUMBER	PRODUCTS SUPPLIED	SALES REP.	DELIVERY DAYS

Hourly Reservations

TIME	NAME	# OF GUESTS	NOTES

Table Count

Week Of: _____

TIME	SUN	MON	TUE	WED	THUR	FRI	SAT
7:00 a.m.							
8:00 a.m.							
9:00 a.m.							
10:00 a.m.							
11:00 a.m.							
11:30 a.m.							
12 Noon							
12:30 p.m.							
1:00 p.m.							
2:00 p.m.							
3:00 p.m.							
4:00 p.m.							
5:00 p.m.							
6:00 p.m.							
6:30 p.m.							
7:00 p.m.							
7:30 p.m.							
8:00 p.m.							
8:30 p.m.							
9:00 p.m.							
10:00 p.m.							
11:00 p.m.							
12:00 Midnight							

Guest Waiting List

TIME	NAME	# OF GUESTS	S/N/E	WAIT QUOTED

Daily Incident Log

Day: _____ Date: _____ Shift: _____

Prepared By: _____ Manager on Duty: _____

Describe Incident: _____ | **TIME INCIDENT OCCURRED:**

_____

Patron's Name: _____ Address: _____

City, State & Zip: _____ Phone Number: _____

Employee(s) Involved: _____

Witness(es) Name(s): _____

Witness(es) Phone Number(s): _____

Describe Incident: _____ | **TIME INCIDENT OCCURRED:**

_____

Patron's Name: _____ Address: _____

City, State & Zip: _____ Phone Number: _____

Employee(s) Involved: _____

Witness(es) Name(s): _____

Witness(es) Phone Number(s): _____

Describe Incident: _____ | **TIME INCIDENT OCCURRED:**

_____

Patron's Name: _____ Address: _____

City, State & Zip: _____ Phone Number: _____

Employee(s) Involved: _____

Witness(es) Name(s): _____

Witness(es) Phone Number(s): _____

Detailed Incident Report

RESTAURANT INFORMATION

Restaurant Name: _____ Date complaint reported:____ /____/____

Address: _____

City: _____ State:_____ Zip Code: _____

Phone Number:_____

CLAIMANT INFORMATION

Name: _____ Date of visit: ____ /____/____

Address: _____

City: _____ State:_____ Zip Code: _____

Phone Number:_____

Number of guests in your party? 1 2 3 4 5 6 7 8 9 10+

WITNESS INFORMATION

Name: _____ Date of visit: ____ /____/____

Address: _____

City: _____ State:_____ Zip Code: _____

Phone Number:_____

Name: _____ Date of visit: ____ /____/____

Address: _____

City: _____ State:_____ Zip Code: _____

Phone Number:_____

INCIDENT INFORMATION

Describe Incident: _____

_____

_____

_____

Specific area where incident occurred: _____

Condition of area where incident occurred: _____

Employee involved: _____

Items involved: _____

Actions taken: _____

Manager on Duty: _____ Signature:_____

Customer Comment Form

Day: SN M T W TH F S **Date:** _____ **Shift:** _____ **Manager:** _____

Prepared By: _____ **Position:** _____

Comments heard about service:

_____

_____

_____

_____

_____

_____

Guest's name (if known): _____

Overall, service comments were: ❑ positive   ❑ negative   ❑ neutral

Comments heard about food:

_____

_____

_____

_____

_____

_____

Guest's name (if known): _____

Overall, food comments were: ❑ positive   ❑ negative   ❑ neutral

Comments heard about physical facility:

_____

_____

_____

_____

_____

_____

Guest's name (if known): _____

Overall, facility comments were: ❑ positive   ❑ negative   ❑ neutral

Customer Satisfaction Survey

SERVICE

1. Were you greeted promptly upon entering the restaurant?
   ❑ Yes ❑ No If no, how long did you wait to be greeted?
   _____

2. Was the host or hostess friendly and made you feel welcome?
   ❑ Yes ❑ No

3. How long did you have to wait to be seated?
   _____

4. Did you feel the wait was too long to be seated?
   ❑ Yes ❑ No

5. How would you rate the overall service provided by the waitperson who served you? On a scale from 1-10, with 1 being very poor and 10 being exceptional (circle one):
   1 2 3 4 5 6 7 8 9 10

6. How would you rate the friendliness of all the staff?
   1 2 3 4 5 6 7 8 9 10

7. Were you satisfied with the pace of the service?
   ❑ Yes ❑ No

Additional comments:
   _____
   _____
   _____
   _____

PHYSICAL FACILITIES

8. Please rate the cleanliness of the dining area:
   1 2 3 4 5 6 7 8 9 10

9. Please rate the cleanliness of the restrooms, if used:
   1 2 3 4 5 6 7 8 9 10

10. Was the lighting too bright?
    ❑ Yes ❑ No

11. Was the lighting too dim?
    ❑ Yes ❑ No

12. Was the temperature comfortable?
    ❑ Yes ❑ No

APPETIZERS

13. Did your server recommend any appetizers?
    ❑ Yes ❑ No

14. Please list any appetizers you ordered:
    _____
    _____
    _____
    _____

15. Were the hot appetizers served hot?
    ❑ Yes ❑ No

16. Were the cold appetizers served cold?
    ❑ Yes ❑ No

17. Please rate the flavor:
    1 2 3 4 5 6 7 8 9 10

18. Please rate the overall quality:
    1 2 3 4 5 6 7 8 9 10

Additional comments:
    _____
    _____
    _____

SALADS

19. What did you order?
    _____
    _____

20. Was the salad the proper temperature (hot salads hot, cold salads cold)?
    ❑ Yes ❑ No

21. Please rate the flavor:
    1 2 3 4 5 6 7 8 9 10

22. Please rate the overall quality:
    1 2 3 4 5 6 7 8 9 10

BEVERAGES

23. What beverages did you order?
    _____
    _____

24. Was there a wide selection of beverages from which to choose?
    ❑ Yes ❑ No

25. Are there other beverages you would like to see on our menu?
    ❑ Yes ❑ No
    If yes, please list: _____

26. Did your server offer you refills in a timely fashion?
    ❑ Yes ❑ No

27. Were the beverages the proper temperature (hot drinks hot, cold drinks cold)?
    ❑ Yes ❑ No

28. Were the drinks served in conjunction with your meal?
    ❑ Yes ❑ No

29. Please rate overall quality:
    1 2 3 4 5 6 7 8 9 10

Customer Satisfaction Survey

ENTRÉES

30. Did your server tell you the daily specials?
❑ Yes ❑ No

31. Was your server knowledgeable and able to answer your questions about the menu?
❑ Yes ❑ No

32. What did you order?
_____
_____
_____

33. Were you pleased with the variety of food on the menu?
❑ Yes ❑ No
If no, please explain:
_____
_____
_____
_____

34. Are there items you would like to see added to the menu?
❑ Yes ❑ No
If yes, please list:
_____
_____
_____
_____

35. Were the cold entrées served on cold plates?
❑ Yes ❑ No

36. Were the cold entrées served cold?
❑ Yes ❑ No

37. Were the hot entrées served on hot plates?
❑ Yes ❑ No

38. Were the hot entrées served hot?
❑ Yes ❑ No

39. Please rate the flavor:
1 2 3 4 5 6 7 8 9 10

40. Please rate overall quality:
1 2 3 4 5 6 7 8 9 10

SIDE ORDERS

41. What did you order?
_____
_____
_____

42. Were you pleased with the side items offered?
❑ Yes ❑ No
If no, please explain:
_____
_____
_____

43. Are there additional side orders you would like to see added to the menu?
❑ Yes ❑ No
If yes, please list:
_____
_____
_____

44. Were the side items the proper temperature (hot items hot, cold items cold)?
❑ Yes ❑ No

45. Please rate the flavor:
1 2 3 4 5 6 7 8 9 10

46. Please rate overall quality:
1 2 3 4 5 6 7 8 9 10

DESSERTS

47. Did your server offer dessert or tell you about any dessert specialties?
❑ Yes ❑ No

48. What did you order?
_____
_____
_____

49. Were the cold desserts served cold?
❑ Yes ❑ No

50. Were the hot desserts served hot?
❑ Yes ❑ No

51. Please rate the flavor:
1 2 3 4 5 6 7 8 9 10

52. Please rate overall quality:
1 2 3 4 5 6 7 8 9 10

SUMMARY

53. Will you dine here again?
❑ Yes ❑ No
If no, please explain:
_____
_____
_____
_____

54. Would you recommend this restaurant to your friends?
❑ Yes ❑ No

55. Please rate overall quality:
1 2 3 4 5 6 7 8 9 10

Additional comments:
_____
_____
_____
_____
_____
_____
_____
_____

Thank you.

Restaurant Shopper's Report

Restaurant: _____ Date of Visit: _____

Reservation Process

The telephone call to make the reservation was answered within three rings.
❑ Yes   ❑ No

The employee answering the phone was pleasant, identified himself/herself and the restaurant.
❑ Yes   ❑ No

The employee taking the reservation was courteous, repeated your reservation information and thanked you.
❑ Yes   ❑ No

The employee taking the reservation was knowledgeable, helpful and able to answer any questions (e.g., directions to restaurant).
❑ Yes   ❑ No

Additional Notes: _____
_____
_____
_____
_____

Restaurant Exterior

The restaurant's sign was easily seen from a distance, easy to read, and in good condition.
❑ Yes   ❑ No

The restaurant's parking lot and grounds were free of debris and well-maintained.
❑ Yes   ❑ No

The area around the dining room was landscaped and well-lit.
❑ Yes   ❑ No

The restaurant had adequate parking.
❑ Yes   ❑ No

Arrival & Seating

You were greeted quickly upon entering.
❑ Yes   ❑ No

The host/hostess was appropriately dressed, smiling and pleasant.
❑ Yes   ❑ No

The host/hostess asked your smoking preference.
❑ Yes   ❑ No

You were seated within a reasonable time.
❑ Yes   ❑ No

The lounge was offered as an alternative if you had to wait for your table.
❑ Yes   ❑ No

The booths and tables were not crowded and easily accessible.
❑ Yes   ❑ No

The table or booth was comfortable and appropriate for your party.
❑ Yes   ❑ No

The host/hostess distributed menus for each guest and they were easily within reach.
❑ Yes   ❑ No

The host/hostess informed you of specials.
❑ Yes   ❑ No

The host/hostess told you the server's name.
❑ Yes   ❑ No

The host/hostess had a pleasant demeanor and treated you graciously.
❑ Yes   ❑ No

Additional Notes: _____
_____
_____

Restaurant Shopper's Report

Menu

The menu was in good, clean condition.
❑ Yes   ❑ No

The menu matched the restaurant's theme.
❑ Yes   ❑ No

The menu size was physically easy to handle.
❑ Yes   ❑ No

Available specials were listed prominently or separately.
❑ Yes   ❑ No

The menu was well-organized, with selections grouped in an easy-to-read and easy-to-find manner.
❑ Yes   ❑ No

The type on the menu was easy to read.
❑ Yes   ❑ No

The number of selections was appropriate.
❑ Yes   ❑ No

Appetizing descriptions were provided for menu items.
❑ Yes   ❑ No

The menu had complete descriptions of side orders included or offered for each item.
❑ Yes   ❑ No

The menu offered additional information as a marketing tool.
❑ Yes   ❑ No

Vegetarian portions were offered.
❑ Yes   ❑ No

Children's portions were offered.
❑ Yes   ❑ No

Senior citizens' portions were offered.
❑ Yes   ❑ No

Additional Notes: _____

_____

_____

Waitstaff

The waiter's or waitress's uniform was clean and attractive.
❑ Yes   ❑ No

The waiter's or waitress's hands and fingernails were clean.
❑ Yes   ❑ No

The waiter or waitress approached your table within three minutes after being seated.
❑ Yes   ❑ No

The waiter or waitress greeted you pleasantly and introduced himself or herself.
❑ Yes   ❑ No

The waiter or waitress smiled, was cordial, and created a genial atmosphere.
❑ Yes   ❑ No

The waiter or waitress was familiar with menu items and able to answer questions.
❑ Yes   ❑ No

The waiter or waitress used suggestive selling techniques, such as offering appetizers, in a friendly and non-offensive manner.
❑ Yes   ❑ No

The waiter or waitress served beverage items promptly and from the left.
❑ Yes   ❑ No

The waiter or waitress served food items in a timely manner and from the left.

The timing between courses was well-spaced.
❑ Yes   ❑ No

The waiter or waitress knew each guest's selections and served them correctly.
❑ Yes   ❑ No

The waiter or waitress returned to the table to check on satisfaction and provide additional service after the main course arrived.
❑ Yes   ❑ No

Restaurant Shopper's Report

Waitstaff (con't)

It was not necessary to summon the waiter or waitress during the meal.
❑ Yes   ❑ No

The waiter or waitress was attentive to guests' needs during the meal.
❑ Yes   ❑ No

The waiter or waitress seemed to enjoy their job.
❑ Yes   ❑ No

Overall, the waiter or waitress did a good job.
❑ Yes   ❑ No

Additional Notes: _____

_____

_____

_____

Bus Staff

The bus person provided water quickly after being seated.
❑ Yes   ❑ No

The bus person made sure water glasses were refilled promptly.
❑ Yes   ❑ No

The bus person was responsive to any service requests.
❑ Yes   ❑ No

The bus person removed dirty dishes quickly, so they were not left sitting on the table after being emptied.
❑ Yes   ❑ No

The bus person removed dirty dishes from the right.
❑ Yes   ❑ No

The bus person removed dirty ashtrays properly and replaced them quickly.
❑ Yes   ❑ No

The bus person was polite and courteous.
❑ Yes   ❑ No

The bus person was presentable, clean and well-groomed.
❑ Yes   ❑ No

The bus person's uniform was clean and attractive.
❑ Yes   ❑ No

The bus person did a good job, and service was not disruptive.
❑ Yes   ❑ No

Additional Notes: _____

_____

_____

Food

Food matched its menu description.
❑ Yes   ❑ No

All items ordered were available.
❑ Yes   ❑ No

Appetizer
Please list appetizer(s) ordered: _____

_____

Appetizing appearance	❑ Yes	❑ No	
Proper temperature	❑ Yes	❑ No	
(hot items hot, cold items cold)			
Tasted good	❑ Yes	❑ No	

Please rate overall appetizer quality:
❑ Excellent   ❑ Good   ❑ Fair   ❑ Poor

Soup
Please list soup(s) ordered: _____

Appetizing appearance	❑ Yes	❑ No	
Proper temperature	❑ Yes	❑ No	
(hot items hot, cold items cold)			
Tasted good	❑ Yes	❑ No	

Please rate overall soup quality:
❑ Excellent   ❑ Good   ❑ Fair   ❑ Poor

Restaurant Shopper's Report

Bread

Please list type of bread(s) ordered: _____

_____

Appetizing appearance	❑ Yes	❑ No
Proper temperature	❑ Yes	❑ No
(hot items hot, cold items cold)		
Tasted good	❑ Yes	❑ No

Please rate overall bread quality:

❑ Excellent   ❑ Good   ❑ Fair   ❑ Poor

Salad

Please list type of salad(s) ordered: _____

_____

Appetizing appearance	❑ Yes	❑ No
Proper temperature	❑ Yes	❑ No
(hot items hot, cold items cold)		
Tasted good	❑ Yes	❑ No
Dressing choices adequate	❑ Yes	❑ No
Dressing amount correct	❑ Yes	❑ No

Please rate overall salad quality:

❑ Excellent   ❑ Good   ❑ Fair   ❑ Poor

Entrée

Please list entrée(s) ordered: _____

_____

_____

Appetizing appearance	❑ Yes	❑ No
Proper temperature	❑ Yes	❑ No
(hot items hot, cold items cold)		
Tasted good	❑ Yes	❑ No
Portions appropriate	❑ Yes	❑ No

Please rate overall entrée quality:

❑ Excellent   ❑ Good   ❑ Fair   ❑ Poor

Side Orders

Please list side order(s) ordered: _____

_____

_____

Appetizing appearance	❑ Yes	❑ No
Proper temperature	❑ Yes	❑ No
(hot items hot, cold items cold)		
Tasted good	❑ Yes	❑ No

Please rate overall side order quality:

❑ Excellent   ❑ Good   ❑ Fair   ❑ Poor

Dessert

Please list dessert(s) ordered: _____

_____

_____

_____

Appetizing appearance	❑ Yes	❑ No
Proper temperature	❑ Yes	❑ No
(hot items hot, cold items cold)		
Tasted good	❑ Yes	❑ No
Portions appropriate	❑ Yes	❑ No

Please rate overall dessert quality:

❑ Excellent   ❑ Good   ❑ Fair   ❑ Poor

Additional Notes: _____

_____

_____

_____

_____

_____

_____

_____

_____

_____

_____

_____

Dining Ambiance

Noise level in dining room is not too loud.
❑ Yes   ❑ No

Music pleasant, not too loud and not distracting.
❑ Yes   ❑ No

Lighting in dining room is not too bright or dim.
❑ Yes   ❑ No

Table decorations are clean and attractive.
❑ Yes   ❑ No

Restaurant Shopper's Report

Dining Ambiance (cont.)

Table decorations are unobtrusive and do not block diners' view of each other.
❑ Yes   ❑ No

The restaurant presented a unified theme in décor, music, employee uniforms and overall atmosphere.
❑ Yes   ❑ No

Decor, furnishings and plants are in good physical condition and tastefully exhibited.
❑ Yes   ❑ No

Additional Notes: _____
_____
_____
_____

Facility Cleanliness

The entrance, lounge, bar and dining room were clean.
❑ Yes   ❑ No

The dining table is clean, in good condition and has no food residue, crumbs or stains.
❑ Yes   ❑ No

Chairs and booths are clean, stain-free and stable.
❑ Yes   ❑ No

Glasses are clean and do not have water spots.
❑ Yes   ❑ No

Flatware is clean and does not have water spots.
❑ Yes   ❑ No

Dishes are clean and do not have water spots.
❑ Yes   ❑ No

Napkins are clean, not stained, and folded nicely.
❑ Yes   ❑ No

The ceiling is clean and in good condition.
❑ Yes   ❑ No

Lighting fixtures are working and clean.
❑ Yes   ❑ No

The walls and floors are clean and well-maintained.
❑ Yes   ❑ No

Additional Notes: _____
_____

Restrooms

Mens' and womens' restrooms clearly marked and in an easy-to-find location.
❑ Yes   ❑ No

The restroom door is clean and well-maintained.
❑ Yes   ❑ No

Overall, the restroom is clean and doesn't have any objectionable odors.
❑ Yes   ❑ No

The restroom lighting is in good working order and sufficiently bright.
❑ Yes   ❑ No

The restroom is adequately stocked with toiletries, soap and disposable paper towels (or a hot-air hand dryer).
❑ Yes   ❑ No

The restroom sink areas and fixtures are clean.
❑ Yes   ❑ No

The restroom mirrors are clean.
❑ Yes   ❑ No

The restroom walls, floors and windows are clean and well-maintained.
❑ Yes   ❑ No

An infant changing area is available, clean and in good condition.
❑ Yes   ❑ No

Additional Notes: _____
_____
_____

Restaurant Shopper's Report

The check was presented in an appropriate and timely manner.
❑ Yes   ❑ No

The check was placed in a discreet location.
❑ Yes   ❑ No

The check is itemized, readable and easy to understand.
❑ Yes   ❑ No

The check is totalled correctly and reflects the items ordered.
❑ Yes   ❑ No

The waiter or waitress informs you that he or she will return for payment at your convenience.
❑ Yes   ❑ No

The waiter or waitress properly tabulated and processed credit card payment.
❑ Yes   ❑ No

The waiter or waitress brought your correct change directly from the cashier.
❑ Yes   ❑ No

The waiter or waitress thanked you upon receiving payment.
❑ Yes   ❑ No

The waiter or waitress thanked you for coming and said "it was a pleasure to server you," and "please come again."
❑ Yes   ❑ No

Exits were well-lit and departure from dining room was free of obstacles.
❑ Yes   ❑ No

Additional Notes: _____
_____
_____
_____

Overall service quality was:
❑ Excellent   ❑ Good   ❑ Fair   ❑ Poor

Overall food quality was:
❑ Excellent   ❑ Good   ❑ Fair   ❑ Poor

Overall dining experience was:
❑ Excellent   ❑ Good   ❑ Fair   ❑ Poor

Please note any areas of service that could be improved:
_____
_____
_____
_____
_____
_____
_____
_____
_____
_____

Please note any areas of service that were exceptional or above ordinary:
_____
_____
_____
_____
_____
_____
_____
_____
_____
_____
_____
_____

Additional Notes: _____
_____
_____
_____

Check-Out Form

Name: _____   **Date:** _____

FOOD & BEVERAGE SALES

FOOD TOTAL	_____	**TOTAL SALES**	_____
Liquor	_____	(-) Charges w/out tips	_____
Beer	_____	(-) Charge tips	_____
Wine	_____	(-) Comp check totals	_____
LIQUOR TOTAL	_____		
Tax	_____		
TOTAL SALES	_____	**CASH TURN-IN**	_____

Name: _____   **Date:** _____

FOOD & BEVERAGE SALES

FOOD TOTAL	_____	**TOTAL SALES**	_____
Liquor	_____	(-) Charges w/out tips	_____
Beer	_____	(-) Charge tips	_____
Wine	_____	(-) Comp check totals	_____
LIQUOR TOTAL	_____		
Tax	_____		
TOTAL SALES	_____	**CASH TURN-IN**	_____

Name: _____   **Date:** _____

FOOD & BEVERAGE SALES

FOOD TOTAL	_____	**TOTAL SALES**	_____
Liquor	_____	(-) Charges w/out tips	_____
Beer	_____	(-) Charge tips	_____
Wine	_____	(-) Comp check totals	_____
LIQUOR TOTAL	_____		
Tax	_____		
TOTAL SALES	_____	**CASH TURN-IN**	_____

Manager's Meeting Organization Form

STAFFING LEVELS

Waitstaff/Restaurant: _____

    ❑ needs _____

Bar/Lounge: _____

    ❑ needs _____

Kitchen: _____

    ❑ needs _____

EMPLOYEE RECOGNITION

Name: _____

Position: _____

Comments: _____

Name: _____

Position: _____

Comments: _____

Name: _____

Position: _____

Comments: _____

EMPLOYEE PROBLEMS

Name: _____

Position: _____

Comments: _____

Name: _____

Position: _____

Comments: _____

Name: _____

Position: _____

Comments: _____

TRAINING NEEDED

Name: _____

Position: _____

Comments: _____

REPAIR/MAINTENANCE NEEDED

_____

_____

_____

_____

SUPPLIES NEEDED

_____

_____

_____

_____

PROFITABILITY

MTD Food Sales $ _____

    Budget $ _____ +/- $_____

MTD Liquor Sales $ _____

    Budget $ _____ +/- $_____

Restaurant Labor _____%

    Budget $ _____% +/- $_____

Bar Labor _____%

    Budget $ _____% +/- $_____

Kitchen Labor _____%

    Budget $ _____% +/- $_____

Food Cost _____

Liquor Cost _____

NOTES

_____

_____

_____

_____

Robbery Description Facial Form

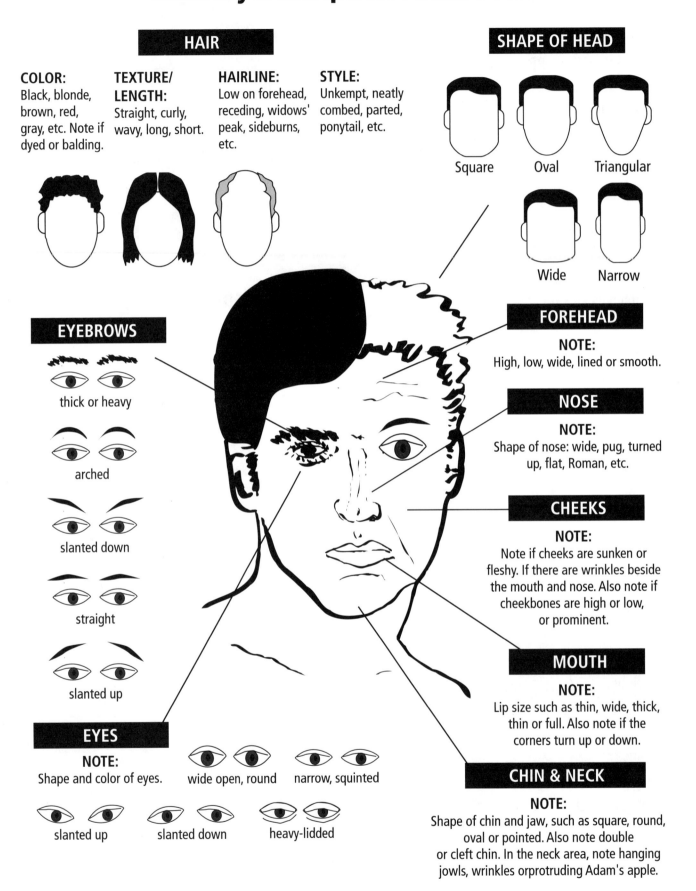

HAIR

COLOR: Black, blonde, brown, red, gray, etc. Note if dyed or balding.

TEXTURE/ LENGTH: Straight, curly, wavy, long, short.

HAIRLINE: Low on forehead, receding, widows' peak, sideburns, etc.

STYLE: Unkempt, neatly combed, parted, ponytail, etc.

SHAPE OF HEAD

Square

Oval

Triangular

Wide

Narrow

EYEBROWS

thick or heavy

arched

slanted down

straight

slanted up

FOREHEAD

NOTE: High, low, wide, lined or smooth.

NOSE

NOTE: Shape of nose: wide, pug, turned up, flat, Roman, etc.

CHEEKS

NOTE: Note if cheeks are sunken or fleshy. If there are wrinkles beside the mouth and nose. Also note if cheekbones are high or low, or prominent.

MOUTH

NOTE: Lip size such as thin, wide, thick, thin or full. Also note if the corners turn up or down.

EYES

NOTE: Shape and color of eyes.

wide open, round

narrow, squinted

slanted up

slanted down

heavy-lidded

CHIN & NECK

NOTE: Shape of chin and jaw, such as square, round, oval or pointed. Also note double or cleft chin. In the neck area, note hanging jowls, wrinkles orprotruding Adam's apple.

Robbery Description Physical Characteristics Form

PHYSICAL DESCRIPTION

Sex _____

Age _____

Race _____

Height _____

Weight _____

Hair _____

Eyes _____

Facial Hair _____

Identifying Marks (scars/tattoos) _____

_____

Complexion _____

Glasses _____

Hat _____

Shirt _____

Coat _____

Pants _____

Shoes _____

Additional Details _____

_____

_____

_____

_____

_____

_____

_____

_____

WEAPONS

❑ Knife

❑ Revolver

❑ Automatic

❑ Rifle

❑ Shotgun

❑ Other (describe)

_____

_____

_____

PISTOL

AUTOMATIC

RIFLE

SHOTGUN

Pest Fumigation Sign

WARNING

All employees — Please be aware that the premises will be fumigated on:

DATE TO SPRAY: _____

TIME TO SPRAY: _____

Opening employees due in at:

Kitchen: _____
Dining Room: _____
Bar: _____

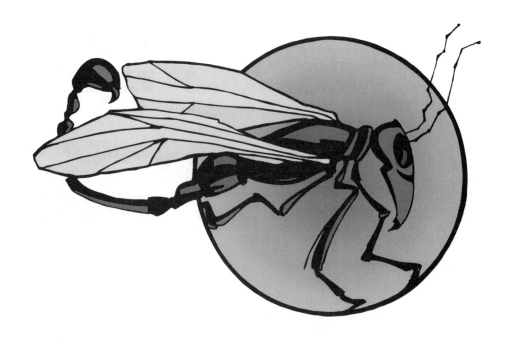

Kitchen Safety Inspection Form

Date Completed: _____ Shift: _____

Prepared By: _____ Manager on Duty: _____

EQUIPMENT

Is all kitchen equipment clean, well-maintained
and in proper working order? ❏ Yes ❏ No

Are grease traps cleaned regularly? ❏ Yes ❏ No

Are the fryers in a separate location, away from
grills, griddles and open flames? ❏ Yes ❏ No

Is all refrigeration equipment free from
dust and grease? ❏ Yes ❏ No

Comments or Corrective Actions Needed: _____

_____

_____

_____

_____

FIRE PREVENTION

Is there a fire-prevention system installed and in good,
working order? ❏ Yes ❏ No

Has the system been inspection by a professional and
been marked with a valid inspection tag? ❏ Yes ❏ No

Are all cooking areas adequately covered by the
fire-suppression system? ❏ Yes ❏ No

Are the fire prevention nozzles aimed correction? ❏ Yes ❏ No

Are fire extinguishers easily accessible? ❏ Yes ❏ No

Are fire extinguishers charged and
inspected yearly? ❏ Yes ❏ No

Has the automatic sprinkler system been
inspected yearly and tagged? ❏ Yes ❏ No

Is the sprinkler system valve open and
in good condition? ❏ Yes ❏ No

Comments or Corrective Actions Needed: _____

_____

_____

_____

_____

VENTILATION SYSTEMS

Are exhaust vents and fans clean and inspected
on a regular basis? ❏ Yes ❏ No

Does the exhaust hood adequately cover all
cooking areas? ❏ Yes ❏ No

Are all the exhaust hood filters clean, well-maintained
and free of grease? ❏ Yes ❏ No

Comments or Corrective Actions Needed: _____

_____

_____

_____

ELECTRICAL

Is the electrical room also used for storage? ❏ Yes ❏ No

Is the fuse box or fuse panels easily accessible? ❏ Yes ❏ No

In the fuse box, are all the breakers
labeled clearly? ❏ Yes ❏ No

Are any of the breaker switches covered
with tape? ❏ Yes ❏ No

Are all electrical switches covered? ❏ Yes ❏ No

Are all electrical outlets covered? ❏ Yes ❏ No

Are all electrical junction boxes
and fittings covered? ❏ Yes ❏ No

Are there any extension cords in use? ❏ Yes ❏ No

Are all exposed electrical cords untangled,
properly insulated and in good condition? ❏ Yes ❏ No

Comments or Corrective Actions Needed: _____

_____

_____

_____

_____

Dining Room Safety Inspection Form

Date Completed: _____ Shift: _____

Prepared By: _____ Manager on Duty: _____

FLOORING, STAIRWAYS & EXITS

Are floor mats in use, especially near wet
or greasy areas? ❏ Yes ❏ No

For high-traffic areas, are rugs and
runners utilized? ❏ Yes ❏ No

Is there adequate lighting in areas with
steps or staircases? ❏ Yes ❏ No

Are steps equipped with handrails
and slip guards? ❏ Yes ❏ No

Do all exits have properly lit exit signs? ❏ Yes ❏ No

Are all exits free from obstructions? ❏ Yes ❏ No

Do all exit doors have with panic bars? ❏ Yes ❏ No

Do all exit doors open easily? ❏ Yes ❏ No

Comments or Corrective Actions Needed: _____

_____

_____

_____

_____

EMERGENCY PROCEDURES

Is there a functional emergency lighting system? ❏ Yes ❏ No

Are all employees instructed in emergency
procedures? ❏ Yes ❏ No

Are the emergency numbers clearly posted for
fire, police, hospital and ambulance? ❏ Yes ❏ No

Are any employees trained in first aid
procedures such as CPR or Heimlich Maneuver? ❏ Yes ❏ No

Comments or Corrective Actions Needed: _____

_____

_____

_____

_____

_____

_____

ELECTRICAL

Are all electrical switches covered? ❏ Yes ❏ No

Are all electrical outlets covered? ❏ Yes ❏ No

Are there any extension cords in use? ❏ Yes ❏ No

Are all exposed electrical cords untangled,
properly insulated and in good condition? ❏ Yes ❏ No

Comments or Corrective Actions Needed: _____

_____

_____

_____

EQUIPMENT

Is all equipment clean, well-maintained and in
good working order? ❏ Yes ❏ No

Do hot beverage machines, such as coffee
urns, have scald warnings posted? ❏ Yes ❏ No

Before using any piece of equipment, are all
employees properly trained? ❏ Yes ❏ No

Comments or Corrective Actions Needed: _____

_____

_____

_____

Worksheet for Your Target Market

RESTAURANT CONCEPT

What overall concept do you envision for your restaurant?

_____

_____

_____

_____

What type of food will you be serving?

_____

_____

_____

_____

How extensive will your menu be?

_____

_____

_____

_____

Estimate your average check price per meal:

Breakfast: _____

Lunch: _____

Dinner: _____

RESTAURANT LOCATION

What area will you be serving within a _____-mile radius?

_____

_____

_____

What is the population of the area? _____

Estimate the population of desired age range in the area:

_____

Are tourists and travelers likely to frequent your location or area?   ❏ Yes   ❏ No

What is the annual estimated tourist and traveler traffic?

_____

CUSTOMER BASE

To what type of clientele will your establishment appeal?

- ❏ Singles
- ❏ Married couples
- ❏ Children and parent groups
- ❏ Senior citizens

What is the age range of your target market? _____

What is the annual income level of your projected customer?

- ❏ Under $25,000
- ❏ $25,000-$50,000
- ❏ $50,000-$75,000
- ❏ $75,000-$125,000
- ❏ $125,000-$200,000
- ❏ over $200,000

List probable occupations of your customer base:

_____

_____

_____

_____

_____

_____

COMPETITORS

List similar or competitive restaurants in the same area:

_____

_____

_____

_____

_____

_____

_____

_____

List notes or concerns:

_____

_____

_____

_____

_____

_____

Restroom Checklist

DATE	TIME	INITIALS
	8:00 a.m.	
	9:00 a.m.	
	10:00 a.m.	
	11:00 a.m.	
	11:30 a.m.	
	12 Noon	
	12:30 p.m.	
	1:00 p.m.	
	2:00 p.m.	
	3:00 p.m.	
	4:00 p.m.	
	5:00 p.m.	
	6:00 p.m.	
	6:30 p.m.	
	7:00 p.m.	
	8:00 p.m.	
	9:00 p.m.	
	10:00 p.m.	
	11:00 p.m.	
	12 Midnight	
	1:00 a.m.	
	2:00 a.m.	
	3:00 a.m.	

ALL OF THESE ITEMS SHOULD BE CHECKED TO ENSURE THE COMFORT OF OUR GUESTS

❑ Fresh, clean odor

❑ Counters clean

❑ Mirrors clean

❑ Floor clean and dry

❑ Hand soap filled

❑ Paper towels filled

❑ Toilet paper stocked

❑ Trash cans empty

❑ Lights and equipment working properly

To ensure the comfort of our guests, we strive to make sure our restrooms are always clean and stocked. Please notify an employee immediately if you find this restroom in an unsatisfactory condition. Thank you!

CHAPTER 5

Menu Management

Menu management is an important component of profit realization in the restaurant industry. Just as you manage your employees, you should manage your menu in order to control costs and increase sales and profit. When pricing menu items, you do need to take food cost, labor and operating expenses into account, but you also have to be aware of what the customer is willing to pay, what the competition is charging and what your establishment offers in comparison to the competition. The bottom line is that your prices have to cover your costs plus provide a profit. The tools in this chapter will help you manage your menu so that you'll see maximum profits.

Standardized Recipe

Menu Item:

INGREDIENTS:

RECIPE YIELD: _____

PORTION SIZE: _____

PORTION COST: _____

PREPARATION:

_____

_____

_____

_____

_____

_____

_____

_____

_____

_____

_____

_____

_____

_____

_____

_____

NOTES:

Standardized Recipe II

MENU ITEM:

INGREDIENT	PORTION	UNIT COST

RECIPE PROCEDURE:

_____

_____

_____

Total Recipe Cost $ _____
Per Serving Cost $ _____
Menu Price $ _____
Food Cost %   _____
Gross Profit $ _____

_____

_____

_____

_____

_____

_____

_____

_____

Standardized Recipe III

Menu Item: _____

TOOLS NEEDED:

☐ _____

☐ _____

☐ _____

☐ _____

☐ _____

☐ _____

☐ _____

☐ _____

☐ _____

photo of finished dish

INGREDIENTS	QUANTITY	PROCEDURE

Standardized Recipe Cost Sheet

MENU ITEM:

RECIPE YIELD: _____

PORTION SIZE: _____

PORTION COST: _____

INGREDIENTS		COST OF INGREDIENTS	
Item	Amount	Unit Cost	Total Cost

Total Recipe Cost: _____ Total Portions: _____

Portion Cost: _____ Date Costed: _____

Previous Portion Cost: _____ Previous Date Costed: _____

Recipe Costing Form

Menu Item: _____ Date: _____

Total Yield: _____ Portion Size: _____

Ingredient	Quantity	COST			Recipe Cost
		A.P. $	Yield %	E.P. $	

TOTAL RECIPE COST $_____
# of Portions $_____
Cost Per Portion $_____

Recipe Cost Chart

Recipe: _____ Number: _____

Date Priced: _____ Total Yield: _____ Number of Servings: _____

Usage: _____ Portion Size: _____

Amount/Unit	Ingredients	Unit Price	Extension

Total Cost $

Portion Cost $

Yield Testing Form

Item: _____ Date: _____

(A.P. information should be found on the invoice.)

A.P. Price: _____

A.P. Weight: _____

TOTAL A.P. COST: _____

TOTAL ITEM YIELD: _____

TOTAL NET COST *(A.P. Cost - Byproduct Value):* _____

NET COST PER LB *(Net Cost ÷ Item Yield):* _____

% of INCREASE *(Net Per Pound ÷ A.P. Cost):* _____

TRIM, WASTE & BYPRODUCTS

Item	Weight	$ Value	Total $ Value

Total Weight	Total Value $

Plate Cost Chart

Menu Item: _____ Date Cost Calculated: _____

Amount/Unit	Ingredients	Unit Price		Extension	

Total Cost $

Menu Item Tally Form

MENU ITEM	SUN	MON	TUE	WED	THUR	FRI	SAT
TOTAL CUSTOMER COUNT							

Menu Item Sales Percentage

To determine the Total Sold of each menu item, use the Menu Item Tally Form on the proceeding page.

Prepared By: _____   Week Of: _____

MENU ITEM	Total Sold	x	Menu Price	=	Item Sales Total	÷	Total Net Sales	=	% Contribution to Sales
		X		=		÷		=	
		X		=		÷		=	
		X		=		÷		=	
		X		=		÷		=	
		X		=		÷		=	
		X		=		÷		=	
		X		=		÷		=	
		X		=		÷		=	
		X		=		÷		=	
		X		=		÷		=	
		X		=		÷		=	
		X		=		÷		=	
		X		=		÷		=	
		X		=		÷		=	
		X		=		÷		=	
		X		=		÷		=	
		X		=		÷		=	
		X		=		÷		=	
		X		=		÷		=	
		X		=		÷		=	
		X		=		÷		=	
		X		=		÷		=	

Food Production Sheet

DATE PREPARED:	PREPARED BY:	CUSTOMER COUNT:

MENU ITEM	Portion Size	Amount to Prepare	Amt. Actually Prepared	Amount Left Over	Amount Used

The Encyclopedia of Restaurant Forms

Menu Item Sales Forecast

DATE PREPARED:	PREPARED BY:	WEEK OF:

MENU ITEM	Sales Estimate	% of Sales	Menu Price	Plate Cost	Contribution	Sales	Food Cost
TOTAL							

Menu Analysis Form

MENU ITEM	# Sold	% Sold	Menu Price	Plate Cost	Gross Profit ($)	Total Gross Profit	Profit Percent
DATE PREPARED:	PREPARED BY:			WEEK OF:			

MENU ITEM	# Sold	% Sold	Menu Price	Plate Cost	Gross Profit ($)	Total Gross Profit	Profit Percent
TOTAL							

The Encyclopedia of Restaurant Forms

Menu Item Weekly Sales History

Prepared By: _____ **Date:** _____

MENU ITEM	SUN	MON	TUE	WED	THUR	FRI	SAT	TOTAL	AVG.
TOTAL									

Sales History Daily Guests

Prepared By: _____   **Date:** _____

SERVING PERIOD	SUN	MON	TUE	WED	THUR	FRI	SAT	TOTAL

SERVING PERIOD	SUN	MON	TUE	WED	THUR	FRI	SAT	TOTAL

Food Sales Recap Report

Prepared By: _____   Date Prepared: _____ Week Of: _____

MENU ITEMS	SUN	MON	TUE	WED	THUR	FRI	SAT	TOTAL
WEATHER CONDITIONS								
ADDITIONAL FACTORS								

Menu Design & Menu Templates

Your menu is one of the first impressions of your restaurant. Menu design is very important as it not only presents your food choices, but conveys the personality of your restaurant. The following 26 pages contain templates you can use to design a professional-looking menu— from daily specials to your wine list. Please note, these templates are also available in color on the CD-Rom accompanying this book.

Before choosing a menu template, you may find it helpful to review some of the menu tips at the right.

Generally, the industry uses four menu formats: single-page, two-page, three-page and multi-page.

Single-panel. The focal point on a single-page menu is the area in the top half of the page. Use this area of the menu to promote your most profitable items.

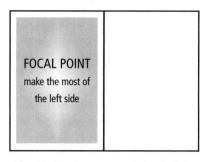

Two-panel. Customers first focus on the left-hand side of the open menu, then continue across the top of the page to the right, and then down the right-hand side. Make the most of the left-hand side.

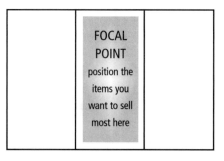

Three-panel. This menu gives you a total of six spaces. With these menus, the eye focuses in the center. Position items you want to sell most on the inside center panel.

Multi-page. It is harder to locate the focal point on a multi-page menu. Each page spread becomes its own "mini-menu," with focal points similar to two-panel menus. Make the most of each mini focal point.

Menu

Eat,

drink,

be merry!

and

Menu

Menu

MENU

menu

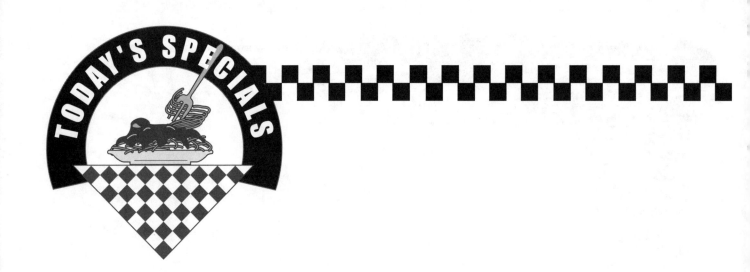

today's Specials

SPECIALS

SPECIALS

FROM THE SEA

CHILDREN'S
menu

Good For Me!!

Kids' Menu

Desserts

Soup & Sandwiches

Wine List

Wine List

CHAPTER 6

Employee Training

Staff is one of your greatest assets as a restaurant owner and/or manager. Your employees have a tremendous influence on how profitable your establishment can be. Of course, how you hire and manage your employees are just as important. The forms in this chapter will help you hire, train and evaluate your staff to create a professional atmosphere and a restaurant that runs smoothly.

Food Service Terminology

2 TOP (OR DEUCE) A table that seats two people.

4 TOP A table that seats four people.

86'D Item has been discontinued and is no longer available.

BEHIND YOU If approaching someone quickly from behind, call out "behind you" to alert them of your presence.

BURIED Exceptionally busy; at peak capacity.

CLEAR After guest departs, to remove all the dirty dishware from a table.

CONDIMENT A substance, such as ketchup, salt, pepper, relish, vinegar or spice, used to flavor or complement food.

CONTAMINATION The presence of an agent on or in a food product, or any object that may come into contact with a food product. This foreign substance is capable of causing an adverse reaction when a person ingests the food.

CONTROL POINT A point, step or procedure that controls food safety hazards, including biological, physical and chemical hazards. Generally a receiving or storage point.

CRITICAL CONTROL POINT A point, step or procedure in the product-handling process where controls can be applied and a food safety hazard can be prevented, eliminated or reduced to safe levels. A measurable factor such as time, temperature, acidity, oxygen availability, food or water activity.

CROSS-CONTAMINATION The transfer of biological, physical or chemical hazards to food products by dirty sanitation rags, contact with other raw food products, contact with previously cooked food, contact with dirty contact surfaces or contact with workers' dirty hands.

DRAGGING Something is incorrect or missing.

DRY STORAGE The area where dry goods, such as cans and paper products, are stored.

COMMON FOOD SERVICE ABBREVIATIONS

M.I.T.
Manager in training

M.O.D
Manager on duty

S.A.
Service assistant

P.P.A.
Per person average sales

W/W
Waiter/waitress

DUMPSTER PAD The area, typically behind the establishment, where the dumpster sits.

FACING The process of aligning cash so all bills are faced in the same direction.

FOLLOW RUNNER The person who follows the runner and assists him or her.

GUEST The customers of the restaurant. It is important to treat them politely and courteously at all times, and provide the best possible service.

HISTORY A past item or event.

IN THE WEEDS Extremely busy (one step below being buried).

MARRY The process of combining partial containers and bottles, such as ketchup, to create full containers.

ON A WAIT When the establishment is at full capacity yet guests continue to come in.

ON THE RAIL Item is needed urgently.

PIVOT POINT The position at a table from which orders are taken in a clockwise manner.

REACH-IN A refrigeration unit you reach into.

RUNNER The person who takes food to a table.

SPEC (OR SPECIFICATION) A description of the correct criteria such as a procedure, product or recipe (typically specified in the recipe book).

STATION The tables or restaurant section on which one server is assigned to wait.

WALK-IN A refrigerator or freezer unit that is large enough to walk into.

WEED EATER A helpful person who assists others "out of the weeds."

WORKING Performing the task requested of you.

Rules to Live By

1 Be cheerful.

2 Praise good work and encourage others.

3 Ask questions. If you don't know how to do something, ask.

4 If you start something, finish it.

5 If you open something, close it.

6 If you turn it on, turn it off.

7 If you break something, fix it (or find someone who can).

8 If you borrow or move something, return it.

9 If you make a mess, clean it up (immediately).

10 You can disagree without being disagreeable.

11 Do your best.

12 Mind your own business.

Server Checklist

To provide quality service, waiters and waitresses should meet the following requirements:

☑ I introduce myself and make guests feel welcome.

☑ I know the menu and beverages thoroughly and can easily answer guests' questions.

☑ I serve food and beverage items promptly and properly.

☑ I keep guests' tables neat throughout the meal by removing any unwanted dishes.

☑ I always use the proper food accompaniments.

☑ I am familiar with our wine list and know proper wine service procedures.

☑ I make sure the water glasses are kept properly filled.

☑ I check at least twice to ensure that everything is fine or to see if I can provide anything else.

☑ I try to anticipate to guests' needs.

☑ I exhibit a sense of teamwork with my co-workers.

☑ I take and show pride in my work.

☑ I have the necessary knowledge to answer guests' questions about all aspects of the restaurant.

☑ I exceed the guests' expectations.

15-Step Opening Guidelines

Following is a 15-step guideline for opening your establishment. You may not follow the sequence exactly, but be sure to make safety the main priority. If you feel that you may enter into an unsafe environment, you should contact the police immediately.

Safety is the First Priority–Check Before You Enter

Upon your arrival, look for any signs of a burglary, such as broken glass, broken windows, unlocked doors, abandoned cars, loiterers or unknown individual(s) inside store, etc.

If you see anything suspicious, call the police immediately. Do not enter the building.

Once you've determined that the building is safe, follow the opening procedures below:

1. Check the exterior of the building for cleanliness and curb appeal. Make sure reader board messages are correct.

2. Unlock the entrance door, enter and deactivate the alarm system.

3. Turn on lights as needed, including outside lights.

4. Check establishment's overall appearance and cleanliness. Note any tasks not satisfactorily completed.

5. Check the previous night's closing paperwork and closing procedures. Note any tasks not completed.

6. Check voice mail and e-mail messages.

7. Check employee status to make sure last night's closers are punched out or signed out.

8. Check daily schedule to make sure all positions are properly filled. Note any additions or changes.

9. Check accuracy of food order to ensure that enough products have been ordered. Check your frequently used products to make sure you have enough for food preparation.

10. Prepare for opening employee's arrival. Unlock front or employee entrance door. Oversee employees as they punch in or sign in. Make sure employees have proper uniforms and are clean and presentable.

11. Assign opening employees their work tasks.

12. Begin accounting procedures. Check safe and set up cash drawers if needed. Check deposit slips and plan coin order.

13. Assign employee cleaning tasks for shift.

14. Check employees' progress and make sure food preparation is being followed according to standards. If all your opening tasks are completed, assist employees where needed.

15. At appointed opening time, unlock doors and turn on "open" sign.

Reservation Procedures

At some point, every employee will answer the phone, so everyone needs to know how to take a dining reservation. Any reservation of six or more should be brought to the manager's attention to be sure we have the proper staffing levels and that the kitchen is aware that the guests are coming.

There are six vital pieces of information needed to ensure we take care of our guests' reservation needs:

 **1 GUEST'S NAME (first and last).**

 **4 PHONE NUMBER (home and work number if possible).**

 **2 NUMBER of people reservation is for.**

 **5 SMOKING PREFERENCE ("S" for smoking, "NS" for nonsmoking, or "E" for either/no preference).**

 **3 TIME of arrival.**

 **6 GROUPS of ten or more. Inquire if it will be separate checks or one check, and if the guests would like the gratuity added.**

Food Server Training Checklist

Initial when completed.

❏ Orientation (policies, procedures, uniform, job description, rate of pay, training materials, etc.)
_____ Trainer _____ Trainee

❏ Employment paperwork completed
_____ Trainer _____ Trainee

❏ Restaurant tour
_____ Trainer _____ Trainee

❏ Co-worker introductions
_____ Trainer _____ Trainee

❏ Uniform issued (if applicable)
_____ Trainer _____ Trainee

❏ Training schedule and procedures explained
_____ Trainer _____ Trainee

❏ Opening responsibilities
_____ Trainer _____ Trainee

❏ Dining table section designations or numbers
_____ Trainer _____ Trainee

❏ Reservation procedures
_____ Trainer _____ Trainee

❏ Correct table set-up
_____ Trainer _____ Trainee

❏ Food items and menu
_____ Trainer _____ Trainee

❏ Alcohol or wine selections and pricing
_____ Trainer _____ Trainee

❏ Alcohol service laws
_____ Trainer _____ Trainee

❏ Wine service
_____ Trainer _____ Trainee

❏ Guest ticket
_____ Trainer _____ Trainee

❏ Point-of-sale computer operations
_____ Trainer _____ Trainee

❏ Separate checks
_____ Trainer _____ Trainee

❏ Carry-out orders
_____ Trainer _____ Trainee

❏ Placing order with kitchen
_____ Trainer _____ Trainee

❏ Service timing
_____ Trainer _____ Trainee

❏ Serving food
_____ Trainer _____ Trainee

❏ Plate presentation
_____ Trainer _____ Trainee

❏ Food quality
_____ Trainer _____ Trainee

❏ Speed of service standard times
_____ Trainer _____ Trainee

❏ Side work (station clean up)
_____ Trainer _____ Trainee

❏ Closing responsibilities
_____ Trainer _____ Trainee

❏ Up-selling
_____ Trainer _____ Trainee

❏ Guest courtesy and treatment
_____ Trainer _____ Trainee

❏ Attitude and teamwork
_____ Trainer _____ Trainee

❏ Table maintenance (pre-bussing)
_____ Trainer _____ Trainee

❏ Check and change procedures
_____ Trainer _____ Trainee

❏ Credit cards
_____ Trainer _____ Trainee

❏ Departure procedures
_____ Trainer _____ Trainee

❏ Employee food
_____ Trainer _____ Trainee

_____

Signature of Manager that training checklist has been successfully completed   Date

Kitchen Training Checklist

Initial when completed.

❏ Orientation (policies, procedures, uniform, job description, rate of pay, training materials, etc.)
_____ Trainer _____ Trainee

❏ Employment paperwork completed
_____ Trainer _____ Trainee

❏ Restaurant tour
_____ Trainer _____ Trainee

❏ Co-worker introductions
_____ Trainer _____ Trainee

❏ Uniform issued (if applicable)
_____ Trainer _____ Trainee

❏ Training schedule and procedures explained
_____ Trainer _____ Trainee

❏ Opening responsibilities
_____ Trainer _____ Trainee

❏ Kitchen work stations
_____ Trainer _____ Trainee

❏ Kitchen duties and organization
_____ Trainer _____ Trainee

❏ Food safety and sanitation
_____ Trainer _____ Trainee

❏ Prep sheets
_____ Trainer _____ Trainee

❏ Recipe book
_____ Trainer _____ Trainee

❏ Food preparation
_____ Trainer _____ Trainee

❏ Proper food labeling
_____ Trainer _____ Trainee

❏ Proper food storage
_____ Trainer _____ Trainee

❏ Kitchenware and cutlery
_____ Trainer _____ Trainee

❏ Correct thawing procedures
_____ Trainer _____ Trainee

❏ Ticket organization
_____ Trainer _____ Trainee

❏ Ticket reading
_____ Trainer _____ Trainee

❏ Ticket timing
_____ Trainer _____ Trainee

❏ Closing procedures
_____ Trainer _____ Trainee

❏ Clean up
_____ Trainer _____ Trainee

❏ Sense of urgency
_____ Trainer _____ Trainee

❏ Safety
_____ Trainer _____ Trainee

❏ Teamwork and productivity
_____ Trainer _____ Trainee

❏ Other _____
_____
_____ Trainer _____ Trainee

❏ Other _____
_____
_____ Trainer _____ Trainee

❏ Other _____
_____
_____ Trainer _____ Trainee

_____   _____

Signature of Manager that training checklist has been successfully completed   Date

Alcohol Service Training

Employee Name: _____

Date Completed: _____ Shift: _____

Prepared By: _____ Manager on Duty: _____

1. Employee can list at least six or more visible signs of intoxication.
   ❑ Yes   ❑ No (if no, note concerns)
   _____
   _____
   _____
   _____

2. The employee is aware of all of the establishment's policies on serving drinks.
   ❑ Yes   ❑ No (if no, note concerns)
   _____
   _____
   _____
   _____

3. The employee consistently checks ID of patrons who appear to be under 30 years old.
   ❑ Yes   ❑ No (if no, note concerns)
   _____
   _____
   _____
   _____

4. The employee will only serve one drink at a time to a customer.
   ❑ Yes   ❑ No (if no, note concerns)
   _____
   _____
   _____
   _____

5. The employee is aware of the the general drink limits.
   ❑ Yes   ❑ No (if no, note concerns)
   _____
   _____
   _____
   _____

6. The employee can track the number of drinks a customer has consumed.
   ❑ Yes   ❑ No (if no, note concerns)
   _____
   _____
   _____
   _____

7. The employee slows service if a customer is nearing intoxication and encourages the patron to order food and nonalcoholic drink.
   ❑ Yes   ❑ No (if no, note concerns)
   _____
   _____
   _____
   _____

8. The employee knows the correct procedures to refuse further alcohol service.
   ❑ Yes   ❑ No (if no, note concerns)
   _____
   _____
   _____
   _____

9. The employee can deal with difficult customers, using the correct procedures.
   ❑ Yes   ❑ No (if no, note concerns)
   _____
   _____
   _____
   _____

10. The employee makes sure intoxicated patrons are not allowed to drive.
    ❑ Yes   ❑ No (if no, note concerns)
    _____
    _____
    _____
    _____

Class Evaluation Form

Name of Class: _____

Instructor: _____ **Date:** _____

This form allows you to evaluate your training session anonymously (you don't need to sign this form). Check the answer below that best describes each category. Please list additional comments at the bottom.

Level of Training
- ❏ Too easy
- ❏ Good
- ❏ Too advanced

Amount of Material
- ❏ Not enough
- ❏ Good
- ❏ Overwhelming

Length of Class
- ❏ Too short
- ❏ Acceptable amount of time
- ❏ Too long

Participation Opportunities
- ❏ Too little
- ❏ Good
- ❏ Too much

Presentation of Class
- ❏ Boring
- ❏ Good
- ❏ Very interesting

Knowledge of Trainer
- ❏ Not very knowledgeable
- ❏ Good
- ❏ Very knowledgeable

Helpfulness of Trainer
- ❏ Not very helpful
- ❏ Helpful
- ❏ Very helpful

Overall Rating of Class
On a scale from 1-10, with 10 being the highest possible score, please rate the class by circling a number below:
1 2 3 4 5 6 7 8 9 10

ADDITIONAL COMMENTS:

Employee Quiz

Employee Name: _____

Job Title: _____ **Date:** _____

Fill in the correct portion sizes for the menu selections listed below:

Menu Item: _____   Menu Item: _____

Portion Size: _____   Portion Size: _____

Menu Item: _____   Menu Item: _____

Portion Size: _____   Portion Size: _____

Menu Item: _____   Menu Item: _____

Portion Size: _____   Portion Size: _____

Menu Item: _____   Menu Item: _____

Portion Size: _____   Portion Size: _____

Menu Item: _____   Menu Item: _____

Portion Size: _____   Portion Size: _____

Menu Item: _____   Menu Item: _____

Portion Size: _____   Portion Size: _____

Menu Item: _____   Menu Item: _____

Portion Size: _____   Portion Size: _____

Menu Item: _____   Menu Item: _____

Portion Size: _____   Portion Size: _____

Menu Item: _____   Menu Item: _____

Portion Size: _____   Portion Size: _____

Menu Item: _____   Menu Item: _____

Portion Size: _____   Portion Size: _____

Employee Training Record

Employee Name: _____

Job Title: _____ Date Employed: _____

DATE OF TRAINING	TYPE OF TRAINING

The Encyclopedia of Restaurant Forms

Sample Time Log

Employee Name: _____

Date: _____   Shift: _____

Start Time	Stop Time	Elapsed Time	Activity Code	Activity	Notes

Service Walk-Through Audit

Employee Name: _____ Date: _____

TASK	SERVICE STATION	PERSON RESPONSIBLE	ACCEPTABLE
			❏ Y ❏ N
			❏ Y ❏ N
			❏ Y ❏ N
			❏ Y ❏ N
			❏ Y ❏ N
			❏ Y ❏ N
			❏ Y ❏ N
			❏ Y ❏ N
			❏ Y ❏ N
			❏ Y ❏ N
			❏ Y ❏ N
			❏ Y ❏ N
			❏ Y ❏ N
			❏ Y ❏ N
			❏ Y ❏ N
			❏ Y ❏ N
			❏ Y ❏ N

Notes: _____

_____

_____

_____

_____

Food Walk-Through Audit

Employee Name: _____

Date: _____ Shift: _____

APPETIZERS

Are appetizers served at the proper temperature (hot appetizers served hot and cold appetizers served cold)?
❑ Yes ❑ No

Are they plated and presented in a visually appealing manner? ❑ Yes ❑ No

Evaluate the flavor:
❑ Excellent ❑ Good ❑ Average ❑ Poor

Comments: _____

_____

_____

SALADS

In cold salads, is the lettuce crisp? ❑ Yes ❑ No

Is the dressing amount adequate? ❑ Yes ❑ No

Are cold salads served on cold plates? ❑ Yes ❑ No

Evaluate the flavor:
❑ Excellent ❑ Good ❑ Average ❑ Poor

Evaluate the salad overall:
❑ Excellent ❑ Good ❑ Average ❑ Poor

Comments: _____

_____

_____

ENTRÉES

Are entrées served at the proper temperature (hot entrées served hot and cold entrées served cold)? ❑ Yes ❑ No

Are cold entrées served on cold plates? ❑ Yes ❑ No

Are hot entrées served on hot plates? ❑ Yes ❑ No

Are they plated and presented in a visually appealing manner? ❑ Yes ❑ No

Evaluate the flavor:
❑ Excellent ❑ Good ❑ Average ❑ Poor

Evaluate overall quality:
❑ Excellent ❑ Good ❑ Average ❑ Poor

Comments: _____

_____

_____

_____

_____

SIDE ORDERS

Are side orders served at the proper temperature (hot side orders served hot and cold side orders served cold)?
❑ Yes ❑ No

Are cold side orders served separately on cold plates? ❑ Yes ❑ No

Are hot side orders served separately on hot plates? ❑ Yes ❑ No

Are they plated and presented in a visually appealing manner? ❑ Yes ❑ No

Evaluate the flavor:
❑ Excellent ❑ Good ❑ Average ❑ Poor

Evaluate overall quality:
❑ Excellent ❑ Good ❑ Average ❑ Poor

Comments: _____

_____

BEVERAGES

Are drinks served at the proper temperature (hot drinks served hot and cold drinks served cold)? ❑ Yes ❑ No

Are drinks served in the proper glasses? ❑ Yes ❑ No

Evaluate the flavor:
❑ Excellent ❑ Good ❑ Average ❑ Poor

Evaluate overall quality:
❑ Excellent ❑ Good ❑ Average ❑ Poor

Comments: _____

_____

DESSERTS

Are desserts served at the proper temperature (hot desserts served hot and cold desserts served cold)? ❑ Yes ❑ No

Are cold desserts served on cold plates? ❑ Yes ❑ No

Are hot desserts served on hot plates? ❑ Yes ❑ No

Are they presented in a visually appealing manner?
❑ Yes ❑ No

Evaluate the flavor:
❑ Excellent ❑ Good ❑ Average ❑ Poor

Evaluate overall quality:
❑ Excellent ❑ Good ❑ Average ❑ Poor

Comments: _____

_____

_____

Service Speed Audit

	■ LUNCH ■ DINNER DATE:									
Server	Tbl #	Greet	Bev.	App.	Salad	Entrée	Ck. Back	Dessert	Check	Change

	■ LUNCH ■ DINNER DATE:									
Server	Tbl #	Greet	Bev.	App.	Salad	Entrée	Ck. Back	Dessert	Check	Change

	■ LUNCH ■ DINNER DATE:									
Server	Tbl #	Greet	Bev.	App.	Salad	Entrée	Ck. Back	Dessert	Check	Change

International Protocol

The customs and practices of other countries often vary from American traditions, and this can affect your restaurant. Following are some general tips to remember when serving international guests.

- Be flexible at all times and follow the leads of your guests.

- Speak clearly, use easy-to-understand phrases, and avoid jargon, slang and colloquialism.

- If you need to address a guest, use titles such as doctor or professor when possible, or common curtesy such as "sir" or "madam."

- Titles are very important to Germans. Do your best to address people by their full, correct title, no matter how long.

- If water is requested, offer bottled water.

- Continental-style dining is a common practice worldwide. The fork is held in the left hand, and the knife in the right hand at all times.

- Do not point with a single finger. Instead, gesture with an open hand, palm up. Hand gestures have different meanings all over the world and you do not want to unintentionally insult a guest. For example, avoid the "OK" sign; in Japan it means money. In Australia, the "thumbs up" sign, or using a crooked index finger to call someone over, are both offensive gestures.

- When serving people from Arab nations, do not serve or offer anything with your left hand. In their culture, the left hand is used only for hygiene.

- Serve politely, with minimal conversation. In Indonesia, talking is impolite while eating dinner. Conversation is reserved for before or after the meal.

- Be aware that even if a person does not speak English, he or she may understand it. Do not make any comments about the person in his or her presence.

- Eye contact is a cultural behavior. The French hold and maintain eye contact longer than Americans. In the Japanese and Korean cultures, direct eye contact is considered intimidating, so avert your eyes and avoid direct eye contact.

- Personal space varies greatly in other cultures. Americans' space bubble extends 12 to 15 inches, or about arm's length. Germans keep a larger personal space around them, approximately 6 inches more space than North Americans do. The Chinese tend to converse very closely together. Other cultures stand much closer. You may be tempted to back up; don't.

- When finished dining, the cutlery is placed at 5 o'clock on the plate. One may assume that the guest has finished dining. When clearing, ask "Sir/Madam, may I remove your plate?" rather than "Are you finished?"

- If possible, use servers and staff who are multi-lingual for the comfort of the guests.

Employee Performance Evaluation Form

NAME: _____ POSITION: _____

INTERVIEWER: _____ DATE: _____

LAST EVALUATION DATE: _____ SALARY: _____

For each of the following categories, grade the employee's performance on a sliding scale of 1 to 10 (see scale below). The overall grade is the average of all scores plus the interviewer's comments.

1-2 poor   3-4 below average   5 average   6-7 above average   8-9 very good   10 exceptional

KNOWLEDGE OF JOB
procedures, paperwork, skill, function

RATING: _____

Comments: _____

_____

_____

QUALITY
up to specification, accuracy, consistency

RATING: _____

Comments: _____

_____

_____

ATTITUDE
towards work, management, other employees, customers

RATING: _____

Comments: _____

_____

_____

LEADERSHIP
ability to give direction

RATING: _____

Comments: _____

_____

_____

RELIABILITY
dependable, on time, follows through on assignments

RATING: _____

Comments: _____

_____

_____

PRODUCTIVITY
volume, utilization of time

RATING: _____

Comments: _____

_____

_____

APPEARANCE
uniform, neat

RATING: _____

Comments: _____

_____

_____

SERVICE
alert, fast

RATING: _____

Comments: _____

_____

_____

OVERALL RATING: _____

SALARY ADJUSTED: ❑ YES ❑ NO

NEW SALARY: _____

Recommendations: _____

_____

_____

Items to be followed up on: _____

_____

_____

_____

CHAPTER 7

One of your greatest assets, or your worst liabilities, is your restaurant staff. A good staff greatly affects your profit potential and a good staff doesn't just happen by accident. As a food service manager or owner, you have a tremendous impact on how good or bad your staff is. This chapter focuses on how to hire and develop a restaurant team.

Human Resource Management

Employment Application

PERSONAL

Last Name _____ First Name _____ Middle _____ Date_____

Street Address _____

City, State, Zip _____

Home Phone _____ Business Phone _____

Social Security Number _____ E-mail _____

Position Desired _____ Pay Expected _____

Are you available for full-time work? ❏ Yes ❏ No   If no, what hours can you work? _____

Will you work overtime if asked? ❏ Yes ❏ No   Are you legally eligible for employment in the United States? ❏ Yes ❏ No

When are you available to begin work? _____

Please list any additional training or skills (languages, certifications, specialty training, etc.): _____

_____

_____

EDUCATION

School	Name and Location of School	Course of Study	Years Completed	Did You Graduate?	Degree or Diploma
GRADUATE				❏ Yes ❏ No	
COLLEGE				❏ Yes ❏ No	
TRADE/TECHNICAL				❏ Yes ❏ No	
HIGH SCHOOL				❏ Yes ❏ No	
ELEMENTARY				❏ Yes ❏ No	

MEMBERSHIPS

Please list professional or civic organizations to which you belong. You may exclude those which may disclose your race, color, religion or ethnic origin.

_____

_____

_____

_____

Employment Application

EMPLOYMENT HISTORY

Starting with your present or most recent employer, give an accurate, complete employment record (include both full-time and part-time). We reserve the right to contact any employer listed below unless you indicate not to do so.

Company Name _____ Telephone_____

Address _____

Employed From (month/year) _____ To _____ Name of Supervisor _____

Weekly Pay Starting _____ Weekly Pay Leaving _____ Job Title _____

Description of Job Duties _____

_____

Reason for Leaving _____ May we contact this employer? ❑ Yes ❑ No

---

Company Name _____ Telephone_____

Address _____

Employed From (month/year) _____ To _____ Name of Supervisor _____

Weekly Pay Starting _____ Weekly Pay Leaving _____ Job Title _____

Description of Job Duties _____

_____

Reason for Leaving _____ May we contact this employer? ❑ Yes ❑ No

---

Company Name _____ Telephone_____

Address _____

Employed From (month/year) _____ To _____ Name of Supervisor _____

Weekly Pay Starting _____ Weekly Pay Leaving _____ Job Title _____

Description of Job Duties _____

_____

Reason for Leaving _____ May we contact this employer? ❑ Yes ❑ No

---

Company Name _____ Telephone_____

Address _____

Employed From (month/year) _____ To _____ Name of Supervisor _____

Weekly Pay Starting _____ Weekly Pay Leaving _____ Job Title _____

Description of Job Duties _____

_____

Reason for Leaving _____ May we contact this employer? ❑ Yes ❑ No

Employment Application

MILITARY

Did you serve in the Armed Forces? ❑ Yes ❑ No   If yes, which branch? _____

Describe any training received relevant to the position for which you are applying.

_____

_____

ADDITIONAL INFORMATION

DO NOT ANSWER ANY QUESTION IN THIS SECTION UNLESS THE BOX IS CHECKED.

If the employer has checked the box next to the question, the information requested is needed for legally permissible reason, including, without limitation, national security considerations, a legitimate occupational qualification or business necessity. The Civil Rights Act of 1964 prohibits discrimination in employment because of color, religion, sex or national origin. Federal law also prohibits discrimination based on age, citizenship and disability. The laws of most states also prohibit some or all of the above types of discrimination as well as some additional types such as discrimination based upon ancestry, marital status or sexual preference.

❑ Provide dates you attended school: Elementary From _____ To _____ High School From _____ To _____
College From _____ To _____ Other (give names and dates) _____

❑ Sex ❑ Male ❑ Female   Number of dependents, including yourself: _____   Are you a Vietnam veteran? ❑ Yes ❑ No

❑ Marital Status ❑ Single ❑ Engaged ❑ Married ❑ Separated ❑ Divorced ❑ Widowed Date of Marriage: _____

❑ What was your previous address? _____
How long at present address? _____ How long at previous address? _____

❑ Have you ever been bonded? ❑ Yes ❑ No   If yes, with what employer(s)? _____

❑ Are you over 18 years of age? ❑ Yes ❑ No   If no, employment is subject to verification of age.

❑ Have you been convicted of a crime in the past ten years, excluding misdemeanors and summary offenses, which has not been annulled, expunged or sealed by a court? ❑ Yes ❑ No   If yes, please describe: _____

SIGNATURE

The information provided in this Application for Employment is true, correct and complete. Any misstatement or omission of fact on this application may result in my dismissal. I understand that acceptance of an offer of employment creates no obligation upon you, the employer, to continue to employ me in the future.

_____   _____
Signature   Date

Employment Application II

PERSONAL INFORMATION

Name (last name first): _____ Social Security Number: _____

Present Address: _____ Apt No.: _____ City: _____ State: _____ Zip: _____

Permanent Address: _____ Apt No.: _____ City: _____ State: _____ Zip: _____

Phone: _____ Are you 18 years or older? ❏ Yes ❏ No

DESIRED EMPLOYMENT

Position: _____ Date you can start: _____ Desired salary: _____

Are you currently employed? ❏ Yes ❏ No   If yes, may we contact your present employer? ❏ Yes ❏ No

Have you applied to this company before? ❏ Yes ❏ No   Where? _____ When? _____

Have you worked for this company before? ❏ Yes ❏ No   Where? _____ When? _____

Reason for leaving: _____

_____

Name of last supervisor at this company: _____

Who referred you to this company? ❏ Employment Agency ❏ Newspaper Ad   ❏ Friend   ❏ State Employment Office
                                 ❏ College Placement Service ❏ Walk In   ❏ Other

EDUCATION

School	Name and Location of School	Course of Study	Years Completed	Did You Graduate?
ELEMENTARY				❏ Yes ❏ No
HIGH SCHOOL				❏ Yes ❏ No
COLLEGE				❏ Yes ❏ No
TRADE/TECHNICAL				❏ Yes ❏ No

GENERAL

Subject of special study or research work	Special training	Special skills
_____	_____	_____
_____	_____	_____
_____	_____	_____
_____	_____	_____
_____	_____	_____

Last

First

Middle

Employment Application II

REFERENCES Please list the names of three persons (not relatives) whom you have known at least one year.

Name	Address	Business	Years Acquainted
_____	_____	_____	_____
_____	_____	_____	_____
_____	_____	_____	_____
_____	_____	_____	_____

FORMER EMPLOYERS Please start with the most recent employer.

Name of Previous Employer: _____ Telephone: _____

Address: _____ City: _____ State: _____ Zip: _____

Employed From (month/year): _____ To: _____ Name of Supervisor: _____

Weekly Starting Salary: _____ Weekly Leaving Salary: _____ May we contact this employer? ❏ Yes ❏ No

Job Title: _____ Description of Job Duties: _____

_____

Reason for Leaving: _____

_____

Name of Previous Employer: _____ Telephone: _____

Address: _____ City: _____ State: _____ Zip: _____

Employed From (month/year): _____ To: _____ Name of Supervisor: _____

Weekly Starting Salary: _____ Weekly Leaving Salary: _____ May we contact this employer? ❏ Yes ❏ No

Job Title: _____ Description of Job Duties: _____

_____

Reason for Leaving: _____

_____

Name of Previous Employer: _____ Telephone: _____

Address: _____ City: _____ State: _____ Zip: _____

Employed From (month/year): _____ To: _____ Name of Supervisor: _____

Weekly Starting Salary: _____ Weekly Leaving Salary: _____ May we contact this employer? ❏ Yes ❏ No

Job Title: _____ Description of Job Duties: _____

_____

Reason for Leaving: _____

_____

Employment Application II

MILITARY SERVICE

Branch of Service	Rank	Discharge Date

ADDITIONAL INFORMATION

Have you ever been convicted of a felony? ❏ Yes ❏ No If yes, please explain (this will not necessarily exclude you from consideration for the position).

_____

_____

_____

_____

_____

AUTHORIZATION

I certify that the information contained in this application is factual, true and complete to the best of my knowledge. I understand that, if employed, falsified statements on this application shall be grounds for immediate dismissal.

I authorize investigation of all statements contained herein and the references and employees listed herein to give you any and all information concerning my previous employment and any pertinent information they may have, personal or otherwise, and release the company from all liability for any damage that may result from the utilization of such information.

I also understand and agree that no representative of the company has the authority to enter into any agreement for employment for any specified period of time, or to make any agreement contrary to the foregoing, unless it is in writing and signed by an authorized company representative.

_____   _____
Signature   Date

Employment Application II

FOR INTERVIEWER'S USE ONLY

Interviewed By: _____ Date: _____

Comments: _____

_____

_____

_____

_____

_____

_____

Interviewed By: _____ Date: _____

Comments: _____

_____

_____

_____

_____

_____

_____

_____

Interviewed By: _____ Date: _____

Comments: _____

_____

_____

_____

_____

_____

_____

_____

Candidate was ❏ Hired ❏ Rejected For Position: _____

Salary: _____ Starting Date: _____

Supervisor: _____

Manager: _____

Comments: _____

_____

_____

Employment Application III

Name _____ Phone Number _____ Date _____

Address _____ City _____ State _____ Zip Code _____

Position Applying For _____ Social Security No. _____ Date of Birth _____

Present or Previous Employer _____ Dates of Employment _____

Address _____ City _____ State _____ Zip Code _____ Phone Number _____

Job Title and Duties _____

Reason for Leaving _____ Starting Salary _____ Ending Salary _____

Present or Previous Employer _____ Dates of Employment _____

Address _____ City _____ State _____ Zip Code _____ Phone Number _____

Job Title and Duties _____

Reason for Leaving _____ Starting Salary _____ Ending Salary _____

	Degree/Course of Study	Dates Attended	Did You Graduate?
Grammar School			❏ Yes ❏ No
High School			❏ Yes ❏ No
College			❏ Yes ❏ No
Other			❏ Yes ❏ No

Reference Name	Address	Occupation	Phone Number
Reference Name	Address	Occupation	Phone Number
Reference Name	Address	Occupation	Phone Number

Applicant's Signature _____

Employment Application IV

Notice to Applicant: We are an Equal Opportunity Employer and do not discriminate on the basis of applicant's race, color, religion, sex, national origin, citizenship, age, physical or mental disability or any other characteristic.

Personal Information (please print)

Name: .... Social Security Number: ....

Address: ....

City:.. State: .... Zip:................................

Phone Number:..

Position Information

Position applied for: ....

Department/Group: ....

Have you ever worked for this organization: ☐ Yes ☐ No   If yes, date(s): ....

Prior position:...

Reason(s) for leaving:...

....

Education (List from present to past)

School/Institution	Major or Area of Study	Degree or Number of Years
....	....	....
....	....	....
....	....	....
....	....	....
....	....	....
....	....	....
....	....	....

Other Information

Name of friends and/or relatives employed by this organization:..

....

....

Position(s) held: ....

....

If you are eligible, are you interested in health insurance? ☐ Yes ☐ No

Employment Application IV

Awards/Achievements

....
....
....
....

References (Please list at least three people who are not related to you)

Name	Occupation	Phone Number

....
....
....
....

Emergency Contact In the event of an emergency, who should we contact?

Name: .... Relationship to applicant:...

Address: ....

City:... State: .... Zip:.......................

Phone Number:..

Name: .... Relationship to applicant:...

Address: ....

City:... State: .... Zip:.......................

Phone Number:..

Acknowledgment (please read carefully)

I hereby certify that the information contained in this application form and in any attachments (hereafter made a part of this application) is true and correct to the best of my knowledge and agree to have any of the statements checked by the organization unless I have indicated to the contrary. I authorize the references listed above to provide the company any and all information concerning my previous employment and any pertinent information that they may have. Further, I release all parties and persons from any and all liability for any damages that may result from furnishing such information to the company as well as from the use or disclosure of such information by the organization or any of its agents, employees or representatives. I understand that any misrepresentation, falsification or material omission of information on this application may result in my failure to receive an offer or, if I am hired, in my dismissal from employment.

....

Applicant's Signature   Date

Employment Application V

We are an Equal Opportunity Employer and do not unlawfully discriminate in employment. No question on this application is used for the purpose of limiting or excluding any applicant from consideration for employment on a basis prohibited by local, state or federal law. Equal access to employment, services and programs is available to all persons. Those applicants requiring reasonable accommodation to the application and/or interview process should notify a representative of the organization.

PERSONAL INFORMATION

Applicant name: _____

Date: _____

Position(s) applied for or type of work desired:

_____

Address: _____

_____

_____

Phone: _____

Social Security No.: _____

Type of employment desired:

❏ Full-time   ❏ Part-time   ❏ Temporary

Date you will be available to start work: _____

Are you able to meet the attendance requirements?

❏ Yes   ❏ No

Do you have any objections to working overtime?

❏ Yes   ❏ No

Can you travel if required by this position?

❏ Yes   ❏ No

Have you ever been previously employed by our organization?

❏ Yes   ❏ No

Can you submit proof of legal employment authorization and identity?

❏ Yes   ❏ No

If you are under 18, can you furnish a work permit if it is required?

❏ Yes   ❏ No

Have you been convicted of a crime in the last 7 years?

❏ Yes   ❏ No

If yes, please explain (a conviction will not automatically bar employment): _____

_____

Driver's license number (if driving is an essential job duty): _____

How were you referred to us? _____

EMPLOYMENT HISTORY

Please provide all employment information for your past three employers, starting with the most recent.

Employer: _____

Position held: _____

Address: _____

Phone: _____

Immediate supervisor and title:

_____

Dates employed: From _____ To _____

Salary: _____

Job summary: _____

Reason for leaving: _____

Employer: _____

Position held: _____

Address: _____

Phone: _____

Immediate supervisor and title:

_____

Dates employed: From _____ To _____

Salary: _____

Job summary: _____

Reason for leaving: _____

Employer: _____

Position held: _____

Address: _____

Phone: _____

Immediate supervisor and title:

_____

Dates employed: From _____ To _____

Salary: _____

Job summary: _____

Reason for leaving: _____

Employment Application V

EDUCATIONAL HISTORY

List school name and location, years completed, course of study and any degrees earned:

High School: _____
_____
_____
_____
_____

College:_____
_____
_____
_____
_____

Technical Training:_____
_____
_____
_____
_____

Other:_____
_____
_____
_____
_____

REFERENCES/OTHER

Other Skills and Qualifications
Summarize any job-related training, skills, licenses, certificates and/or other qualifications:
_____
_____
_____
_____
_____

References
List 3 reference names, phone numbers and years known (do not include relatives or employers):
Name: _____
Occupation: _____
Relationship: _____
Phone: _____

Name: _____
Occupation: _____
Relationship: _____
Phone: _____

Name: _____
Occupation: _____
Relationship: _____
Phone: _____

I hereby authorize the potential employer to contact, obtain and verify the accuracy of information contained in this application from all previous employers, educational institutions and references. I also hereby release from liability the potential employer and its representatives for seeking, gathering and using such information to make employment decisions and all other persons or organizations for providing such information.

I understand that any misrepresentation or material omission made by me on this application will be sufficient cause for cancellation of this application or immediate termination of employment if I am employed, whenever it may be discovered.

If I am employed, I acknowledge that there is no specified length of employment and that this application does not constitute an agreement or contract for employment. Accordingly, either I or the employer can terminate the relationship at will, with or without cause, at any time, so long as there is no violation of applicable federal or state law.

I understand that it is the policy of this organization not to refuse to hire or otherwise discriminate against a qualified individual with a disability because of that person's need for a reasonable accommodation as required by the ADA.

I also understand that if I am employed, I will be required to provide satisfactory proof of identity and legal work authorization within three days of being hired. Failure to submit such proof within the required time shall result in immediate termination of employment.

I represent and warrant that I have read and fully understand the foregoing, and that I seek employment under these conditions.

_____
Applicant's Signature

_____
Date

C7

Consent for Drug & Alcohol Screen Testing

Employee Name: _____

Test Date: _____

Social Security Number: _____

Department: _____

Employee Start Date: _____

Supervisor: _____

I, _____, freely give my consent for this drug

and/or alcohol test. I have been fully informed of the reason for this urine test and I

understand that the results will be forwarded to my supervisor.

If the test results are positive, I will be given the opportunity to explain the results before any

action is taken.

Signature: _____

Date: _____

Employment Interview

Applicant: _____

Job Title: _____   ❑ General Interview   ❑ Promotion Interview

Interviewer: _____   Title: _____

❑ 1st Interview   ❑ 2nd Interview   ❑ 3rd Interview

PERSONALITY TRAITS

Briefly list the personality traits the ideal candidate for this position would possess:

_____

_____

_____

❑ Great for this position.
❑ Good for this position.
❑ Acceptable for this position.
❑ Not very good for this position.
❑ Not acceptable for this position.

Comments: _____

_____

_____

_____

EXPERIENCE

Briefly list the ideal type of experience and training the best candidate for this position would possess:

_____

_____

_____

❑ Exceptional experience and background.
❑ Above-average experience and background.
❑ Average experience and background.
❑ Below-average experience and background.
❑ No experience and background not applicable.

Comments: _____

_____

_____

JOB FAMILIARITY

❑ Exceptional familiarity; no training needed.
❑ Above-average familiarity.
❑ Rudimentary familiarity, but able to meet job performance standards.
❑ Below-average familiarity; training needed.
❑ Applicant has no familiarity in this field.

Comments: _____

_____

_____

WORK FIELD UNDERSTANDING

❑ Exceptional understanding of the field.
❑ Above-average knowledge and understanding.
❑ Average knowledge of this field.
❑ Below-average knowledge of this field.
❑ Poor knowledge and understanding in this field.

Comments: _____

_____

_____

MOTIVATION

❑ Very strong desire to work; excellent level of motivation.
❑ High level of interest in job.
❑ Basic desire to work.
❑ Interest in the position is minimal.
❑ Little or no interest in the position.

Comments: _____

_____

_____

Employment Interview

AMBITION & ENTHUSIASM

❑ Extremely high; very resourceful.

❑ Positive drive to succeed.

❑ Average goals.

❑ Lacks goals and enthusiasm.

❑ Relies on others; no goals or ambition.

Comments: _____

_____

_____

ORIGINALITY & APTITUDE

❑ Exceptional creativity; seems original and proposes new ideas.

❑ Above-average creativity.

❑ Average level of creativity.

❑ Few ideas or suggestions.

❑ Poor creativity—little or no suggestions.

Comments: _____

_____

_____

POISE & COMPOSURE

❑ Very self-assured and capable.

❑ Able to handle problems well.

❑ Fair composure and control.

❑ Below-average composure.

❑ Seemly unstable.

Comments: _____

_____

_____

_____

APPEARANCE

❑ Neat and very well-groomed.

❑ Above-average personal appearance.

❑ Average personal appearance.

❑ Disheveled, disregard for personal appearance.

Comments: _____

_____

OVERALL

❑ Excellent for this position.

❑ Highly possible for other position.

❑ A possible candidate.

❑ An unlikely candidate.

❑ Unsatisfactory.

Comments: _____

_____

_____

_____

RATE THE APPLICANT:

Carefully consider all factors in this evaluation. Then rate the candidate on a scale from 1 to 10, with 10 being the highest possible score.

1 2 3 4 5 6 7 8 9 10

Other position this applicant seems to have experience for: _____

Comments: _____

_____

_____

_____

_____

Interviewer's Signature   Date

Employment Interview Questions & Analysis

Applicant: _____ Job Desired: _____

REFERENCE CHECK

Company Name _____ Telephone _____

Person Contacted _____

Results _____

_____

_____

Company Name _____ Telephone _____

Person Contacted _____

Results _____

_____

_____

Company Name _____ Telephone _____

Person Contacted _____

Results _____

_____

_____

TEST RESULTS

Tested Administered	Raw Score	Rating	Analysis and Comments

Employment Interview Questions & Analysis

INTERVIEW QUESTIONS

Interviewer: _____ Title: _____

❑ 1st Interview   ❑ 2nd Interview   ❑ 3rd Interview

1. What are your strengths? _____

2. What are your weaknesses? _____

3. How would your current (or last) boss describe you? _____

4   What were your boss's responsibilities? _____

5. What's your opinion of him or her? _____

6. How would your co-workers or subordinates describe you professionally? _____
_____

7. Why do you want to leave your present employer? _____

8. Why should we hire you over the other finalists? _____

9. What qualities or talents would you bring to the job? _____

10. Tell me about your accomplishments. _____

11. What is your most important contribution to your last (or current) employer? _____

12. How do you perform under deadline pressure? Give me an example. _____

13. How do you react to criticism? _____

14. Describe a conflict or disagreement at work in which you were involved. How was it resolved? _____
_____

15. What are two of the biggest problems you've encountered at your last (or current) job and how did you overcome them? _____
_____

16. Think of a major crisis you've faced at work and explain how you handled it. _____

17. Give me an example of a risk that you took at your last (or current) job and how it turned out. _____
_____

18. What's your managerial style like? _____

19. Have you ever hired employees, and, if so, have they lived up to your expectations? _____

20. What type of performance problems have you encountered in people who report to you, and how did you motivate them to improve?
_____

21. Describe a typical day at your current (or last) job. _____

22. What do you see yourself doing five years from now? _____

Other _____
_____
_____
_____

Employment Interview Questions & Analysis

APPEARANCE

- ❑ Neat, well-groomed, very presentable.
- ❑ Pays extra attention to personal appearance.
- ❑ Standard personal appearance.
- ❑ Neglects details in personal appearance.
- ❑ Not groomed and untidy.

Notes:_____
_____
_____

PERSONALITY TRAITS (His/her personality suitable for position)

- ❑ Exceptional for this position.
- ❑ Good for this position.
- ❑ Workable for this position.
- ❑ Personality may not fit this position.
- ❑ Unsuitable for this position.

Notes:_____
_____
_____

COMPOSURE

- ❑ Good control; very calm; thrives under pressure.
- ❑ Appears to handle problems well.
- ❑ Typical composure.
- ❑ Seems bothered or stressed.
- ❑ Uneasy; shows concern.

Notes:_____
_____
_____

MOTIVATION

- ❑ Very motivated; strong desire to work.
- ❑ Quite interested in job.
- ❑ Desires to work.
- ❑ Low level of interest in position.
- ❑ Impassive and not interested in position.

Notes:_____
_____
_____

INITIATIVE

- ❑ Driven to succeed and sets very high goals.
- ❑ Possesses confidence and makes an effort.
- ❑ Takes some initiative; has goals.
- ❑ Rather irresponsible; few goals.
- ❑ Little direction; minimal goals, relies on others too often.

Notes:_____
_____
_____

JOB EXPERIENCE

- ❑ Excellent experience, education and background.
- ❑ Good experience and background.
- ❑ Standard experience and background.
- ❑ Has some background experience.
- ❑ Background not relevant to position.

Notes:_____
_____
_____

JOB KNOWLEDGE

- ❑ Highly knowledgeable; little training needed.
- ❑ Very efficient; may need some training.
- ❑ Basic; training required.
- ❑ Extensive training needed.
- ❑ Not related to this position.

Notes:_____
_____
_____

GENERAL WORK FIELD INFORMATION

- ❑ Very knowledgeable and high level of understanding in this field.
- ❑ Above-average knowledge and understanding.
- ❑ Average work field knowledge.
- ❑ Slight understanding of field.
- ❑ Very poor knowledge and understanding.

Notes:_____
_____
_____

OVERALL

- ❑ Exceptional—highly recommended.
- ❑ Above average.
- ❑ Average.
- ❑ Below average.
- ❑ Unsatisfactory.

Notes:_____
_____
_____

ANALYSIS

- ❑ Applicant is recommended for position.
- ❑ A possible candidate for the position.
- ❑ A very unlikely candidate.

Notes:_____
_____
_____
_____

Interviewer's Signature: _____ **Date:** _____

Avoiding Interview-Related Lawsuits

Interviews are designed to determine the best candidate for your position. However, asking illegal or improper questions (even inadvertently) can result in compliance actions or lawsuits. Unfortunately, there is no way to guarantee that you will never be sued. However, the risk can be minimized by following some basic guidelines:

Review laws carefully. Do some research on federal, state and local laws on proper interview questions. Use the Internet, bookstores or the local library for references.

Know what questions to ask. Develop a list of pre-planned questions. Ask the same question of every applicant, and document responses. Even informal "chatting" can be a problem if questions are asked about marital status or children.

Document each step. The interview should be documented in two ways: with notes taken during the interview and recap documentation. Inform the applicant that you will be taking notes. Once the interview is complete, your recap documentation is an overall analysis and recommendation. All records should be carefully maintained and preserved, and ready-made forms used when possible.

Treat each applicant respectfully. This applies not only to the interview, but specifically to your rejection methods. Be as professional, respectful and kind as possible.

Be aware of bias. A biased individual has a tendency to find traits and attitudes that fulfill preconceived beliefs. If you know a manager is biased, do not allow him or her to conduct interviews, as their personal opinions and beliefs may be inadvertently communicated to the applicant in the interview.

Consider rejected applicants' challenges. Take the time to review all rejected applicants' challenges and provide a method for rejected applicants to voice their dissatisfaction. If there is error on the part of the company, rectify the error.

Be aware of staffing. It's much better to do an internal review of hiring practices than have a third party review your records after a complaint. Don't just review the process annually for the affirmative action plan. Know what your selection rates are. If there appears to be an adverse impact, fully investigate the matter, advise management of risks and enlist managers in finding solutions.

Employee Reference Check

REFERENCE CHECK

TO:

Company Name: _____ Telephone: _____

Address: _____ City: _____ State: _____ Zip: _____

Attention: _____ Title: _____

FROM:

Company Name: _____ Telephone: _____

Address: _____ City: _____ State: _____ Zip: _____

Name: _____ Title: _____

TO BE FILLED OUT BY APPLICANT

Previous employer: I have made application for employment with the company above. I authorize you to furnish this company with any information requested concerning my employment records, character, habits and ability. I do hereby release (fill in previous employer's company name) _____ from any claims, suits and liabilities for any damage resulting from their actions and conduct in responding to this request and supplying the information.

Name While in Your Employ: _____

Social Security Number: _____

Dates of Employment: _____ Department : _____

Start Position: _____ Salary: _____ Per ❏ hour ❏ week ❏ month ❏ annual

End Position: _____ Salary: _____ Per ❏ hour ❏ week ❏ month ❏ annual

Immediate Supervisor: _____

_____
Signature

TO BE FILLED OUT BY EMPLOYER

Was the applicant employed by your company? ❏ Yes ❏ No

Is all the information stated above correct? ❏ Yes ❏ No

If no, what is incorrect? _____

_____

What were the applicant's responsibilities? _____

_____

_____

Employee Reference Check

Please rate the applicant's performance in the following areas:

Attendance	❑ Above Average	❑ Average	❑ Below Average
Reliability	❑ Above Average	❑ Average	❑ Below Average
Quality of Work	❑ Above Average	❑ Average	❑ Below Average
Teamwork & Cooperation	❑ Above Average	❑ Average	❑ Below Average
Skill Level	❑ Above Average	❑ Average	❑ Below Average
Enthusiasm & Initiative	❑ Above Average	❑ Average	❑ Below Average
Productivity	❑ Above Average	❑ Average	❑ Below Average

While working for your company, what were this person's strong points? _____
_____
_____

What were his or her weak points? _____
_____
_____

Would you consider rehiring this person? ❑ Yes ❑ No Why or why not?_____

What was his or her reason for leaving?_____
_____
_____

Additional Comments:
_____
_____
_____
_____

Completed By:_____ Date: _____

Company:_____

Employee Reference Check II

APPLICANT: ....

POSITION:..

Reference:...

Company: ....

Address: ....

....

Phone: ....

Dates of Employment: ....

Job Title: ....

Duties: ....

....

....

Why did the applicant leave your employment?

....

....

....

What were the applicant's best job skills? ....

....

....

....

In what areas could the applicant improve? ....

....

....

....

Did the applicant get along with supervisors?

❏ Yes   ❏ No   With peers? ❏ Yes   ❏ No

In comparison to others with the same position, please rate the applicant:

❏ Above average   ❏ Average   ❏ Below average

Following is a list of personal characteristics. Using a scale from 1 to 10 (with 10 being the highest), please rate the applicant, based on your experience working together.

Punctual	1	2	3	4	5	6	7	8	9	10
Pleasant	1	2	3	4	5	6	7	8	9	10
Honest	1	2	3	4	5	6	7	8	9	10
Flexible	1	2	3	4	5	6	7	8	9	10
Organized	1	2	3	4	5	6	7	8	9	10
Composed	1	2	3	4	5	6	7	8	9	10
Reliable	1	2	3	4	5	6	7	8	9	10
Competent	1	2	3	4	5	6	7	8	9	10
Professional	1	2	3	4	5	6	7	8	9	10
Safety-Conscious	1	2	3	4	5	6	7	8	9	10
Team Player	1	2	3	4	5	6	7	8	9	10
Lazy	1	2	3	4	5	6	7	8	9	10
Inconsistent	1	2	3	4	5	6	7	8	9	10
Inattentive	1	2	3	4	5	6	7	8	9	10
Temperamental	1	2	3	4	5	6	7	8	9	10
Antagonistic	1	2	3	4	5	6	7	8	9	10

Would you rehire this person? ❏ Yes   ❏ No

Why or why not? ....

....

....

Do you have any additional comments on this individual's character or work habits? ....

....

....

....

....

CHECKED BY: ....

DATE: ....

GOOD CANDIDATE ❏ YES   ❏ NO

Co-worker Reference Check

APPLICANT: ....
POSITION:...

Reference:...
Company: ....
Address: ....
....
Phone: ....

How long did you work with the applicant? ....

What was your job? ....

What was the applicant's job? ....
....

What were the applicant's principal duties?..............
....
....

What did you like about working with the applicant?
....
....
....

What did you dislike about working with the applicant?
....
....
....

Was this person easy to get along with? ....
....
....
....

Following is a list of personal characteristics. Using a scale from 1 to 10 (with 10 being the highest), please rate the applicant, based on your experience working together.

Punctual	1	2	3	4	5	6	7	8	9	10
Pleasant	1	2	3	4	5	6	7	8	9	10
Honest	1	2	3	4	5	6	7	8	9	10
Flexible	1	2	3	4	5	6	7	8	9	10
Organized	1	2	3	4	5	6	7	8	9	10
Composed	1	2	3	4	5	6	7	8	9	10
Reliable	1	2	3	4	5	6	7	8	9	10
Competent	1	2	3	4	5	6	7	8	9	10
Professional	1	2	3	4	5	6	7	8	9	10
Safety-Conscious	1	2	3	4	5	6	7	8	9	10
Team Player	1	2	3	4	5	6	7	8	9	10
Lazy	1	2	3	4	5	6	7	8	9	10
Inconsistent	1	2	3	4	5	6	7	8	9	10
Inattentive	1	2	3	4	5	6	7	8	9	10
Temperamental	1	2	3	4	5	6	7	8	9	10
Antagonistic	1	2	3	4	5	6	7	8	9	10

Would you like to work with this person again?
❏ Yes   ❏ No   Why or why not? ....
....
....

Do you have any additional comments on this individual's character or work habits? ....
....
....
....
....

CHECKED BY: ....
DATE: ....
GOOD CANDIDATE ❏ YES   ❏ NO

Grounds for Immediate Dismissal

1 Misuse or abuse of property or equipment belonging to the restaurant.

2 Theft of money, equipment or personal or restaurant property.

3 Altering a guest's charge to add a gratuity without management approval.

4 Requesting or approaching guest about a gratuity.

5 Falsifying or changing a charge after the guest has signed it.

6 Use of alcohol or illegal drugs during working hours or reporting to work under the influence of such.

7 Missing a scheduled shift without prior management approval.

8 Falsifying application information, paperwork or time cards.

9 Threatening, attempting or doing bodily harm to another.

10 Intentionally not charging for any food or liquor items.

11 Animosity, rudeness or unkindness to a guest.

12 Serving alcohol to a minor or an obviously intoxicated guest.

13 Violating any safety procedures in food preparation or service.

14 Disclosure or use of confidential information.

Job Description & Specifications

Position: _____

Prepared By: _____ **Date Prepared:** _____

Salary Range: _____ Department/Supervisor: _____

Primary Tasks

1._____
2._____
3._____
4._____
5._____
6._____
7._____
8._____
9._____
10. _____
11. _____
12. _____

Personality Traits or Characteristics Required

1._____
2._____
3._____
4._____
5._____

Notes

_____
_____
_____

Job Description Template

Job Title: _____   Company Job Code: _____

FLSA Status: _____   Division/Department: _____

EEO Code: _____   Reports To: _____

Salary Grade/Band: _____   Last Revision Date: _____

SUMMARY

This section provides an overview or summary of the job.

ADDITIONAL RESPONSIBILITIES

This section provides additional functions of the job that are desirable but not required. Since these duties are not "essential functions," an applicant who cannot perform these duties will still be considered for the position.

KNOWLEDGE AND SKILL REQUIREMENTS

Specific knowledge and skill requirements are listed here. Examples would include sales techniques, generally accepted accounting principles and physical requirements. Also listed here are the years of experience needed and/or education requirements.

PRIMARY RESPONSIBILITIES

This section lists the primary job functions. Responsibilities should be listed in order of importance and/or time spent. Duties listed here should be considered "essential" to help define "essential functions" for the purposes of the Americans with Disabilities Act. If an applicant cannot perform most, if not all, of the essential functions, the applicant will not be considered.

WORKING CONDITIONS

This section contains information on non-standard working conditions such as extensive travel, high noise levels and frequent lifting of over "_____" pounds.

ACKNOWLEDGMENT

The dated signature lines for the manager/supervisor and employee provides a record that the employee was shown and understands the job responsibilities.

Manager's Name (print):_____   Signature:_____   Date:_____

Employee's Name (print):_____   Signature:_____   Date:_____

Uniform Purchase Agreement

Employee: _____ **Date:** _____

ITEM	# PURCHASED	PRICE EACH	TOTAL

❑ Items have been paid in full

❑ Cost of uniforms to be deducted from payroll
check for the week ending _____

TOTAL DUE

I agree to reimburse the company in full for the above items. In addition, I authorize my employer
to withhold any salary due to me until all items have been paid for or returned.

_____   _____
Employee's Signature   Date

_____   _____
Manager's Signature   Date

Employee Schedule

Shift: _____ **Date:** _____

Labor Category: _____ **Labor Budget:** _____

EMPLOYEE	SCHEDULE	HOURS SCHEDULED	RATE	TOTAL COST
TOTAL				

Work Schedule

Week Of: _____ Department: _____

Date Prepared: _____ Prepared By: _____

POSITION	NAME	SUN	MON	TUE	WED	THUR	FRI	SAT
	scheduled lunch break here →							
	scheduled lunch break here →							
	scheduled lunch break here →							
	scheduled lunch break here →							
	scheduled lunch break here →							
	scheduled lunch break here →							
	scheduled lunch break here →							
	scheduled lunch break here →							
	scheduled lunch break here →							
	scheduled lunch break here →							
	scheduled lunch break here →							

Work Schedule II

Prepared By: _____   **Week Of:** _____

Approved By: _____

EMPLOYEE	SUN	MON	TUE	WED	THUR	FRI	SAT	TOTAL

Work Schedule III

Employee	Sunday	Monday	Tuesday	Wednesday	Thursday	Friday	Saturday

WEEK OF:

Work Schedule IV

Week Of: _____

Employee	PH #	SUN	MON	TUE	WED	THUR	FRI	SAT

Work Schedule V

DATE														
EMPLOYEE	L	D	L	D	L	D	L	D	L	D	L	D	L	D

Employee Vacation Request

EMPLOYEE INFORMATION

Name: _____ Date: _____

Employee Number: _____ Department: _____

Vacation Days Available: _____ As Of (Date): _____

VACATION REQUEST

Dates/Times Requested Off: _____ ❑ Approved ❑ Denied

_____ ❑ Approved ❑ Denied

_____ ❑ Approved ❑ Denied

_____ ❑ Approved ❑ Denied

_____ ❑ Approved ❑ Denied

Alternative Days Requested, If Denied:

_____ ❑ Approved ❑ Denied

_____ ❑ Approved ❑ Denied

_____ ❑ Approved ❑ Denied

Employee's Signature: _____ **Date:** _____

Manager's Signature: _____ **Date:** _____

Comments: _____

_____

_____

_____

_____

_____

_____

_____

_____

Employee Attendance Record

Name: _____ Date of Employment: _____ Year: 20_____

Employee Number: _____ Department: _____

Mark each instance of missing work below with the reason for the absence.

| **S** = Sick **V** = Vacation **H** = Holiday **I** = Injury **D** = Death in the Family **J** = Jury Duty |
| **L** = Leave Without Pay **U** = Unexcused **P** = Personal Time **F** = Maternity Leave/Family Leave Act |

	Jan	Feb	March	April	May	June	July	Aug	Sept	Oct	Nov	Dec
1												
2												
3												
4												
5												
6												
7												
8												
9												
10												
11												
12												
13												
14												
15												
16												
17												
18												
19												
20												
21												
22												
23												
24												
25												
26												
27												
28												
29												
30												
31												

Absence Summary

S _____ V _____ H _____ I _____ D _____

J _____ L _____ U _____ P _____ F _____

Absence Report

Name: _____ Date of Employment: _____

Employee Number: _____ Department: _____

First Date Absent: _____ Expected Return Date: _____

REASON FOR ABSENCE

❏ Sick ❏ Vacation ❏ Holiday ❏ Injury

❏ Death in the Family ❏ Jury Duty ❏ Leave Without Pay ❏ Unexcused

❏ Personal Time ❏ Maternity Leave/Family Leave Act ❏ Suspension

❏ Other _____

Explanation _____

_____

_____

_____

ABSENCE DETAIL

This absence was:

Expected in Advance ❏ Yes ❏ No

Reported in Advance of Shift ❏ Yes ❏ No

Considered by Supervisor as ❏ Unexcused ❏ Excused

_____
Signature of Supervisor or Manager   Date

Payroll Adjustment

Name: _____ Date of Employment: _____

Employee Number: _____ Payroll Number: _____

Date Payroll Adjustment Effective: _____

Authorized By: _____

NEW ADDRESS

Street Address: _____

City, State, Zip: _____

Home Phone: _____

FOR NEW EMPLOYEES ONLY Social Security Number: _____ Date of Birth: _____

CHANGE (existing employees only)

JOB From: _____ To: _____

SHIFT From: _____ To: _____

DEPARTMENT From: _____ To: _____

PAY From: _____ To: _____

REASON FOR CHANGE

❏ Hired   ❏ Rehired   ❏ Promotion   ❏ Demotion

❏ Transfer   ❏ Merit Increase   ❏ Resignation   ❏ Layoff

❏ Termination   ❏ Probation Completed ❏ Retirement   ❏ Union Contract

❏ Other _____

LEAVE OF ABSENCE

From: _____ To: _____

Charged to Vacation ❏ Yes ❏ No   Family Leave Act ❏ Yes ❏ No

_____   _____
Signature of Supervisor or Manager   Date

Today's Issues

Date: _____   Manager: _____

TODAY'S SPECIALS

_____

_____

_____

_____

_____

_____

_____

TODAY'S SOUPS

_____

_____

_____

_____

_____

TODAY'S TOPICS:

SPECIAL RECOGNITION:

SERVICE TOPICS:

SALES:

PROFITS:

TEAMWORK:

TIP FOR THE DAY:

Production Schedule

DATE PREPARED: _____ PREPARED BY: _____

ITEM	SALES FORECAST	PRIOR DAY CARRYOVER	NEW PRODUCTION	TOTAL AVAILABLE	# SOLD	CARRYOVER

Special Instructions:

Employee Accident Report

EMPLOYEE INVOLVED

Name:_____

Address: _____

Phone: _____

Date of birth: _____

SS#: _____

Emergency contact: _____

ACCIDENT DETAILS

Date of accident occurred: _____

Time of accident occurred: _____

Location accident occurred: _____

Manager on duty: _____

Date reported: _____

Time reported:_____

EMPLOYMENT STATEMENT

To whom was the accident reported? _____

_____

Specify work area where accident occurred:

_____

_____

Part of body injured: _____

_____

Specify machine, appliance, substance or object
connected with accident: _____

_____

Describe what you were doing when accident occurred:

_____

_____

_____

_____
Employee's Signature   Date

SUPERVISOR'S DESCRIPTION OF ACCIDENT

_____

_____

_____

_____

_____

_____

_____

_____

INJURY DETAILS

Disabling injury   ❏ Yes ❏ No

Sent to hospital   ❏ Yes ❏ No

Return to regular job   ❏ Yes ❏ No

Return to light duty   ❏ Yes ❏ No

Estimated days of disability: _____

Date to return to work: _____

Initial medical diagnosis: _____

_____
Manager's Signature   Date

Sample Confidentiality Agreement

This CONFIDENTIALITY AGREEMENT (herein referred to as "Agreement") is made this _____ day of _____, 20___, by and between _____ (herein referred to as the "Company") and _____ (herein referred to as "Beneficiary").

WHEREAS, the Beneficiary would like to be associated with the Company's business and desires to learn about, and participate in the Company's services and confidential information in pursuit of a business relationship and/or the consummation of a transaction between the Beneficiary and the Company.

WHEREAS, the Beneficiary agrees that they will be in receipt of confidential information created, ordered by and conceived by the Company or prepared by a third party such as a client, attorney, partner, employee or representative for the Company's business purposes.

WHEREAS, the Beneficiary agrees that the distribution, broadcasting or circulation of such information to any has the potential to significantly harm to the Company.

WHEREAS, the Company is willing to disclose information to the Beneficiary subject to the conditions and terms contained herein.

The Beneficiary hereby agrees as follows:

1. **CONFIDENTIAL INFORMATION**

   For purposes of this Agreement, Confidential Information shall mean all Company information including but not limited to: written and oral communications, strategic plans, products, services, financial statements, pricing, business plans, business records, client lists, correspondence, market reports, employee information, suppliers and vendors lists, recipes, formulas, manuals, policies, procedures, ideas, concepts, systems, practices, methods, processes, technologies, inventions, discoveries or theory and all other information which may be disclosed by the Company or to which the Beneficiary may be provided access by the Company or others in accordance with this Agreement, or which is generated as a result of the Company's business purposes which is not made publically available.

2. **BENEFICIARY'S OBLIGATIONS**

   Beneficiary agrees to keep the Confidential Information, including any such information developed by Beneficiary for the Company, confidential. Beneficiary also agrees:

   a. not to use any of the Confidential Information except for express Company business purposes.

   b. to protect Confidential Information against unauthorized use, publication or disclosure.

   c. not to, directly or indirectly, reveal, publish, disclose, broadcast or otherwise use any of the

Sample Confidentiality Agreement

Confidential Information except as specifically authorized by the Company in this Agreement.

d. to keep all Confidential Information furnished by the Company, and to return all Confidential Information received in written or tangible form, including copies or reproductions, upon request of the Company, within fifteen (15) days of such request.

e. that in the event that Beneficiary becomes legally ordered by deposition, subpoena or similar process to disclose any of the information, the Beneficiary will provide the Company with prior written notice so the Company may seek an appropriate remedy and/or waive compliance with the terms of this Agreement. If the Company does not legally block release of the information, the Beneficiary agrees to supply only the portion of the Confidential Information legally required.

f. that Beneficiary cannot assign its rights under this Agreement without the written consent of the Company.

3. EXCEPTIONS

The confidentiality obligations shall not apply to:

a. information that the Company waives the Beneficiary's duty as to the confidentiality in writing.

b. information which is, or later becomes, legally obtainable from other non-confidential sources.

c. information of which Beneficiary knew prior to Company's disclosure to Beneficiary; evidenced by written records.

4. NO RIGHT TO CONFIDENTIAL INFORMATION

Beneficiary hereby agrees that no license, either expressed or implied, is granted to Beneficiary by the Company to use any of the Confidential Information. All Confidential Information, even if created by Beneficiary, shall be the exclusive property of the Company. The Beneficiary has no right, license or title to such information.

Sample Confidentiality Agreement

5. REMEDIES

Beneficiary agrees that the Confidential Information is unique and that breaching this Agreement would cause the Company irreparable harm which cannot be adequately compensated for in damages in a legal action. Therefore, the Company shall be entitled to injunctive relief for such breach in addition to any other rights or legal remedies.

6. INDEMNIFICATION

Beneficiary agrees to indemnify and exempt from liability the Company and its directors, shareholders, employees and agents from and against any losses, damages, liabilities or expenses incurred by the Company as a result of Beneficiary's breach of this Agreement.

7. NO IMPLIED WAIVER

Company's failure to insist upon strict performance of the terms of this Agreement shall not be construed as a waiver of any right. The failure of the Company to take action at the earliest possible time to redress any action shall not deprive the Company of the right to take action at any later date.

8. SEVERABILITY

If any term of this Agreement is deemed by a court to be invalid or unenforceable, then this Agreement and all of the remaining terms, shall remain in full effect as if such invalid or unenforceable term had never been included.

9. LEGAL FEES

If any legal action is needed to enforce or interpret this Agreement, the prevailing party in such action shall be entitled to reasonable attorney's fees, expert witness fees and other costs in addition to any other entitled relief.

10. TERM AND TERMINATION

This Agreement is legally binding when signed by the Beneficiary and shall be effective as of the date that the Beneficiary first received any Confidential Information. Beneficiary's obligations towards the Confidential Information shall remain in full effect until further written notice from Company.

11. GOVERNING LAW

This Agreement shall be construed in accordance with the laws of the United States. Beneficiary consents to the exclusive jurisdiction of the state courts and United States federal courts for resolution of any dispute arising out of this Agreement.

Sample Confidentiality Agreement

IN WITNESS THEREOF, the undersigned parties hereby executed this Agreement through their duty-authorized representatives as of the date first written above.

_____

Organization

_____

Signature

_____

Name

_____

Title

_____

Organization

_____

Signature

_____

Name

_____

Title

(This Confidentiality Agreement is only an example document only and is in no way intended to substitute for the advice of an attorney. The user should consult with legal counsel in his or her own jurisdiction or county when drafting any legal document.)

Sample Independent Contractor's Agreement

This Independent Contractor's Agreement ("Agreement") is made this ___ day of _____, 20___, by and between _____, a _____ company ("Company"), and _____, an independent contractor ("Contractor"), in consideration of the mutual promises made herein, as follows:

ARTICLE 1   TERM OF AGREEMENT

This Agreement will become effective on _____, 20___, and will continue in effect until the services provided for herein have been performed, or for a period of _____ years, unless sooner terminated.

ARTICLE 2   SERVICES TO BE PERFORMED BY CONTRACTOR

2.a.   **Specific Services.** Contractor agrees to perform the services specified in the "Description of Services" attached to this Agreement as Exhibit A and incorporated herein by this reference.

2.b.   **Method of Performing Services.** Contractor will determine the method and means of performing the services as attached to this Agreement in Exhibit A.

2.c.   **Assistants.** At Contractor's own expense, Contractor may employ assistants as needed to perform the services required of Contractor by this Agreement. Company may not directly supervise, or control in any manner, the Contractor's assistants or employees in the performance of specified services.

ARTICLE 3   COMPENSATION *(choose the method of payment best suited for your needs)*

3.a.   **Hourly Compensation with Stated Maximum and Minimum.** For the services to be performed by Contractor, Company agrees to pay to Contractor the sum of _____ Dollars ($_____) per hour. In no event, however, will the compensation paid to Contractor be less than _____ Dollars ($_____) per hour, or more than _____ Dollars ($_____) per hour. Contractor will submit to Company a statement of services rendered at the end of each month. Company agrees to pay the amount due to Contractor for services on or before the thirtieth (30th) day of the following month.

OR

Flat Rate. For the services to be performed by Contractor, Company agrees to pay Contractor the sum of _____ Dollars ($_____).

Sample Independent Contractor's Agreement

OR

Retainer. Company agrees to pay Contractor for the services set forth in "Description of Services" attached to this Agreement as Exhibit A, the sum of _____ Dollars ($_____) as a retainer at the time of execution of this Agreement.

ARTICLE 4   OBLIGATIONS OF CONTRACTOR

4.a.   **Hours of Service.** Contractor agrees to perform the services attached to this Agreement as Exhibit A on Company's premises during Company's regular business hours.

4.b.   **Minimum Amount of Service.** Contractor agrees to devote a minimum of _____ (____) hours per month to the performance of the services described herein.

4.c.   **Service for Other Parties.** In Contractor's sole discretion, Contractor may perform services for and be employed by additional clients, persons or companies as Contractor sees fit.

4.d.   **Workers' Compensation.** Contractor agrees to provide workers' compensation insurance for Contractor's employees and agents. Contractor agrees to hold Company harmless for any claims of injury, disability or death of any of Contractor's employees or agents.

4.e.   **Tools and Equipment.** Contractor will supply all tools and equipment needed to perform the services under this Agreement.

4.f.   **Liability Insurance.** Contractor agrees to maintain a policy of insurance in the minimum amount of _____ Dollars ($_____) for any negligent acts performed by Contractor or Contractor's employees or agents while carrying out duties under this Agreement. Contractor agrees to hold Company harmless from any claims arising from any such negligent act or omission.

OR

Limited Liability. Company will indemnify and hold Contractor harmless from any costs, claims, judgments, attorneys' fees and attachments in any way connected with the services rendered to Company under the terms of this Agreement, unless Contractor is judged by a court to be guilty of willful misconduct. Contractor will not be liable to Company, or to anyone who claims any right due to a relationship with Company, for any acts or omissions in the performance of services under the terms of this Agreement or on the part of employees or agents of Contractor unless such acts or omissions are due to willful misconduct.

Sample Independent Contractor's Agreement

4.g. **Assignment.** This Agreement, and any obligations under this Agreement, may not be assigned by Contractor without the prior written consent of Company.

ARTICLE 5 OBLIGATIONS OF COMPANY

5.a. **Assignment.** This Agreement, and any obligations under this Agreement, may not be assigned by Company without the prior written consent of Contractor.

5.b. **Company Cooperation.** Company agrees to provide access to all documents and comply with all reasonable requests of Contractor relating to the performance of Contractor's duties under this Agreement.

5.c. **Work Space.** Company agrees to accommodate and furnish space on Company's premises for use by Contractor while performing the above-described services.

ARTICLE 6 TERMINATION OF AGREEMENT

6.a. **Termination Upon Notice.** Notwithstanding any other provisions of this Agreement, either the Company or Contractor may terminate this Agreement at any time by giving thirty (30) days' written notice to the other party. Unless otherwise terminated as provided herein, this Agreement shall continue in force for a period of _____(____) months or until the services have been performed.

OR

Agreement Expiration. Unless otherwise terminated as provided herein, this Agreement shall continue in force for a period of _____(____) months (until the services provided for herein have been fully and completely performed) and shall thereupon terminate unless renewed in writing by both parties.

6.b. **Termination by Bankruptcy.** This Agreement shall terminate automatically if either party files for bankruptcy.

6.c. **Termination by Sale of Business.** This Agreement shall terminate automatically by the sale of the business of either party.

6.d. **Termination by Death.** This Agreement shall terminate automatically upon the death of the Contractor.

Sample Independent Contractor's Agreement

6.e.   **Termination by Improper Assignment.** This Agreement shall terminate automatically on assignment of this Agreement by either the Contractor or Company without the express written consent of the other party.

6.f.   **Termination by Company for Default of Contractor.** In the event that Contractor defaults in the performance of this Agreement or materially breaches any of its provisions, the Company, at Company's option, may terminate this Agreement by giving ten (10) days' written notice to Contractor. For the purposes of this clause, material breach of this Agreement shall include, but not be limited to,

_____ .

6.g.   **Termination by Contractor for Default of Company.** In the event that the Company defaults in the performance of this Agreement or materially breach any of its provisions, Contractor, at Contractor's option, may terminate this Agreement by giving ten (10) days' written notice to Company. For the purposes of this paragraph, material breach of this Agreement shall include, but not be limited to, _____ .

6.h.   **Termination for Non-Payment.** Should Company fail to pay Contractor all or any part of the compensation set forth in Paragraph 3.a. of this Agreement by the date due, Contractor, at Contractor's option, may terminate this Agreement if payment is not made by Company within thirty (30) days from the date payment is due.

ARTICLE 7   GENERAL PROVISIONS

7.a.   **Entire Agreement.** This Agreement supersedes any agreements, either oral or in writing, between the parties hereto regarding the performance of services by Contractor for Company, and contains all of the covenants and agreements between the parties with respect to the rendering of such services. Contractor and Company acknowledges that no promises, representations, inducements or agreements, orally or otherwise, have been made by any party, or anyone acting on behalf of any party, which are not contained herein, and that no other agreement or statement not contained in this Agreement shall be valid or binding. The only modifications effective to this Agreement will be made in writing and signed by both Contractor and Company.

7.b.   **Personal Notices.** Any notices to be given by either party to the other may be effected either by personal delivery. Notices delivered personally shall be deemed communicated as of the date of actual receipt.

7.c.   **Mailed Notices.** Any notices to be given by either party to the other may be effected by mail, registered or certified, postage prepaid with return receipt requested. Mailed notices shall be

Sample Independent Contractor's Agreement

addressed to the parties at the addresses appearing in the introductory paragraph of this Agreement, but each party may change that address by written notice in accordance with this paragraph. Mailed notices shall be deemed communicated as of three (3) days after the date of mailing.

7.d.   **Partial Invalidity.** If any provision of this Agreement is held by a court of competent jurisdiction to be invalid, void or unenforceable, the remaining provisions shall continue in full force without being invalidated in any way.

7.e.   **Payment of Monies Due Deceased Contractor.** If Contractor dies prior to the completion of this Agreement, any monies due Contractor from Company under this Agreement as of the date of death shall be paid to Contractor's executors, administrators, heirs, successors and assigns.

(OPTIONAL)

7.f.   **Arbitration.** Any controversy or claim relating to this Agreement or the breach thereof will be settled by arbitration in accordance with the rules of the American Arbitration Association, and judgment upon the award rendered by the arbitrator(s) may be entered in any court having jurisdiction thereof.

OR

In the event of a dispute, each party will appoint one person to hear and determine the dispute, and if they are unable to agree, then the two chosen persons will select a third impartial arbitrator whose decision will be final and conclusive on both parties. The cost of such arbitration will be determined by the arbitrators.

(OPTIONAL)

7.g.   **Liquidated Damages.** In the event of a breach of this Agreement by Contractor, it would be extremely difficult to fix the actual damages and, therefore, Contractor will pay to Company as liquidated damages and not as a penalty, the sum of _____ Dollars ($_____), which represents a reasonable compensation for the loss incurred because of the breach.

7.h.   **Attorneys' Fees.** If any action at law or in equity, is brought to enforce or interpret the terms of this Agreement, the prevailing party shall be entitled to reasonable attorneys' fees, in addition to any other relief to which that party may be entitled.

Sample Independent Contractor's Agreement

Executed at _____, _____, on the date and year first written above.

_____
Contractor Name

_____
Signature

_____
Name

_____
Title

_____
Company Name

_____
Signature

_____
Name

_____
Title

_____

_____

This Independent Contractor's Agreement is for basic informational purposes only.
Consult with legal counsel when drafting your own version of this document

Employee Development & Performance Plan

The Employee Development & Performance Plan is a detailed, step-by-step program designed to improve communication between employees and supervisors, enhance customer service, increase overall productivity and boost company morale. It is divided into three sections: preview, preparation and feedback. Each section can be specifically tailored for any establishment by adding company-specific details.

STEP 1: PREVIEW SESSION

The first step of the Employee Development & Performance Plan (EDPP) is the Preview Session, where the supervisor schedules a time to discuss with the employee the program details. It is appropriate to schedule the Preview Session one week prior to the Feedback Session to allow the employee appropriate preparation for the EDPP.

The employee's immediate supervisor is designated the evaluator, unless the employee is a member of a self-managed work team and has no supervisor. In that case, an evaluator must be decided prior to the EDPP.

Follow the steps below for the Preview Session:

1. Review all EDPP instructions carefully. Discuss each step of the process and answer any questions the employee may have. Next, incorporate any specific company evaluation policies into the EDPP.

2. Establish a timeline for the EDPP.

3. Review the employee's job description to make sure duties and responsibilities are accurate and up to date.

4. Review the employee's Personal Performance Standards. The Performance Standards should include particular behaviors, special assignments, specific goals or results, special training, etc., that relate directly to the employee.

5. Review the Performance Elements listed on the following page. Determine which are relevant to the employee's job and what may need to be added. Unlike Performance Standards (which are more personal), the Performance Elements should be used universally for all employees in that work unit to which they are applicable.

STEP 2: EDPP PREPARATION

The employee and the supervisor should each draft their own individual responses to Parts I through III of the EDPP. The responses should be based on performance of the employee's duties and responsibilities, Personal Performance Standards and the relevant Performance Elements.

Both the employee and supervisor should demonstrate how the employee's job and performance standards relate to the organization's goals, values, objectives and quality improvement efforts.

Finally, Part IV of the EDPP is completed by the employee only. This is the employee's opportunity to give the supervisor feedback on the supervisor's effectiveness, communication and leadership.

STEP 3: FEEDBACK SESSION

After completing Parts I through III of the EDPP, the employee and supervisor meet to discuss their individual responses. An open and constructive discussion is the main objective. This conversation should result in a clear understanding of the employee's past performance, future expectations and development objectives. Finally, the employee should present his or her review of the supervisor from Part IV. If the employee is uncomfortable doing this personally, it can be presented to the supervisor in writing after the Feedback Session.

If any problems or conflicts occur during the feedback session, another manager should function as a mediator at the request of either the supervisor or the employee.

Once the Feedback Session is complete, the supervisor compiles a final review form for the employee to review and sign. This form should contain all comments from Parts I through IV of the EDPP. The supervisor also signs the EDPP, and then gives the form to the reviewer whose signature indicates that the EDPP has been completed properly. The reviewer does not make changes or comments relative to the employee's performance. The supervisor gives the employee a copy and places the original in the employee's personnel file.

Employee Development & Performance Plan

The following Performance Elements should be considered, where applicable, in assessing employee performance (Part I) and determining future performance expectations and development needs (Parts II and III). Other performance elements may be added as needed.

PERFORMANCE ELEMENTS

PERSONAL MANAGEMENT TRAITS

- Using work time effectively.
- Punctuality.
- Possessing integrity and honesty.
- Following company rules and procedures.
- Absences and attendance record.
- Being open to constructive feedback for self and others.
- Proper use of equipment and resources.
- Proper maintenance of equipment.
- Proper safety procedures.
- Seeking and fulfilling additional responsibilities as suitable.
- Treating others with respect and dignity.
- Focusing on the situation, problem or behavior rather than on the person.
- Other: _____
  _____
  _____
  _____

TEAMWORK

- Communicating with others openly and honestly.
- Working with others towards the team's and organization's goals.
- Realizing the benefits of teamwork.
- Offering assistance to others and recognizing the contributions of others.
- Viewing the organization's success as more important than individual achievement.
- Working towards team cohesion and productivity.
- Sharing information internally and externally.
- Other: _____
  _____
  _____

WORK PROCESSES & RESULTS

- Achieving results.
- Establishing and adhering to priorities.
- Using sound judgment.
- Meeting productivity standards and deadlines.
- Working accurately with minimal supervision.
- Providing products and services above or beyond the customers' needs and expectations.
- Being aware of customer satisfaction.
- Utilizing problem-solving to improve processes.
- Evaluating information to make informed decisions.
- Striving for efficiency in the use of resources.
- Informing supervisor of problems and offering solutions.
- Other: _____
  _____
  _____
  _____

INNOVATION AND CHANGE

- Looking for creative and innovative ways to contribute to organizational and individual goals.
- Adapting willingly to new situations.
- Striving to be open to new ideas and explore different options.
- Avoiding being overly defensive.
- Seeking ways to improve work processes.
- Helping others adapt to changes.
- Other: _____
  _____
  _____
  _____

Employee Development & Performance Plan

PERFORMANCE ELEMENTS (CONTINUED)

GROWTH & PROGRESSION

- Actively striving for ways to increase knowledge.
- Participating in opportunities that are offered by the organization to enhance skills.
- Developing or upgrading knowledge and skills independent of job position through self-initiative.
- Actively applying new skills acquired from developmental opportunities.
- Teaching others new processes or systems.
- Using technology effectively, when appropriate.
- Other: _____

_____

_____

_____

COMMUNICATION

- Actively participating in meetings.
- Interacting with others in a cooperative and courteous manner.
- Giving oral presentations before groups in clear and effective manner.
- Competently communicating verbally in small groups and one-on-one.
- Writing clearly and concisely.
- Responding quickly and properly to other's verbal requests or e-mail, phone messages and mail.
- Other: _____

_____

_____

_____

CUSTOMER SERVICE

- Being responsive to customers' needs.
- Striving to be accessible, timely and responsive to customers.
- Handling customer inquiries promptly and politely.
- Dealing with customer complaints courteously and in a non-judgmental manner.
- Expending extra effort to satisfy customer needs and expectations.
- Other: _____

_____

_____

SUPERVISORY PERFORMANCE

- Offering clear directions to staff.
- Giving regular, ongoing feedback to staff.
- Clearly communicating organization's goals and mission to employees.
- Supporting staff's efforts to succeed.
- Facilitating and coaching employees.
- Recognizing individual's efforts and performance.
- Recognizing team efforts and performance.
- Supporting workplace diversity.
- Following through on instructions.
- Making appropriate decisions regarding employee selection and promotions.
- Other: _____

_____

_____

_____

Employee Development & Performance Plan

Name: _____ Date of Employment: _____

Job Position: _____ Date of Preview Session: _____

Evaluated By: _____ Evaluation Period: _____

Purpose of Evaluation: ❑ Annual Review ❑ Trial Service Review ❑ Probationary Review ❑ Other

PART I: PERFORMANCE FEEDBACK

1. Assess the employee's overall performance in relation to carrying out job responsibilities and performance standards.

2. Evaluate the employee's contribution to helping the organization achieve its goals and be successful.

3. Review all Performance Elements and describe how well the employee has done in relation to each relevant area.

PART II: PERFORMANCE EXPECTATIONS

1. Review the employee's Personal Performance Standards in relation to job duties, special assignments and skills the employee needs to focus on in order to further his/her success and contribution to the organization.

2. Note any areas in which the employee could improve.

PART III: FUTURE TRAINING & DEVELOPMENT

1. Identify training and development opportunities that could improve and enhance the employee's existing skills and performance.

PART IV: ORGANIZATIONAL SUPPORT
(TO BE COMPLETED BY THE EMPLOYEE)

1. Please list at least five ways your supervisor, co-workers and company can support you in your present job and with future career goals.

2. What do you perceive as your supervisor's greatest strength?

3. Are there any areas in which your supervisor could improve?

PART V: COMMENTS AND SIGNATURES

By signing below, the evaluator agrees that this report is based on his or her judgment. By signing below, the employee agrees that he or she has had an opportunity to review and discuss this report.

_____

Evaluator's Signature

_____

Title   Date

_____

Employee's Signature

_____

Title   Date

I have reviewed this report and, in my judgment, the process has been properly followed.

_____

Reviewer's Signature

_____

Title   Date

Upon completion of this report and signatures of evaluator, employee and reviewers, a final copy should be provided to the employee and the original report placed in the employee's personnel file.

C7

Human Resources Audit

Auditor: _____ Date: _____

MINIMUM WAGE LAW & WORKING CONDITIONS

Is there a regularly scheduled payday?
❏ Yes   ❏ No

Are minimum wage laws, both federal and state, upheld?
❏ Yes   ❏ No

Are payroll deductions made for Social Security, federal and state income taxes and Medicare?
❏ Yes   ❏ No

Upon termination, are employees paid in a timely manner?
❏ Yes   ❏ No

If an employee works 6 hours or longer, is a 30-minute meal break given?
❏ Yes   ❏ No

For each 4-hour work period, do employees get to take 10-minute work breaks?
❏ Yes   ❏ No

Are 14- and 15-year-olds limited to working only 3 hours per school day?
❏ Yes   ❏ No

Are 14- and 15-year-olds limited to working only 8 hours on a non-school day?
❏ Yes   ❏ No

Are working hours for 14- and 15-year-olds limited to between 7 a.m. and 9 p.m.?
❏ Yes   ❏ No

Are 14- to 17-year-olds working with prohibited equipment, such as a slicer?
❏ Yes   ❏ No

Are working conditions for minors regarding breaks and meal periods being met?
❏ Yes   ❏ No

Comments _____

_____

_____

OSHA

Is an OSHA information poster posted in a clear and visible area?
❏ Yes   ❏ No

Are MSDS forms for all chemicals used in the establishment available to employees?
❏ Yes   ❏ No

Are all chemicals stored in proper containers and labeled correctly?
❏ Yes   ❏ No

Are pesticides stored in their original labeled container?
❏ Yes   ❏ No

Do suitable facilities (located within the work area for immediate emergency use) exist for quick drenching or flushing of the eyes and body if exposure to injurious corrosive material occurs?
❏ Yes   ❏ No

Do any potentially hazardous conditions exist?
❏ Yes   ❏ No

Have employees sustained serious injuries while working that results in missed days of work?
❏ Yes   ❏ No

Have all workers been trained in and practice proper lifting procedures?
❏ Yes   ❏ No

Is personal protective equipment, such as gloves, eye goggles, and special aprons, provided for employees?
❏ Yes   ❏ No

Do the facilities meet OSHA standards for safety?
❏ Yes   ❏ No

Comments _____

_____

_____

_____

Human Resources Audit

AMERICANS WITH DISABILITIES ACT (ADA) COMPLIANCE

Have all employment tests been checked to make sure they are not discriminatory against disabled persons?
❏ Yes ❏ No

Do job descriptions have reasonable accommodations for the disabled?
❏ Yes ❏ No

Do physical facilities comply with ADA regulations?
❏ Yes ❏ No

Have physical facilities been inspected by an ADA regulation specialist?
❏ Yes ❏ No

Are health insurance considerations a reason for rejecting qualified potential employees with disabilities?
❏ Yes ❏ No

Comments _____

_____

_____

EQUAL EMPLOYMENT OPPORTUNITY COMMISSION (EEOC) CONSIDERATIONS

Are interview questions non-discrimatory and legal?
❏ Yes ❏ No

Are all pre-employment tests directly related to the job?
❏ Yes ❏ No

Are employees of both genders hired?
❏ Yes ❏ No

For corresponding work, are both genders are paid equally?
❏ Yes ❏ No

Are promotions awarded based upon job performance that is quantifiable and verifiable?
❏ Yes ❏ No

Comments _____

_____

_____

FAMILY AND MEDICAL LEAVE ACT

Does the employer/employee qualify for the Family and Medical Leave Act? (Employees are eligible to take FMLA leave if they have worked for their employer for at least 12 months, and have worked for at least 1,250 hours over the previous 12 months, and work at a location where at least 50 employees are employed by the employer within 75 miles.)
❏ Yes ❏ No

Are employees allowed to take up to a total of 12 weeks of unpaid leave during any 12-month period?
❏ Yes ❏ No

Upon returning to work, are employees returned to their previous position, or an equivalent position?
❏ Yes ❏ No

During leave, are health care benefits continued?
❏ Yes ❏ No

Comments _____

_____

_____

_____

IMMIGRATION REFORM ACT

Does employer possess, utilize and complete 1-9 forms when needed?
❏ Yes ❏ No

Does employer obtain verification of citizenship for 1-9 forms?
❏ Yes ❏ No

Does employer discriminate against people who are not citizens of the United States?
❏ Yes ❏ No

Comments _____

_____

_____

_____

_____

Human Resources Audit

SEXUAL HARASSMENT

Are all employees aware of what constitutes sexual harassment, including:

- The victim as well as the harasser may be a woman or a man. The victim does not have to be of the opposite sex.

- The harasser can be the victim's supervisor, an agent of the employer, a supervisor in another area, a co-worker or a non-employee.

- The victim does not have to be the person harassed but could be anyone affected by the offensive conduct.

- Unlawful sexual harassment may occur without economic injury to or discharge of the victim.

- The harasser's conduct must be unwelcome.

❏ Yes   ❏ No

Were any sexual harassment claims made during the past year?
❏ Yes   ❏ No

If any sexual harassment claims were made, were they investigated immediately?
❏ Yes   ❏ No

Was disciplinary action taken for any sexual harassment claims?
❏ Yes   ❏ No

Does establishment have a written procedure established for reporting sexual harassment claims?
❏ Yes   ❏ No

Is the written sexual harassment policy posted for all employees?
❏ Yes   ❏ No

Comments _____

_____

_____

_____

TIP-REPORTING REQUIREMENTS

Is employer using Form 8027 for tip allocation?
❏ Yes   ❏ No

Does employer collect income tax, employee Social Security tax and employee Medicare tax on tips reported by employees?
❏ Yes   ❏ No

Are employees using Form 4070A?
❏ Yes   ❏ No

Is a good-faith agreement being used?
❏ Yes   ❏ No

Are employees aware of IRS tip-reporting requirements and trained to report all tips?
❏ Yes   ❏ No

Comments _____

_____

_____

_____

_____

CHAPTER 8

Maintaining and controlling inventory is one of the keys to a successful food service operation. Effective inventory management begins with planning. You need to collect, organize and interpret your inventory which will impact your bottom line. This is not a job that can be delegated, because these numbers are your controls.

Inventory Control

Purchase Order

COMPANY INFORMATION

| |
| PURCHASE ORDER NUMBER |

Company Name: _____

Address: _____

_____

_____

Phone: _____

Fax: _____

Date Issued: _____

Issued By: _____

SUPPLIER INFORMATION

Company Name: _____

Contact/Representative: _____

Address: _____

_____

_____

Phone: _____

Fax: _____

Required Delivery Date: _____

Terms: _____

_____

Freight Charges: ❏ Collect $_____   ❏ FOB   ❏ Pre-paid

ITEMS

ITEM DESCRIPTION	QUANTITY	UNIT	UNIT COST	EXTENSION

TOTAL $

AUTHORIZED SIGNATURE:

Purchase Order II

Company A: _____

Company B: _____

Company C: _____

PURCHASE ORDER #

Order Date: _____

Delivery Date: _____

ITEM	QTY	COMPARE QUOTES			ITEM COST	ITEM TOTAL
		VENDOR A	VENDOR B	VENDOR C		

SPECIAL INSTRUCTIONS:

SUBTOTAL: _____

SHIPPING: _____

TAX: _____

TOTAL: _____

NAME: AUTHORIZED SIGNATURE:

Purchase Order III

Vendor Name: _____

Contact/Representative: _____

Address: _____

_____

_____

Phone: _____

Fax:_____

Required Delivery Date: _____

Ordered By: _____

Order Date: _____

Ship To: _____

_____

_____

Delivery Instructions: _____

_____

_____

	ITEM PURCHASED	SPEC #	QTY ORDERED	QUOTED PRICE	EXT PRICE
1					
2					
3					
4					
5					
6					
7					
8					
9					
10					
11					
12					
13					
14					
15					

COMMENTS:

TOTAL $

Par Order Sheet

FOOD CATEGORY:	PURVEYOR:

ITEM & DESCRIPTION	LOW-LEVEL PAR	DELIVERY DATES				

Daily Inventory Order Sheet

VENDOR	ITEM	UNIT	Sunday			Monday			Tuesday			Wednesday			Thursday			Friday			Saturday		
			PAR	INV	BUY	PAR	INV	BUY	PAR	INV	BUY	PAR	INV	BUY	PAR	INV	BUY	PAR	INV	BUY	PAR	INV	BUY

Miscellaneous Order Sheet

DELIVERY DATE:	PURVEYOR:	PHONE #:

PRODUCT #	ORDER	ITEM & DESCRIPTION

Bid Order Sheet

Ordered By: _____

Date Ordered: _____ Delivery Date: _____

Vendor A: _____

Vendor B: _____

Vendor C: _____

ITEM	Quantity	VENDOR A		VENDOR B		VENDOR C	
		Unit	Total	Unit	Total	Unit	Total
Individual Invoice Total:							

Bid Sheet

Ordered By: _____ **Date:** _____

ITEM	Quantity	VENDORS (fill in names below)		

Par Amount Requisition

Date: _____   Req. #: _____

Time: _____   Department: _____

Prepared By: _____   Priced By: _____

Delivered By: _____   Received By: _____

Approved By: _____

Item Description	Par	On Hand	Order	Price		Extension	

Total $

General Requisition

Date: _____   Req. #: _____

Time: _____   Department: _____

Prepared By: _____   Priced By: _____

Delivered By: _____   Received By: _____

Approved By: _____

Item Description	Unit	Quantity	Price		Extension	

Total $

Food Requisition Form

| Date: _____ | Date Needed: _____ | Requested By: _____ |

Qty. Ordered	Ingred. #	Item Description	Qty Issued	Unit Cost		Unit Total	

The Encyclopedia of Restaurant Forms

Credit Memo

Credit Memo #: _____   Date Issued: _____

Vendor: _____   Vendor Invoice Number: _____

Vendor Representative: _____

Explanation: _____

_____

ITEM	Quantity	Correction		Price	Credit Amount
		Short	Refused		

Credit Memo II

Sold To: _____ Date: _____

Customer Number: _____

Invoice Number: _____ Invoice Date: _____

Instructions:

❏ Pickup Order Only

❏ Pickup and Credit Order

❏ Credit Only

ITEM	PRODUCT CODE	QUANTITY	PACKAGE	PRICE	AMOUNT

AUTHORIZED SIGNATURE: DATE:

Receiving Checklist

Received By: _____ **Date:** _____

ITEM

_____

Actual Temp. _____ °F   Packaging Intact ❏ Yes ❏ No
Valid Use-By Date ❏ Yes ❏ No
❏ **ACCEPTED** ❏ **STORED** ❏ **REJECTED**

ITEM

_____

Actual Temp. _____ °F   Packaging Intact ❏ Yes ❏ No
Valid Use-By Date ❏ Yes ❏ No
❏ **ACCEPTED** ❏ **STORED** ❏ **REJECTED**

ITEM

_____

Actual Temp. _____ °F   Packaging Intact ❏ Yes ❏ No
Valid Use-By Date ❏ Yes ❏ No
❏ **ACCEPTED** ❏ **STORED** ❏ **REJECTED**

ITEM

_____

Actual Temp. _____ °F   Packaging Intact ❏ Yes ❏ No
Valid Use-By Date ❏ Yes ❏ No
❏ **ACCEPTED** ❏ **STORED** ❏ **REJECTED**

ITEM

_____

Actual Temp. _____ °F   Packaging Intact ❏ Yes ❏ No
Valid Use-By Date ❏ Yes ❏ No
❏ **ACCEPTED** ❏ **STORED** ❏ **REJECTED**

ITEM

_____

Actual Temp. _____ °F   Packaging Intact ❏ Yes ❏ No
Valid Use-By Date ❏ Yes ❏ No
❏ **ACCEPTED** ❏ **STORED** ❏ **REJECTED**

ITEM

_____

Actual Temp. _____ °F   Packaging Intact ❏ Yes ❏ No
Valid Use-By Date ❏ Yes ❏ No
❏ **ACCEPTED** ❏ **STORED** ❏ **REJECTED**

ITEM

_____

Actual Temp. _____ °F   Packaging Intact ❏ Yes ❏ No
Valid Use-By Date ❏ Yes ❏ No
❏ **ACCEPTED** ❏ **STORED** ❏ **REJECTED**

ITEM

_____

Actual Temp. _____ °F   Packaging Intact ❏ Yes ❏ No
Valid Use-By Date ❏ Yes ❏ No
❏ **ACCEPTED** ❏ **STORED** ❏ **REJECTED**

ITEM

_____

Actual Temp. _____ °F   Packaging Intact ❏ Yes ❏ No
Valid Use-By Date ❏ Yes ❏ No
❏ **ACCEPTED** ❏ **STORED** ❏ **REJECTED**

ITEM

_____

Actual Temp. _____ °F   Packaging Intact ❏ Yes ❏ No
Valid Use-By Date ❏ Yes ❏ No
❏ **ACCEPTED** ❏ **STORED** ❏ **REJECTED**

ITEM

_____

Actual Temp. _____ °F   Packaging Intact ❏ Yes ❏ No
Valid Use-By Date ❏ Yes ❏ No
❏ **ACCEPTED** ❏ **STORED** ❏ **REJECTED**

ITEM

_____

Actual Temp. _____ °F   Packaging Intact ❏ Yes ❏ No
Valid Use-By Date ❏ Yes ❏ No
❏ **ACCEPTED** ❏ **STORED** ❏ **REJECTED**

ITEM

_____

Actual Temp. _____ °F   Packaging Intact ❏ Yes ❏ No
Valid Use-By Date ❏ Yes ❏ No
❏ **ACCEPTED** ❏ **STORED** ❏ **REJECTED**

Receiving Report

Supplier: _____ Date: _____

Representative: _____ Delivery Date: _____

Item Description	Quantity	Notes	Unit Price	

Receiving Report II

Received By: _____ **Date:** _____

Distribution Key: 1. _____ 2. _____

3. _____ 4. _____

Invoice #	Supplier	Item	Unit Price	# of Units	Total Cost	Distribution			
						1	2	3	4

Inventory Valuation Sheet

Inventory Date: _____ Extended By: _____

Counted By: _____

ITEM	ITEM AMOUNT	ITEM VALUE	INVENTORY VALUE
PAGE TOTAL			

Paper Goods Inventory

Date:_____   Department:_____

Time:_____   Location:_____

Inventoried By:_____   Priced By:_____

Approved By:_____   Extended By:_____

Item Description	Unit	Quantity	Price		Extension	

Notes:

Total $ _____

China & Flatware Inventory

Inventory Date: _____	Extended By: _____
Counted By: _____	Approved By: _____

ITEM	Par	Inventory					Total	+ or - Balance
		A	B	C	D	E		

Equipment Inventory

Inventory Date: _____ Department: _____

Counted By: _____ Approved By: _____

Item Description (Name & Serial #)	Unit Count	Office Count	Difference	Explanation

Notes: _____

_____

_____

_____

Perpetual Inventory Chart

Location: _____

Item: _____ Unit: _____

Date	Beginning	Additions	Deletions	Ending	Unit Price	Extension	Initials

The Encyclopedia of Restaurant Forms

General Inventory Form

Date: _____	Department: _____
Time: _____	Location: _____
Taken By: _____	Priced By: _____
Approved By: _____	Extended By: _____

Item Description	Unit	Quantity	Price		Extension	

Notes:

Total $

Inventory Count Sheet

Date Inventoried: _____ Month Of: _____

Item Description	Unit	Counts	Total	Cost	Total Value
PAGE TOTAL $					

CHAPTER 9

Financial Management

All restaurants are in business to make a profit. In order to plan financially, you must first set up a long-range plan detailing how much money you want the restaurant to return and when. This financial plan is the restaurant's budget. You will also need to know the procedures for projecting actual operating costs, and how to recognize, analyze and resolve cost problems. The forms in this chapter cover all aspects of financial planning, from payroll to sales forecasting.

Financial Management

Commonly Used Costing Formulas

Standard Accounting

Liabilities (+) Owner's equity = Assets

Current assets (÷) Current liabilities = Current ratio

Current assets (-) Current liabilities = Working capital

Total liabilities (÷) Total assets = Debt-to-assets ratio

Profit (÷) Sales = Return on sales (ROS)

Sales (÷) Working capital = Working capital ratio

Total sales (÷) Average amount of accounts receivable =
Accounts receivable turnover

Profit (÷) Total invested = Return on investment (ROI)

Profit (÷) Average owner's equity =
Return on owner's equity

Profit (÷) Average total assets = Return on assets

Income & Expenses

Income (-) Expense = Profit
Part (÷) Whole = Percent
Expense (÷) Income = Expense %
Profit (÷) Income = Profit %
Actual (÷) Budget = % of budget

Managing Food & Beverage

Issues today (÷) Sales today = Beverage cost estimate today

Cost in product category (÷) Total cost in all categories =
Proportion of total product cost

Cost of product (÷) Desired product cost % = Selling price

100 (÷) Desired product cost % = Pricing factor

Pricing factor (x) Product cost = Selling price

Product cost (+) Contribution margin desired = Selling price

EP weight (÷) AP weight = Product yield %

AP price per pound (÷) Product yield % =
Cost per servable pound

Sales Volume

Total sales (÷) # of guests served = Average sales per guest

Labor Costs

Cost of labor (÷) Sales = Labor cost %

Sales (÷) Labor hours used = Sales per labor hour

Guest served (÷) Cost of labor =
Guests served per labor dollar

Cost of labor (÷) Guests served =
Dollars expended per guest served

Guest served (÷) Labor hours used =
Guests served per labor hour

Food & Beverage Costs

Total # of specific menu items sold (÷)
Total # of all menu items sold =
Percent selecting

# of expected guests (x) % selecting = Predicted # sold

Yield desired (÷) Current yield = Conversion factor

Product loss (÷) AP weight = Waste %

1.00 (-) Waste % = Yield %

EP required (÷) Yield % = AP required

AP required (x) Yield % = EP required

Item amount (x) Item value = Inventory value

Beginning inventory (+) Purchases = Goods avail. for sale

Goods available for sale (-) Ending inventory
(-) Employee meals =
Cost of food consumed

Cost of food consumed (÷) Sales = Food cost %

Cost of beverages consumed (÷) Beverages sales =
Beverage cost %

Item dollar sales (÷) Total sales = Item's % of total sales

Sales Forecast Work Sheet

RESTAURANT NAME: _____ SEATING CAPACITY: _____

PREPARED BY: _____ DATE: _____

BREAKFAST

ESTIMATED DAILY SALES REVENUE

_____ Seats (x) _____ Customer turnover = _____

(-) $1/3$ Vacant seat factor = _____

(x) $ _____ Average menu price = _____

BREAKFAST DAILY SALES $ _____

30-DAY SALES ESTIMATE

30 days serving (x) $_____ Daily sales = $ _____

LUNCH

ESTIMATED DAILY SALES REVENUE

_____ Seats (x) _____ Customer turnover = _____

(-) $1/3$ Vacant seat factor = _____

(x) $ _____ Average menu price = _____

LUNCH DAILY SALES $ _____

30-DAY SALES ESTIMATE

30 days serving (x) $_____ Daily sales = $ _____

DINNER

ESTIMATED DAILY SALES REVENUE

_____ Seats (x) _____ Customer turnover = _____

(-) $1/3$ Vacant seat factor = _____

(x) $ _____ Average menu price = _____

DINNER DAILY SALES $ _____

30-DAY SALES ESTIMATE

30 days serving (x) $_____ Daily sales = $ _____

MONTHLY & ANNUAL SALES

ESTIMATED BEVERAGE SALES (30 DAYS)

Liquor $ _____ _____ %

Wine $ _____ _____ %

TOTAL $ _____ _____ %

ESTIMATED FOOD SALES (30 DAYS)

Breakfast $ _____ _____ %

Lunch $ _____ _____ %

Dinner $ _____ _____ %

TOTAL $ _____ _____ %

TOTAL FOOD & BEVERAGE SALES

$_____ Total beverage sales (+)

$_____ Total food sales =

$ _____

30-DAY SALES PROJECTION

$_____ 30-Day sales projection (x) 12 =

$ _____

PROJECTED ANNUAL REVENUE

Sales Graph

MONTH: _____	YEAR: _____
PREPARED BY: _____	DATE: _____

Day of Week ☐☐☐☐☐☐☐☐☐☐☐☐☐☐☐☐☐☐☐☐☐☐☐☐☐☐☐☐☐☐☐

Date: 1 2 3 4 5 6 7 8 9 10 11 12 13 14 15 16 17 18 19 20 21 22 23 24 25 26 27 28 29 30 31

MONETARY VALUE ($)

25
24
23
22
21
20
19
18
17
16
15
14
13
12
11
10
9
8
7
6
5
4
3
2
1K
900
800
700
600
500
400
300
200
100
50
0

Cost of Sales Analysis

PERIOD: _____ DATE: _____

PREPARED BY: _____

FOOD COST

Total Food Sales	$_____
Beginning Inventory (+)	$_____
(=)	$_____
Purchases (-)	$_____
Ending Inventory (=)	$_____
Cost of Sales	$_____
Percent of Sales	_____%

LIQUOR COST

Total Liquor Sales	$_____
Beginning Inventory (+)	$_____
(=)	$_____
Purchases (-)	$_____
Ending Inventory (=)	$_____
Cost of Sales	$_____
Percent of Sales	_____%

Sales Projection Form

DATE	# OF EACH	AVG # DINNERS	SUB-TOTAL
MONDAY			
TUESDAY			
WEDNESDAY			
THURSDAY			
FRIDAY			
SATURDAY			
SUNDAY			
HOLIDAYS			

BREAKFAST TOTAL _____

LUNCH TOTAL _____

DINNER TOTAL _____

GRAND TOTAL _____

Grand Total x % Growth/Loss = Projected Volume x Check Avg. = Projected Sales

DIVISION OF SALES

	TOTAL PROJECTED SALES x	% SALES DIVISION	= SALES DIVISION
FOOD			
LIQUOR			
WINE			

HOLIDAYS THAT MUST BE CONSIDERED:

- Washington's Birthday
- Easter
- Mothers' Day
- Memorial Day
- Fourth of July

- Labor Day
- Thanksgiving
- Christmas Eve
- Christmas
- New Year's Eve

- New Year's Day
- Halloween
- Valentine's Day
- Graduation Day
- Fathers' Day

Operational Budget Form

ITEM	BUDGETED	%	ACTUAL	%
SALES				
Food				
Liquor				
Wine				
TOTAL SALES				
MATERIALS				
Food Costs				
Liquor Costs				
Wine Costs				
TOTAL COSTS				
GROSS PROFIT				
LABOR				
Manager Salary				
Employee				
Overtime				
TOTAL LABOR COSTS				
Controller Oper. Costs				
China & Utensils				
Glassware				
Kitchen Supplies				
Bar Supplies				
Dining Room Supplies				
Uniforms				
Laundry/Linen				
Services				
Trash Pick-Up				
Laundry Cleaning				
Protection				
Freight				
Accounting				
Maintenance				
Payroll				
TOTAL THIS PAGE				

Comprehensive Budget Form

MONTH: _____ YEAR: _____

Day	Date	SUPPLIES Budget $_____		REPAIRS Budget $_____		Budget $_____		Budget $_____	
		Spent MTD	Remaining	Spent MTD	Remaining	Spent MTD	Remaining	Spent MTD	Remaining

Performance to Budget Summary

PERIOD: _____ DATE: _____

PREPARED BY: _____

Item Description	Budget	Actual	% of Budget
Meals Served			
Income			
Food Expense			
Labor Expense			
Other Expenses (list below)			
Total Expenses			
PROFIT			

Depreciation Worksheet

Description of Property	Date Placed in Service	Cost or Other Basis	Business/ Investment Use %	Section 179 Deduction and Special Allowance	Depreciation Prior Years	Basis for Depreciation	Method/ Convention	Recovery Period	Rate or Table %	Depreciation Deduction

Depreciation Worksheet & Record

DATE	DESCRIPTION	METH	LIFE	NEW/ USED	AC RS%	COST	SALVAGE	ADDIT. 1st YEAR

Depreciation Worksheet & Record (continued)

BALANCE	DEPREC 20	BALANCE	DEPREC 20	BALANCE

IRS Form 4562 Depreciation & Amortization

Form **4562**	**Depreciation and Amortization** (Including Information on Listed Property)	OMB No. 1545-0172 **2003**
Department of the Treasury Internal Revenue Service	▶ **See separate instructions.**　▶ **Attach to your tax return.**	Attachment Sequence No. **67**

Name(s) shown on return	Business or activity to which this form relates	Identifying number

Part I　Election To Expense Certain Property Under Section 179
Note: *If you have any listed property, complete Part V before you complete Part I.*

1	Maximum amount. See page 2 of the instructions for a higher limit for certain businesses	**1**	$100,000
2	Total cost of section 179 property placed in service (see page 2 of the instructions)	**2**	
3	Threshold cost of section 179 property before reduction in limitation	**3**	$400,000
4	Reduction in limitation. Subtract line 3 from line 2. If zero or less, enter -0-	**4**	
5	Dollar limitation for tax year. Subtract line 4 from line 1. If zero or less, enter -0-. If married filing separately, see page 2 of the instructions	**5**	

(a) Description of property	(b) Cost (business use only)	(c) Elected cost	
6			

7	Listed property. Enter the amount from line 29	**7**	
8	Total elected cost of section 179 property. Add amounts in column (c), lines 6 and 7	**8**	
9	Tentative deduction. Enter the **smaller** of line 5 or line 8	**9**	
10	Carryover of disallowed deduction from line 13 of your 2002 Form 4562	**10**	
11	Business income limitation. Enter the smaller of business income (not less than zero) or line 5 (see instructions)	**11**	
12	Section 179 expense deduction. Add lines 9 and 10, but do not enter more than line 11	**12**	
13	Carryover of disallowed deduction to 2004. Add lines 9 and 10, less line 12 ▶	**13**	

Note: *Do not use Part II or Part III below for listed property. Instead, use Part V.*

Part II　Special Depreciation Allowance and Other Depreciation (Do not include listed property.)

14	Special depreciation allowance for qualified property (other than listed property) placed in service during the tax year (see page 3 of the instructions)	**14**	
15	Property subject to section 168(f)(1) election (see page 4 of the instructions)	**15**	
16	Other depreciation (including ACRS) (see page 4 of the instructions)	**16**	

Part III　MACRS Depreciation (Do not include listed property.) (See page 4 of the instructions.)

Section A

17	MACRS deductions for assets placed in service in tax years beginning before 2003	**17**	
18	If you are electing under section 168(i)(4) to group any assets placed in service during the tax year into one or more general asset accounts, check here ▶ ☐		

Section B—Assets Placed in Service During 2003 Tax Year Using the General Depreciation System

(a) Classification of property	(b) Month and year placed in service	(c) Basis for depreciation (business/investment use only—see instructions)	(d) Recovery period	(e) Convention	(f) Method	(g) Depreciation deduction
19a　3-year property						
b　5-year property						
c　7-year property						
d　10-year property						
e　15-year property						
f　20-year property						
g　25-year property			25 yrs.		S/L	
h　Residential rental property			27.5 yrs.	MM	S/L	
			27.5 yrs.	MM	S/L	
i　Nonresidential real property			39 yrs.	MM	S/L	
				MM	S/L	

Section C—Assets Placed in Service During 2003 Tax Year Using the Alternative Depreciation System

20a　Class life					S/L	
b　12-year			12 yrs.		S/L	
c　40-year			40 yrs.	MM	S/L	

Part IV　Summary (see page 6 of the instructions)

21	Listed property. Enter amount from line 28	**21**	
22	**Total.** Add amounts from line 12, lines 14 through 17, lines 19 and 20 in column (g), and line 21. Enter here and on the appropriate lines of your return. Partnerships and S corporations—see instr.	**22**	
23	For assets shown above and placed in service during the current year, enter the portion of the basis attributable to section 263A costs	**23**	

For Paperwork Reduction Act Notice, see separate instructions.　Cat. No. 12906N　Form **4562** (2003)

IRS Form 4562 Depreciation & Amortization

Form 4562 (2003) Page **2**

Part V **Listed Property** (Include automobiles, certain other vehicles, cellular telephones, certain computers, and property used for entertainment, recreation, or amusement.)

Note: *For any vehicle for which you are using the standard mileage rate or deducting lease expense, complete only 24a, 24b, columns (a) through (c) of Section A, all of Section B, and Section C if applicable.*

Section A—Depreciation and Other Information (Caution: *See page 7 of the instructions for limits for passenger automobiles.*)

24a Do you have evidence to support the business/investment use claimed? ☐ **Yes** ☐ **No** **24b** If "Yes," is the evidence written? ☐ **Yes** ☐ **No**

(a) Type of property (list vehicles first)	(b) Date placed in service	(c) Business/ investment use percentage	(d) Cost or other basis	(e) Basis for depreciation (business/investment use only)	(f) Recovery period	(g) Method/ Convention	(h) Depreciation deduction	(i) Elected section 179 cost
25 Special depreciation allowance for qualified listed property placed in service during the tax year and used more than 50% in a qualified business use (see page 6 of the instructions)						**25**		
26 Property used more than 50% in a qualified business use (see page 6 of the instructions):								
		%						
		%						
		%						
27 Property used 50% or less in a qualified business use (see page 6 of the instructions):								
		%				S/L –		
		%				S/L –		
		%				S/L –		
28 Add amounts in column (h), lines 25 through 27. Enter here and on line 21, page 1 .						**28**		
29 Add amounts in column (i), line 26. Enter here and on line 7, page 1 .							**29**	

Section B—Information on Use of Vehicles

Complete this section for vehicles used by a sole proprietor, partner, or other "more than 5% owner," or related person.

If you provided vehicles to your employees, first answer the questions in Section C to see if you meet an exception to completing this section for those vehicles.

	(a) Vehicle 1		(b) Vehicle 2		(c) Vehicle 3		(d) Vehicle 4		(e) Vehicle 5		(f) Vehicle 6	
30 Total business/investment miles driven during the year (**do not** include commuting miles—see page 2 of the instructions)												
31 Total commuting miles driven during the year												
32 Total other personal (noncommuting) miles driven												
33 Total miles driven during the year. Add lines 30 through 32.												
	Yes	No	Yes	No	Yes	No	Yes	No	Yes	No	Yes	No
34 Was the vehicle available for personal use during off-duty hours?												
35 Was the vehicle used primarily by a more than 5% owner or related person?												
36 Is another vehicle available for personal use?												

Section C—Questions for Employers Who Provide Vehicles for Use by Their Employees

Answer these questions to determine if you meet an exception to completing Section B for vehicles used by employees who **are not** more than 5% owners or related persons (see page 8 of the instructions).

	Yes	No
37 Do you maintain a written policy statement that prohibits all personal use of vehicles, including commuting, by your employees?		
38 Do you maintain a written policy statement that prohibits personal use of vehicles, except commuting, by your employees? See page 8 of the instructions for vehicles used by corporate officers, directors, or 1% or more owners		
39 Do you treat all use of vehicles by employees as personal use?		
40 Do you provide more than five vehicles to your employees, obtain information from your employees about the use of the vehicles, and retain the information received?		
41 Do you meet the requirements concerning qualified automobile demonstration use? (See page 9 of the instructions.). .		

Note: *If your answer to 37, 38, 39, 40, or 41 is "Yes," do not complete Section B for the covered vehicles.*

Part VI **Amortization**

(a) Description of costs	(b) Date amortization begins	(c) Amortizable amount	(d) Code section	(e) Amortization period or percentage	(f) Amortization for this year
42 Amortization of costs that begins during your 2003 tax year (see page 9 of the instructions):					
43 Amortization of costs that began before your 2003 tax year			**43**		
44 **Total.** Add amounts in column (f). See page 9 of the instructions for where to report . . .			**44**		

✱ Form **4562** (2003)

15

Financial Management

Break-Even Analysis Graphic Representation

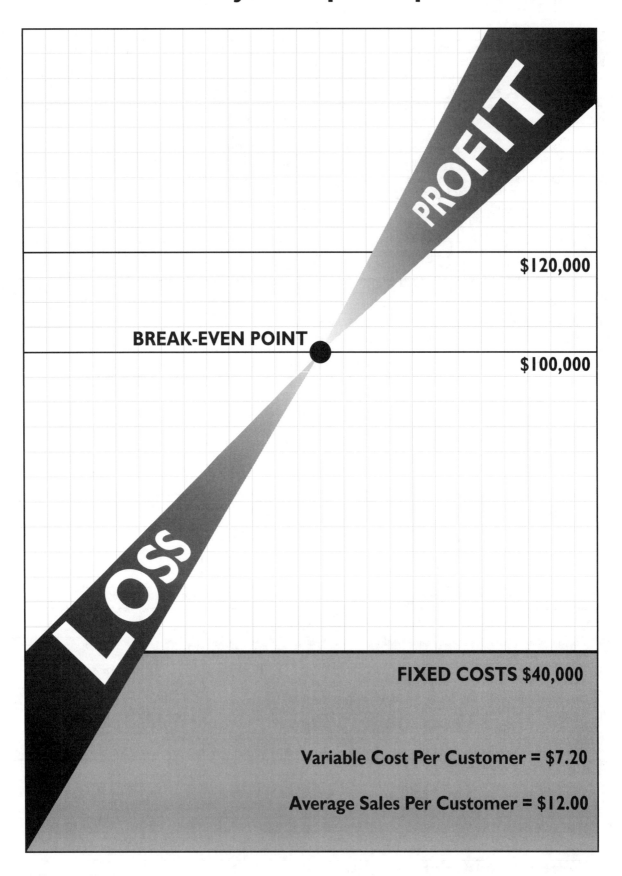

Break-Even Cost Analysis

COST	TYPE	FIXED	VARIABLE	TOTAL

Materials Cost Projection Form

MONTH _____

FOOD

Beginning Inventory   _____

Purchases   _____

Comp/Manager   _____

Ending Inventory   _____

Cost   _____

Sales   _____

TOTAL FOOD COST PERCENTAGE _____

WINE

Beginning Inventory   _____

Purchases   _____

Comp/Manager   _____

Ending Inventory   _____

Cost   _____

Sales   _____

TOTAL WINE COST PERCENTAGE _____

LIQUOR

Beginning Inventory   _____

Purchases   _____

Comp/Manager   _____

Ending Inventory   _____

Cost   _____

Sales   _____

TOTAL LIQUOR COST PERCENTAGE _____

Operational Supplies Cost Projection Form

PAGE _____ **MONTH** _____

CATEGORY _____ **#** _____

    Beginning Inventory _____

    Purchases _____

    Ending Inventory _____

    Cost _____

    Sales _____

    TOTAL COST PERCENTAGE _____

CATEGORY _____ **#** _____

    Beginning Inventory _____

    Purchases _____

    Ending Inventory _____

    Cost _____

    Sales _____

    TOTAL COST PERCENTAGE _____

CATEGORY _____ **#** _____

    Beginning Inventory _____

    Purchases _____

    Ending Inventory _____

    Cost _____

    Sales _____

    TOTAL COST PERCENTAGE _____

CATEGORY _____ **#** _____

    Beginning Inventory _____

    Purchases _____

    Ending Inventory _____

    Cost _____

    Sales _____

    TOTAL COST PERCENTAGE _____

Cashier's Report

Prepared By: _____

Date: _____ **Day:** _____ **Shift:** _____

		BAR REGISTER		SERVICE REGISTER		TOTAL
		Day	Night	Day	Night	All Shifts
1	**BANK DEPOSIT** Part I					
2	Currency					
3	Silver					
4	Checks					
5	**SUB TOTAL**					
6	**CREDIT CARDS:**					
7	MasterCard/Visa					
8	American Express					
9	Diners Club					
10	Other					
11	**OTHER RECEIPTS:**					
12	**TOTAL BANK DEPOSIT**					
13	**CASH SUMMARY** Part II					
14	Sales per Register					
15	Sales Tax per Register					
16	**ADJUSTMENTS:**					
17	Over/Under Rings					
18	Other: Complimentaries					
19	Other					
20	**TOTAL ADJUSTMENTS**					
21	Sales to Be Accounted For					
22	Sales Tax to Be Acctd. For					
23	Accounts Collected					
24	Other Receipts:					
25						
26						
27	**TIPS CHARGED:**					
28	MasterCard/Visa					
29	American Express					
30	Diners Club					
31	Other					
32	House Accounts-Tips					
33	**TOTAL RECEIPTS**					
34	**DEDUCT: PAID OUTS**					
35	Tips Paid Out					
36	House Charges					
37	Total Deductions					
38	**NET CASH RECEIPTS**					
39	**BANK DEPOSIT** (Line 12)					
40	**OVER or SHORT**					

Cashier's Report II

DATE: _____ DAY: _____ SHIFT: _____

CASHIER: _____ PREPARED BY: _____

Total Cash/Check Guest Checks	_____
Total Charged Guest Checks	_____
TOTAL RECEIPTS	_____
Total Cash Guest Checks	_____
Total Cash Turned In	_____
DIFFERENCE (note + or -)	_____

REASON FOR DIFFERENCE: _____

_____

_____

_____

REGISTER READING (Taken by Manager Only)

End Reading	_____
Beginning Reading	_____
DIFFERENCE (note + or -)	_____
REGISTER READING	_____
TOTAL RECEIPTS	_____
DIFFERENCE (note + or -)	_____

REASON FOR DIFFERENCE: _____

_____

_____

_____

Cashier's Log

DATE	DAY	LOCATION	SHIFT	AMOUNT RECEIVED	CASHIER'S NAME	INITIALS

Change Funds

DATE: _____ PREPARED BY: _____

BILLS

Large Bills	$ _____
$20.00 Bills	$ _____
$10.00 Bills	$ _____
$5.00 Bills	$ _____
$1.00 Bills	$ _____
TOTAL BILLS	**$ _____**

CHANGE

Half-Dollars	$ _____
Quarters	$ _____
Dimes	$ _____
Nickels	$ _____
Pennies	$ _____
TOTAL CHANGE	**$ _____**

OTHER

Register Banks	$ _____
_____	$ _____
_____	$ _____
_____	$ _____
TOTAL OTHER	**$ _____**

CHECKS (list by name)

_____	$ _____
_____	$ _____
_____	$ _____
_____	$ _____
_____	$ _____
_____	$ _____
_____	$ _____
_____	$ _____
_____	$ _____
_____	$ _____
_____	$ _____
_____	$ _____
_____	$ _____
_____	$ _____
_____	$ _____
_____	$ _____
_____	$ _____
_____	$ _____
_____	$ _____
_____	$ _____
_____	$ _____
_____	$ _____
_____	$ _____
TOTAL CHECKS	**$ _____**

TOTAL CASH ON HAND: _____

_____
Signature of Manager

Cash Report

DATE: _____ DAY: _____ SHIFT: _____

CASHIER: _____ PREPARED BY: _____

ITEM	NUMBER	$ AMOUNT
BEGINNING BANK		
CURRENCY		
$100.00		
$50.00		
$20.00		
$10.00		
$5.00		
$1.00		
COINS		
$0.50		
$0.25		
$0.10		
$0.05		
$0.01		
TOTAL CURRENCY & COINS		
Checks		
Subtotal		
Less Bank		
TOTAL TURN-IN		
Notes:		

Cash Turn-In Report

CASHIER NAME: _____

SHIFT: _____

DATE: _____

BILLS:	$100		
	$50		
	$20		
	$10		
	$5		
	$1		
COINS:	$.50		
	$.25		
	$.10		
	$.05		
	$.01		
CHECKS & VOUCHERS:			
Total Amount Enclosed:			
- Due Back			
= Deposit			
- Deposit (from cash sheet)			
DIFFERENCE (over/short)			

Closing Bank Account Form

CASHIER NAME: _____

SHIFT: _____

DATE: _____

BILLS:	$100		
	$50		
	$20		
	$10		
	$5		
	$1		
COINS:	$.50		
	$.25		
	$.10		
	$.05		
	$.01		
SUBTOTAL:			
+ DUE BACK:			
= TOTAL BANK:			

Credit Voucher

DEPARTMENT: _____

ISSUED BY: _____

DATE: _____

ACCOUNT NUMBER: _____

Credit Issued To:		
Date:		
Symbol:		
Amount:		
Explanation:		

Charge Voucher

DEPARTMENT:	
ISSUED BY:	
DATE:	
ACCOUNT NUMBER:	

Charged By:		
Date:		
Symbol:		
Amount:		
Explanation:		

Check Log

Check #	Amount	Date	Written To	Invoice #	Deposit	Acct. Balance

Guest Check Control

Issued To	Check #s Issued		Check #s Returned		Checks Used	# Accounted For	# Missing
	From	To	From	To			

UNACCOUNTED CHECKS

Check #	Issued To	Explanation	Manager's Initials

Guest Check Record

Date	Table	Server	Guests	Check Number

Guest Check Daily Record

DAY: _____ DATE: _____

PREPARED BY: _____

Server	Server #	Beginning Check #	End Check #	# Checks Used	# By Actual Count	# Missing	Initials

Guest Check Daily Record II

DATE: _____ PREPARED BY: _____

SERVER: _____ **SHIFT:** _____ **DATE:** _____

Beginning Check _____ Time Issued _____ Sequence # of Unused Check(s) _____

Ending Check _____ Time Returned _____ Sequence # of Missing Check(s) _____

_____

Signature of Server

SERVER: _____ **SHIFT:** _____ **DATE:** _____

Beginning Check _____ Time Issued _____ Sequence # of Unused Check(s) _____

Ending Check _____ Time Returned _____ Sequence # of Missing Check(s) _____

_____

Signature of Server

SERVER: _____ **SHIFT:** _____ **DATE:** _____

Beginning Check _____ Time Issued _____ Sequence # of Unused Check(s) _____

Ending Check _____ Time Returned _____ Sequence # of Missing Check(s) _____

_____

Signature of Server

SERVER: _____ **SHIFT:** _____ **DATE:** _____

Beginning Check _____ Time Issued _____ Sequence # of Unused Check(s) _____

Ending Check _____ Time Returned _____ Sequence # of Missing Check(s) _____

_____

Signature of Server

SERVER: _____ **SHIFT:** _____ **DATE:** _____

Beginning Check _____ Time Issued _____ Sequence # of Unused Check(s) _____

Ending Check _____ Time Returned _____ Sequence # of Missing Check(s) _____

_____

Signature of Server

Daily Payroll Form

DATE _____ MONTH _____ YEAR _____

H = HOURS   **G = GROSS**

EMPLOYEE	RATE	H	G	H	G	H	G	H	G	H	G	H	G	H	G	H	G	TOTAL

TOTAL

Payroll Budget Estimate

DATE PREPARED: _____ WEEK OF: _____

PREPARED BY: _____

EMPLOYEE NAME	POSITION	PAY RATE	HOURS	OVERTIME	TOTAL EARNED
TOTAL					

Allowance for Social Security, Medicare, Federal & State Unemployment Taxes:

Total Hourly Wages _____ x Rate _____ = _____

EMPLOYEE MEALS & TOTALS

Estimated Number of Meals _____ Cost _____ **Total Cost Meals** _____

Total (Wages & Meals) _____

Estimated Sales for Week _____

Estimated Payroll Cost Percentage for Week _____

Payroll Cost Percentage Goal _____

Payroll Cost Sheet

DATE PREPARED: _____   WEEK OF: _____

PREPARED BY: _____

HOURLY EMPLOYEES

EMPLOYEE NAME	POSITION	PAY RATE	HOURS	OVERTIME	TOTAL EARNED
TOTAL					

Allowance for Taxes*: Total Hourly Wages _____ x Rate _____ = _____

SALARIED EMPLOYEES

EMPLOYEE NAME	POSITION	PAY RATE	HOURS	OVERTIME	TOTAL EARNED
TOTAL					

Allowance for Taxes*: Total Salaries _____ x Rate _____ = _____

TOTAL (HOURLY + SALARIED)

* Taxes to be allowed for include: Social Security, Medicare, Federal & State Unemployment

Payroll Cost Report

DATE PREPARED: _____ WEEK OF: _____

PREPARED BY: _____

TOTAL PAYROLL COST

Total Gross Wages	$	_____
(+) Total Employee Meals	$	_____
(=) **Total Payroll Cost**	$	_____

PAYROLL COST PERCENTAGE

Total Payroll Cost	$	_____
(÷) Total Gross Sales	$	_____
(_____ x 100 =) **Payroll Cost**	%	_____

SALES PER PERSON PER HOUR

Total Gross Sales	$	_____
(÷) Total Hours Worked	$	_____
(=) **Sales Per Person Per Hour**	$	_____

Employee Turnover Rate & Cost Chart

PREPARED BY: _____

DATE: _____

EMPLOYEE TURNOVER RATE

Number of Completed W-2s   _____

(-)

Current Number of Employees   _____

(=)

Number of Past Employees   _____

Number of Past Employees   _____

(÷)

Average Number of Employees Employed   _____

(x 100)

Employee Turnover Rate Percentage   _____%

COST OF EMPLOYEE TURNOVER

Number of Past Employees   _____

(x)

Cost to Hire Each Employee $ _____

(=)

Cost of Employee Turnover $ _____

Labor Analysis Form

	DAY	DATE	DAILY SALES	DAILY PAYROLL BUDGET	DAILY PAYROLL ACT	DAILY PAYROLL OV/UND	%	MONTH TO DATE	MONTH-TO-DATE PAYROLL BUDGET	MONTH-TO-DATE PAYROLL ACT	MONTH-TO-DATE PAYROLL OV/UND	%
1												
2												
3												
4												
5												
6												
7												
7-DAY TOTAL												
8												
9												
10												
11												
12												
13												
14												
14-DAY TOTAL												
15												
16												
17												
18												
19												
20												
21												
21-DAY TOTAL												
22												
23												
24												
25												
26												
27												
28												
28-DAY TOTAL												
29												
30												
31												
TOTAL												

Employee's Daily Record of Tips/Employer Report

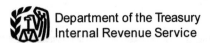 **Department of the Treasury**
Internal Revenue Service

Publication 1244
(Rev. June 1999)

Employee's Daily
Record of Tips
and
Report to Employer

This publication contains:

Form 4070A, Employee's Daily Record of Tips

Form 4070, Employee's Report of Tips to Employer

_____

For the period

beginning .... , ... and

ending .... , ...

_____

Name and address of employee

_____

Publication 1244 (Rev. 6-99)   Cat. No. 44472W

Instructions

You must keep sufficient proof to show the amount of your tip income for the year. A daily record of your tip income is considered sufficient proof. Keep a daily record for each workday showing the amount of cash and credit card tips received directly from customers or other employees. Also keep a record of the amount of tips, if any, you paid to other employees through tip sharing, tip pooling or other arrangements, and the names of employees to whom you paid tips. Show the date that each entry is made. This date should be on or near the date you received the tip income. You may use Form 4070A, Employee's Daily Record of Tips, or any other daily record to record your tips.

Reporting Tips to Your Employer. If you receive tips that total $20 or more for any month while working for one employer, you must report the tips to your employer. Tips include cash left by customers, tips customers add to credit card charges, and tips you receive from other employees. You must report your tips for any one month by the 10th of the month after the month you receive the tips. If the 10th day falls on a Saturday, Sunday, or legal holiday, you may give the report to your employer on the next business day that is not a Saturday, Sunday, or legal holiday.

You must report tips that total $20 or more every month regardless of your total wages and tips for the year. You may use Form 4070, Employee's Report of Tips to Employer, to report your tips to your employer. See the instructions on the back of Form 4070.

You must include all tips, including tips not reported to your employer, as wages on your income tax return. You may use the last page of this publication to total your tips for the year.

Your employer must withhold income, social security, and Medicare (or railroad retirement) taxes on tips you report. Your employer usually deducts the withholding due on tips from your regular wages.

(continued on inside of back cover)

Form **4070A** (Rev. June 1999) Department of the Treasury Internal Revenue Service	Employee's Daily Record of Tips This is a voluntary form provided for your convenience. See instructions for records you must keep.			OMB No. 1545-0065
Employee's name and address	Employer's name			Month and year
	Establishment name (if different)			

Date tips rec'd.	Date of entry	a. Tips received directly from customers and other employees	b. Credit card tips received	c. Tips paid out to other employees	d. Names of employees to whom you paid tips
1					
2					
3					
4					
5					
Subtotals					

For Paperwork Reduction Act Notice, see Instructions on the back of Form 4070.   Page 1

Employee's Daily Record of Tips/Employer Report

Date tips rec'd.	Date of entry	a. Tips received directly from customers and other employees	b. Credit card tips received	c. Tips paid out to other employees	d. Names of employees to whom you paid tips
6					
7					
8					
9					
10					
11					
12					
13					
14					
15					
Subtotals					

Page 2

Date tips rec'd.	Date of entry	a. Tips received directly from customers and other employees	b. Credit card tips received	c. Tips paid out to other employees	d. Names of employees to whom you paid tips
16					
17					
18					
19					
20					
21					
22					
23					
24					
25					
Subtotals					

Page 3

Date tips rec'd.	Date of entry	a. Tips received directly from customers and other employees	b. Credit card tips received	c. Tips paid out to other employees	d. Names of employees to whom you paid tips
26					
27					
28					
29					
30					
31					
Subtotals from pages 1, 2, and 3					
Totals					

1. Report total cash tips (col. a) on Form 4070, line 1.
2. Report total credit card tips (col. b) on Form 4070, line 2.
3. Report total tips paid out (col. c) on Form 4070, line 3.

Page 4

Employee's Daily Record of Tips/Employer Report

Form **4070**
(Rev. June 1999)
Department of the Treasury
Internal Revenue Service

Employee's Report of Tips to Employer

▶ For Paperwork Reduction Act Notice, see back of form.

OMB No. 1545-0065

Employee's name and address

Social security number

Employer's name and address (include establishment name, if different)

1 Cash tips received

2 Credit card tips received

3 Tips paid out

Month or shorter period in which tips were received

from , , to ,

4 Net tips (lines 1 + 2 - 3)

Signature

Date

Purpose. Use this form to report tips you receive to your employer. This includes cash tips, tips you receive from other employees, and credit card tips. You must report tips every month regardless of your total wages and tips for the year. However, you do not have to report tips to your employer for any month you received less than $20 in tips while working for that employer.

Report tips by the 10th day of the month following the month that you receive them. If the 10th day is a Saturday, Sunday, or legal holiday, report tips by the next day that is not a Saturday, Sunday, or legal holiday.

See Pub. 531, Reporting Tip Income, for more details.

You can get additional copies of Pub. 1244, Employee's Daily Record of Tips and Report to Employer, which contains both Forms 4070A and 4070, by calling 1-800-TAX-FORM (1-800-829-3676).

Paperwork Reduction Act Notice. We ask for the information on these forms to carry out the Internal Revenue laws of the United States. You are required to give us the information. We need it to ensure that you are complying with these laws and to allow us to figure and collect the right amount of tax.

You are not required to provide the information requested on a form that is subject to the Paperwork Reduction Act unless the form displays a valid OMB control number. Books or records relating to a form or its instructions must be retained as long as their contents may become material in the administration of any Internal Revenue law. Generally, tax returns and return information are confidential, as required by Code section 6103.

The time needed to complete Forms 4070 and 4070A will vary depending on individual circumstances. The estimated average times are: Recordkeeping—Form 4070, 7 min.; Form 4070A, 3 hr. and 23 min.; Learning about the law—each form, 2 min.; Preparing Form 4070, 13 min.; Form 4070A, 55 min.; and Copying and providing Form 4070, 10 min.; Form 4070A, 28 min.

If you have comments concerning the accuracy of these time estimates or suggestions for making these forms simpler, we would be happy to hear from you. You can write to the Tax Forms Committee, Western Area Distribution Center, Rancho Cordova, CA 95743-0001.

Employee's Daily Record of Tips/Employer Report

Instructions (continued)

Unreported Tips. If you received tips of $20 or more for any month while working for one employer but did not report them to your employer, you must figure and pay social security and Medicare taxes on the unreported tips when you file your tax return. If you have unreported tips, you must use Form 1040 and Form 4137, Social Security and Medicare Tax on Unreported Tip Income, to report them. You may not use Form 1040A or 1040EZ. Employees subject to the Railroad Retirement Tax Act cannot use Form 4137 to pay railroad retirement tax on unreported tips. To get railroad retirement credit, you must report tips to your employer.

If you do not report tips to your employer as required, you may be charged a penalty of 50% of the social security and Medicare taxes (or railroad retirement tax) due on the unreported tips unless there was reasonable cause for not reporting them.

Additional Information. Get Pub. 531, Reporting Tip Income, and Form 4137 for more information on tips. If you are an employee of certain large food or beverage establishments, see Pub. 531 for tip allocation rules.

Recordkeeping. If you do not keep a daily record of tips, you must keep other reliable proof of the tip income you received. This proof includes copies of restaurant bills and credit card charges that show amounts customers added as tips.

Keep your tip income records for as long as the information on them may be needed in the administration of any Internal Revenue law.

Instructions (continued)

Use this space to total your tips for the year

Employee's Daily Record of Tips/Employer Report

Form **8027**

Department of the Treasury
Internal Revenue Service

Employer's Annual Information Return of Tip Income and Allocated Tips

▶ **See separate instructions.**

OMB No. 1545-0714

20**03**

Use IRS label. Make any necessary changes. Otherwise, please type or print.

Name of establishment

Number and street (see instructions)

City or town, state, and ZIP code

Employer identification number

Type of establishment (check only one box)

- [ ] 1 Evening meals only
- [ ] 2 Evening and other meals
- [ ] 3 Meals other than evening meals
- [ ] 4 Alcoholic beverages

Employer's name (same name as on Form 941)

Number and street (P.O. box, if applicable)

Apt. or suite no.

Establishment number (see instructions)

City, state, and ZIP code (if a foreign address, see instructions)

Does this establishment accept credit cards, debit cards, or other charges?   Yes [ ]   No [ ]   (lines 1 and 2 **must** be completed)

Check **if:** Amended Return [ ]
Final Return [ ]

1 Total charged tips for calendar year 2003	**1**	
2 Total charge receipts showing charged tips (see instructions)	**2**	
3 Total amount of service charges of less than 10% paid as wages to employees	**3**	
4a Total tips reported by indirectly tipped employees	**4a**	
b Total tips reported by directly tipped employees	**4b**	

Note: Complete the **Employer's Optional Worksheet for Tipped Employees** on page 4 of the instructions to determine potential unreported tips of your employees.

c Total tips reported (add lines 4a and 4b)	**4c**	
5 Gross receipts from food or beverage operations (not less than line 2—see instructions) .	**5**	

6 Multiply line 5 by 8% (.08) or the lower rate shown here ▶ _____ granted by the IRS. (Attach a copy of the IRS determination letter to this return.) **6**

Note: If you have allocated tips using other than the calendar year (semimonthly, biweekly, quarterly, etc.), mark an **"X"** on line 6 and enter the amount of allocated tips from your records on line 7.

7 Allocation of tips. If line 6 is more than line 4c, enter the excess here **7**

▶ This amount must be allocated as tips to tipped employees working in this establishment. Check the box below that shows the method used for the allocation. (Show the portion, if any, attributable to each employee in box 8 of the employee's Form W-2.)

a Allocation based on hours-worked method (see instructions for restriction). . . . [ ]

Note: If you marked the checkbox in line 7a, enter the average number of employee hours worked per business day during the payroll period. (see instructions) _____

b Allocation based on gross receipts method . . . . [ ]

c Allocation based on good-faith agreement (Attach a copy of the agreement.) . . . [ ]

8 Enter the total number of directly tipped employees at this establishment during 2003 ▶

Under penalties of perjury, I declare that I have examined this return, including accompanying schedules and statements, and to the best of my knowledge and belief, it is true, correct, and complete.

Signature ▶

Title ▶

Date ▶

For Privacy Act and Paperwork Reduction Act Notice, see page 4 of the separate instructions.

Cat. No. 49989U

Form **8027** (2003)

Labor Tracking

DATE PREPARED: _____ WEEK OF: _____

PREPARED BY: _____

MONDAY

	GOAL	FORECAST	ACTUAL
Labor Hours			
Total Sales			
Labor Dollars			
Labor %			

FRIDAY

	GOAL	FORECAST	ACTUAL
Labor Hours			
Total Sales			
Labor Dollars			
Labor %			

TUESDAY

	GOAL	FORECAST	ACTUAL
Labor Hours			
Total Sales			
Labor Dollars			
Labor %			

SATURDAY

	GOAL	FORECAST	ACTUAL
Labor Hours			
Total Sales			
Labor Dollars			
Labor %			

WEDNESDAY

	GOAL	FORECAST	ACTUAL
Labor Hours			
Total Sales			
Labor Dollars			
Labor %			

SUNDAY

	GOAL	FORECAST	ACTUAL
Labor Hours			
Total Sales			
Labor Dollars			
Labor %			

THURSDAY

	GOAL	FORECAST	ACTUAL
Labor Hours			
Total Sales			
Labor Dollars			
Labor %			

Monetary Labor Performance

SERVERS

	MON	TUES	WED	THURS	FRI	SAT	SUN	TOTALS
AM SHIFT								$
PM SHIFT								$
TOTAL								$

HOST

	MON	TUES	WED	THURS	FRI	SAT	SUN	TOTALS
AM SHIFT								$
PM SHIFT								$
TOTAL								$

COOKS

	MON	TUES	WED	THURS	FRI	SAT	SUN	TOTALS
AM SHIFT								$
PM SHIFT								$
TOTAL								$

PREP

	MON	TUES	WED	THURS	FRI	SAT	SUN	TOTALS
AM SHIFT								$
PM SHIFT								$
TOTAL								$

	MON	TUES	WED	THURS	FRI	SAT	SUN	TOTALS
AM SHIFT								$
PM SHIFT								$
TOTAL								$

	MON	TUES	WED	THURS	FRI	SAT	SUN	TOTALS
AM SHIFT								$
PM SHIFT								$
TOTAL								$

TOTALS

	MON	TUES	WED	THURS	FRI	SAT	SUN	TOTALS
								$

Labor Performance by Position

DATE PREPARED: _____ WEEK OF: _____

PREPARED BY: _____

POSITION:

	MON	TUES	WED	THURS	FRI	SAT	SUN	TOTALS
HOURS								$
RATE								$
TOTAL								$

POSITION:

	MON	TUES	WED	THURS	FRI	SAT	SUN	TOTALS
HOURS								$
RATE								$
TOTAL								$

POSITION:

	MON	TUES	WED	THURS	FRI	SAT	SUN	TOTALS
HOURS								$
RATE								$
TOTAL								$

POSITION:

	MON	TUES	WED	THURS	FRI	SAT	SUN	TOTALS
HOURS								$
RATE								$
TOTAL								$

POSITION:

	MON	TUES	WED	THURS	FRI	SAT	SUN	TOTALS
HOURS								$
RATE								$
TOTAL								$

TOTALS

	MON	TUES	WED	THURS	FRI	SAT	SUN	TOTALS
								$

Labor Budget

DATE PREPARED: _____ MONTH OF: _____

PREPARED BY: _____

	Sales Forecast	Labor Cost Standard	Labor Expense Budget
Week One			
Week Two			
Week Three			
Week Four			
TOTAL			

ACTUAL LABOR VS. BUDGETED LABOR COST

	Sales			Labor Costs			Labor Cost %	
	Budgeted	Actual	% of Budget	Budgeted	Actual	% of Budget	Budgeted	Actual
Week One								
Week Two								
Week Three								
Week Four								
TOTAL								

Waitstaff Production

DATE: _____ DAY: _____ SHIFT: _____
PREPARED BY: _____

SERVER: _____

Total Sales: _____ Hours Worked: _____

Total # of Customers: _____ Station #: _____

Sales per Person-Hour: _____
(Divide Total Sales by Hours Worked)

Average Customer Sale: _____
(Divide Total Sales by Total Number of Customers)

Sales–Item %: _____

Sales–Item %: _____

Sales–Item %: _____

SERVER: _____

Total Sales: _____ Hours Worked: _____

Total # of Customers: _____ Station #: _____

Sales per Person-Hour: _____
(Divide Total Sales by Hours Worked)

Average Customer Sale: _____
(Divide Total Sales by Total Number of Customers)

Sales–Item %: _____

Sales–Item %: _____

Sales–Item %: _____

SERVER: _____

Total Sales: _____ Hours Worked: _____

Total # of Customers: _____ Station #: _____

Sales per Person-Hour: _____
(Divide Total Sales by Hours Worked)

Average Customer Sale: _____
(Divide Total Sales by Total Number of Customers)

Sales–Item %: _____

Sales–Item %: _____

Sales–Item %: _____

SERVER: _____

Total Sales: _____ Hours Worked: _____

Total # of Customers: _____ Station #: _____

Sales per Person-Hour: _____
(Divide Total Sales by Hours Worked)

Average Customer Sale: _____
(Divide Total Sales by Total Number of Customers)

Sales–Item %: _____

Sales–Item %: _____

Sales–Item %: _____

SERVER: _____

Total Sales: _____ Hours Worked: _____

Total # of Customers: _____ Station #: _____

Sales per Person-Hour: _____
(Divide Total Sales by Hours Worked)

Average Customer Sale: _____
(Divide Total Sales by Total Number of Customers)

Sales–Item %: _____

Sales–Item %: _____

Sales–Item %: _____

SERVER: _____

Total Sales: _____ Hours Worked: _____

Total # of Customers: _____ Station #: _____

Sales per Person-Hour: _____
(Divide Total Sales by Hours Worked)

Average Customer Sale: _____
(Divide Total Sales by Total Number of Customers)

Sales–Item %: _____

Sales–Item %: _____

Sales–Item %: _____

Shift Productivity Chart

DATE: _____ DAY: _____ SHIFT: _____
PREPARED BY: _____

Hours of Operation	Sales per Hour	Covers per Hour	Person-Hours	❶ Sales per Person-Hour	❷ Covers per Person-Hour	Mishaps per Hour	❸ Mishap %
Shift Average							

❶ Sales per Hour ÷ Person Hours   ❸ Mishaps per Hour - Covers per Hour

❷ Covers per Hour ÷ Person Hours

Sales & Labor Report

WEEK OF: _____ DATE PREPARED: _____

PREPARED BY: _____

ITEM	MON	TUES	WED	THURS	FRI	SAT	SUN	TOTAL
Food Sales								
Month to Date								
Beverage Sales								
Month to Date								
Total Sales								
Month to Date								
Service Labor								
Beverage Labor								
Kitchen Labor								
Management Labor								
Total Labor								
Labor % to Sales								

NOTES:

Daily Sales Report Form

	DAY	DATE	FOOD SALES		LIQUOR SALES		WINE SALES		TOTAL SALES	MONTH-TO-DATE	
			AMT $	INV #	AMT $	INV #	AMT $	INV #		ACTUAL	BUDGET
1											
2											
3											
4											
5											
6											
7											
7-DAY TOTAL											
8											
9											
10											
11											
12											
13											
14											
14-DAY TOTAL											
15											
16											
17											
18											
19											
20											
21											
21-DAY TOTAL											
22											
23											
24											
25											
26											
27											
28											
28-DAY TOTAL											
29											
30											
31											
TOTAL											

Food Itemization Form

ITEM	USE A ✔ MARK TO DESIGNATE ONE SOLD	TOTALS
	TOTAL	

Food Sales Recap

WEEK OF: _____ DATE PREPARED: _____

PREPARED BY: _____

MENU ITEM	MON	TUES	WED	THURS	FRI	SAT	SUN	TOTAL

Sales History — Average Sales Per Guest

PREPARED BY: _____   DATE PREPARED: _____

WEEK OF:

	DATE	SALES	GUESTS SERVED	SALES PER GUEST
Monday				
Tuesday				
Wednesday				
Thursday				
Friday				
Saturday				
Sunday				
TOTAL FOR WEEK				

WEEK OF:

	DATE	SALES	GUESTS SERVED	SALES PER GUEST
Monday				
Tuesday				
Wednesday				
Thursday				
Friday				
Saturday				
Sunday				
TOTAL FOR WEEK				

Daily Sales Report

DATE: _____ DAY: _____ APPROVED BY: _____

PREPARED BY: _____

REGISTER READINGS

DEPARTMENT	SHIFT	END READING	BEGINNING READING	DIFFERENCE

TOTAL RECEIPTS

DEPARTMENT	SHIFT	CASH	CHARGE	TOTAL	OVER/SHORT

SALES BREAKDOWN

DEPARTMENT	SHIFT	FOOD SALES	BAR SALES	TOTAL SALES

Weekly Sales History

PREPARED BY: _____   **DATE PREPARED:** _____

WEEK OF:

	DATE	SALES	SALES TO DATE
Monday			
Tuesday			
Wednesday			
Thursday			
Friday			
Saturday			
Sunday			
TOTAL FOR WEEK			

WEEK OF:

	DATE	SALES	SALES TO DATE
Monday			
Tuesday			
Wednesday			
Thursday			
Friday			
Saturday			
Sunday			
TOTAL FOR WEEK			

Monthly Food Production Productivity Chart

DATE PREPARED: _____ MONTH: _____ YEAR: _____

PREPARED BY: _____

Day/Date	Shift	Av. Sales per Hour	Av. Covers per Hour	Av. Person-Hours	❶ Av. Sales per Person-Hour	❷ Av. Covers per Person-Hour	Av. Mishaps per Hour	❸ Av. Mishap %

❶ Av. Sales per Hour ÷ Av. Person Hours   ❸ Av. Mishaps per Hour - Av. Covers per Hour

❷ Av. Covers per Hour ÷ Av. Person Hours

Quarterly Sales History

FIRST QUARTER

	Current Year's Sales	Last Year's Sales	Variance	% Variance
January				
February				
March				
TOTAL				

SECOND QUARTER

	Current Year's Sales	Last Year's Sales	Variance	% Variance
April				
May				
June				
TOTAL				

THIRD QUARTER

	Current Year's Sales	Last Year's Sales	Variance	% Variance
July				
August				
September				
TOTAL				

FOURTH QUARTER

	Current Year's Sales	Last Year's Sales	Variance	% Variance
October				
November				
December				
TOTAL				

Quarterly Sales Forecast

DATE: _____ DAY: _____ APPROVED BY: _____

PREPARED BY: _____

CUSTOMER COUNTS

Month/Year	Last Year	Projected % Increase	Total Expected
Quarter Total			

CHECK AVERAGE

Month/Year	Last Year	Projected Increase	Check Av. Forecast
Quarter Total			

PROJECTED SALES

First Quarter	Second Quarter	Third Quarter	Fourth Quarter

Quarterly Sales Projection

PREPARED BY: _____ DATE PREPARED: _____

FIRST QUARTER			
	Last Year's Sales	Forecasted Change	Projected Sales Increase
January			
February			
March			
TOTAL			

SECOND QUARTER			
	Last Year's Sales	Forecasted Change	Projected Sales Increase
April			
May			
June			
TOTAL			

THIRD QUARTER			
	Last Year's Sales	Forecasted Change	Projected Sales Increase
July			
August			
September			
TOTAL			

FOURTH QUARTER			
	Last Year's Sales	Forecasted Change	Projected Sales Increase
October			
November			
December			
TOTAL			

Annual Food Production Productivity Report

DATE PREPARED: _____ YEAR: _____

PREPARED BY: _____

Month/Year	Shift	Av. Sales per Hour	Av. Covers per Hour	Av. Person-Hours	❶ Av. Sales per Person-Hours	❷ Av. Covers per Person-Hour	Av. Mishaps per Hour	❸ Av. Mishap %

❶ Av. Sales per Hour ÷ Av. Person Hours   ❸ Av. Mishaps per Hour - Av. Covers per Hour

❷ Av. Covers per Hour ÷ Av. Person Hours

Purchase Ledger

COMPANY _____ MONTH _____

DATE	INV #	AMT $	INV #	AMT $	INV #	AMT $	PAID OUTS
GRAND TOTAL							

PAGE TOTAL

Invoice

INVOICE NUMBER	DATE

SHIP TO:

BILL TO:

DATE	ATTENTION	TERMS

Quantity	Description of Item or Service	Unit	Amount	Total
		SUBTOTAL		
		TAX		
		TOTAL DUE		

Invoice II

ACCOUNT NUMBER   INVOICE DATE   INVOICE NUMBER

Remit To: _____

Bill To: _____

DATE	DESCRIPTION	QTY	PRICE	AMOUNT

SUBTOTAL	
TAX	
TOTAL	

Invoice Payment Schedule

Date:_____   Department: _____

Period Ending: _____   Quarter: _____

Prepared By: _____

Approved By: _____

Supplier	Invoice Number	Date	Amount		Total Amount	

Notes:

Total $

Invoice Log

DATE: _____ MONTH: _____

PREPARED BY: _____

Date	Supplier	Invoice #	Total	Expense Category
				❑ Food ❑ Beverage ❑ Office ❑ Repairs ❑ Supplies ❑ Other
				❑ Food ❑ Beverage ❑ Office ❑ Repairs ❑ Supplies ❑ Other
				❑ Food ❑ Beverage ❑ Office ❑ Repairs ❑ Supplies ❑ Other
				❑ Food ❑ Beverage ❑ Office ❑ Repairs ❑ Supplies ❑ Other
				❑ Food ❑ Beverage ❑ Office ❑ Repairs ❑ Supplies ❑ Other
				❑ Food ❑ Beverage ❑ Office ❑ Repairs ❑ Supplies ❑ Other
				❑ Food ❑ Beverage ❑ Office ❑ Repairs ❑ Supplies ❑ Other
				❑ Food ❑ Beverage ❑ Office ❑ Repairs ❑ Supplies ❑ Other
				❑ Food ❑ Beverage ❑ Office ❑ Repairs ❑ Supplies ❑ Other
				❑ Food ❑ Beverage ❑ Office ❑ Repairs ❑ Supplies ❑ Other
				❑ Food ❑ Beverage ❑ Office ❑ Repairs ❑ Supplies ❑ Other
				❑ Food ❑ Beverage ❑ Office ❑ Repairs ❑ Supplies ❑ Other
				❑ Food ❑ Beverage ❑ Office ❑ Repairs ❑ Supplies ❑ Other
				❑ Food ❑ Beverage ❑ Office ❑ Repairs ❑ Supplies ❑ Other
				❑ Food ❑ Beverage ❑ Office ❑ Repairs ❑ Supplies ❑ Other
				❑ Food ❑ Beverage ❑ Office ❑ Repairs ❑ Supplies ❑ Other
				❑ Food ❑ Beverage ❑ Office ❑ Repairs ❑ Supplies ❑ Other
				❑ Food ❑ Beverage ❑ Office ❑ Repairs ❑ Supplies ❑ Other
				❑ Food ❑ Beverage ❑ Office ❑ Repairs ❑ Supplies ❑ Other
				❑ Food ❑ Beverage ❑ Office ❑ Repairs ❑ Supplies ❑ Other
				❑ Food ❑ Beverage ❑ Office ❑ Repairs ❑ Supplies ❑ Other
				❑ Food ❑ Beverage ❑ Office ❑ Repairs ❑ Supplies ❑ Other

Expense Report

EMPLOYEE: _____ DATE: _____

LOCATIONS VISITED: _____ PURPOSE OF TRIP: _____

ITEM	MON	TUES	WED	THURS	FRI	SAT	SUN	TOTAL
Airfare								
Breakfast								
Lunch								
Dinner								
Lodging								
Parking/Toll								
Transportation								
Postage								
Supplies								
Telephone								
Other								
Other								
TOTAL								

	MON	TUES	WED	THURS	FRI	SAT	SUN	TOTAL
Mileage ($. per mile)								

ADDITIONAL EXPENSES	DETAILS	AMOUNT

TOTAL EXPENSES: _____ (- Any Advance) _____ TOTAL DUE EMPLOYEE: $ _____

Purchase Order

PURCHASE ORDER NUMBER	DATE

SHIP TO:

BILL TO:

DATE	ATTENTION		TERMS	
Quantity	Description of Item or Service	Unit	Amount	Total

Authorized By: _____ Title: _____

_____

Signature

SUBTOTAL	
TAX	
TOTAL DUE	

Inter-Department Transfer

PREPARED BY: _____   DATE PREPARED: _____

FROM: **TO:**

DATE	ITEM TRANSFERRED	AMOUNT	COST	TOTAL

FROM: **TO:**

DATE	ITEM TRANSFERRED	AMOUNT	COST	TOTAL

CHAPTER 10

Catering is another unique aspect of the food service industry. One of the keys to a successful catering operation is organization and written contracts and procedures. You also need to be able to multitask and prioritize your time with military precision. The forms in this chapter will help define and streamline catering.

Catering/Banquet Management

Booking Inquiry Call Log

CALL TAKEN BY: _____

DATE: _____

Name of Group/Party: _____

Name of Person Calling: _____

Address: _____

_____

City, State, Zip: _____

Phone Number: _____

Posting Instructions : _____

_____

_____

BOOKING INSTRUCTIONS

Date: _____

Alternative Date: _____

Hours: _____

Function: _____

Room: _____

Approximate Number of People Attending : _____

Rate:_____

Booking is: ❏ Tentative   ❏ Definite   ❏ Inquiry

Notes: _____

_____

_____

_____

Inquiry Report

Inquiry Received By: _____ File #: _____

Date of Inquiry: _____ Type of Inquiry: ❑ Phone ❑ Letter ❑ Personal Meeting

EVENT INFORMATION

❑ New Business   ❑ Repeat Business   ❑ On-Premise Event   ❑ Off-Premise Event

Type of Function: _____

Date(s): _____ Guest Count: _____

Additional Notes: _____

_____

_____

CONTACT INFORMATION

Contact Person: _____

Organization/Company: _____

Address: _____

City: _____ State: _____ Zip: _____

Phone: _____ Fax: _____ E-mail: _____

Additional Comments: _____

_____

_____

_____

_____

_____

Table Sizes

TABLE TYPE	TABLE SIZE	TABLECLOTH SIZE
Round	2-1/2 feet cocktail	54" x 54"
Round	3 feet cocktail	64" x 64"
Round	4-1/2 feet cocktail	64" x 64"
Round	5 feet, 10 person	84" x 84"
Round	5-1/2 feet, 10 person	90" x 90"
Round	6 feet, 12 person	90" x 90"
Rectangular	6 feet x 18 inches	
Rectangular	6 feet x 24 inches	
Rectangular	6 feet x 30 inches	
Rectangular	6 feet x 36 inches	
Rectangular	5 feet x 30 inches	
Rectangular	4 feet x 30 inches	
Square	30 inches x 30 inches	
Half-Round	5 feet x 30 inches	
Quarter-Round	30 inches x 30 inches	
Crescent	6 feet x 36 inches	

COMBINATIONS:

Large oval table to seat 16
Combine two half-rounds with four rectangular 6-feet x 30-inch tables.

Hollow buffet table
Combine four crescent tables with sufficient number of 3-foot rectangular tables.

Clover leaf buffet table with large center
Combine half-round tables with rectangular and square table.

Place Settings

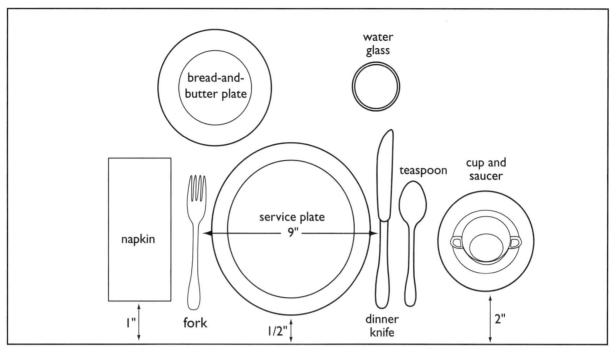

"Table Cover Setup" using 16" x 12" doily and showing space allowance for a 24" cover arrangement.

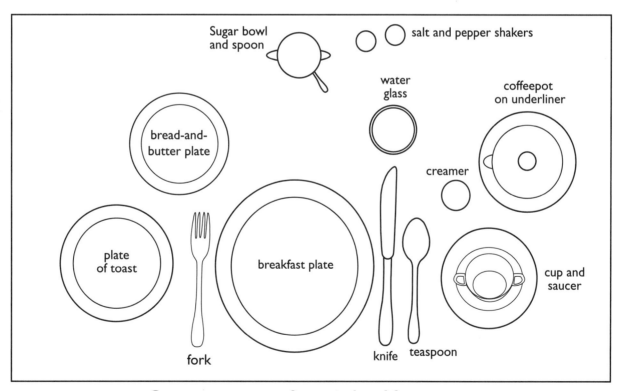

Cover arrangement for main breakfast course.

Place Settings

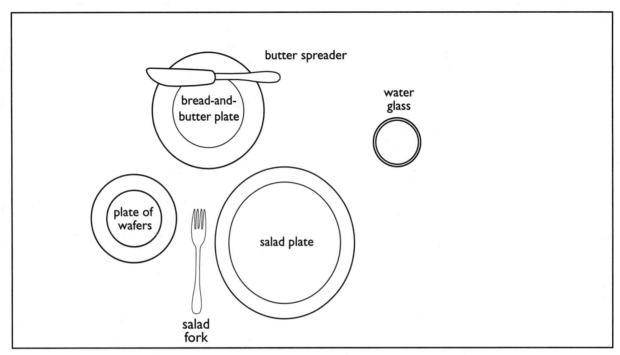

Cover arrangement when a dinner salad is served as separate course.

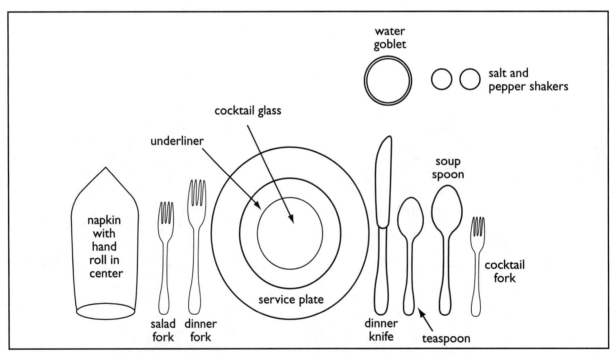

Cover arrangement for appetizer course of a formal dinner.

Place Settings

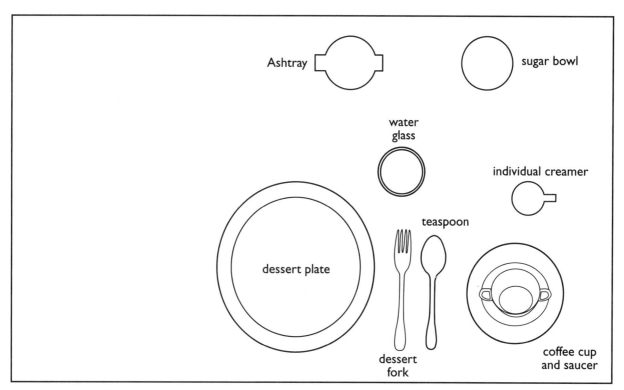

Cover arrangement for dessert course for luncheon or dinner.

Reception Drink Estimator

DRINKS PER GUEST

# of Guests	30 Minutes	1 Hour	90 Minutes	2 Hours
25-59	2	$3^{1}/_{2} - 4$	$4 - 4^{1}/_{2}$	$4^{1}/_{2} - 5$
60-104	2	$3^{1}/_{2} - 4$	4	$4^{1}/_{2} - 5$
105-225	2	3	4	$4^{1}/_{2} - 5$
226-500	$1^{1}/_{2} - 2$	$2^{1}/_{2} - 3$	3	$3^{1}/_{2} - 4$
over 500	$1^{1}/_{2} - 2$	$2^{1}/_{2} - 3$	3	$3^{1}/_{2} - 4$

DRINKS PER BOTTLE

Bottle Size	Drink Size	# of Drinks
$^{4}/_{5}$ Quart	1 ounce	25
$^{4}/_{5}$ Quart	$1^{1}/_{4}$ ounce	20
$^{4}/_{5}$ Quart	$1^{1}/_{2}$ ounce	17
Quart	1 ounce	31
Quart	$1^{1}/_{4}$ ounce	25
Quart	$1^{1}/_{2}$ ounce	21

RECEPTION STAFF ESTIMATE

# of Guests	# of Bartenders	# of Waiters w/Food	# of Waiters wo/Food
25-100	1	2	1
101-200	2	3	2
201-300	3	3	2
301-500	4	4	3
over 500	6	6	4

Event Ordering Sheet

Customer: _____ Contact: _____

Phone Number: _____

Event Date: _____

Event Location: _____

Number of Guests: _____ Set-Up Time: _____

Event Type: _____

_____

SCHEDULE:

_____ a.m./p.m. _____

_____ a.m./p.m. _____

_____ a.m./p.m. _____

_____ a.m./p.m. _____

_____ a.m./p.m. _____

MENU:

_____

_____

_____

_____

_____

_____

RENTALS:

_____

_____

NOTES:

_____

_____

Event Organizational Form

Date Requested: _____ Date of Event: _____

Time Guests Arrive: _____ Time to Serve: _____

Room or Location: _____

Contact Name: _____

Address: _____ Phone Number: _____

Occasion: _____

Number of Guests: _____

Deposit: _____ Gratuity: _____ Tax: _____

MENU	NOTES

_____

Signature

Detailed Catering Contract

CATERING COMPANY

Catering Company Name _____

Contact Name _____

Address _____

City, State, Zip _____

Phone _____ Fax _____ E-mail _____

CLIENT

Name _____

Organization _____

Address _____

City, State, Zip _____

Phone _____ Fax _____ E-mail _____

EVENT INFORMATION

Date _____ Day _____

Location _____

Type of Event _____

Arrival Time _____

Cocktails Served _____

Hor d'oeuvres Served _____

Food Served _____

Bar Time from _____ to _____

Entertainment from _____ to _____

Speaker(s) from _____ to _____

Dancing from _____ to _____

Photography from _____ to _____

Videography from _____ to _____

Departure Time _____

GUEST INFORMATION

Estimated Number of Guests _____

Guaranteed Number of Guests _____

Date for Final Guaranteed Guests _____

Confirmed Number of Guests _____

Table Arrangements _____

_____

Seating Arrangements _____

_____

(diagram on separate sheet if necessary)

Additional Notes _____

_____

_____

_____

_____

_____

Detailed Catering Contract

MENU INFORMATION

Menu Type: ❑ Full-Service   ❑ Buffet   Menu Theme: _____

Menu Selections: _____

_____

_____

_____

_____

_____

_____

Special Cake: _____

Beverage Selection: (Alcoholic/Nonalcoholic) _____ ❑ Open Bar   ❑ Cash Bar   ❑ Combination

ACCESSORY DETAILS (check all that apply)

❑ Linen (_____ tablecloths, _____ napkins, _____ skirting, _____ chair covers)

❑ Floral Decor (_____ centerpieces, _____ baskets, _____ plants, _____ sprays)

❑ Decorations (_____ room, _____ table)   ❑ Sound System/Microphone _____

❑ Background Music _____   ❑ Ice Sculptures _____

❑ Beverage Fountain(s) _____   ❑ Valet Parking   ❑ Entertainment _____

❑ Head Table ❑ Table Numbers ❑ Candles ❑ Registration Desk ❑ Speaker Podium ❑ Lectern

❑ Stage ❑ Tripod ❑ Easel ❑ Projector Screen/VCR ❑ Dance Floor ❑ Balloons ❑ Photography

AGREEMENT OF CHARGES

Date: _____

Guaranteed Guest Count of _____ People @ $ _____ per Guest for a Total of $ _____

Accessory Charges (list) _____ $ _____

_____ $ _____

The final charge will be for the guaranteed guest count or the confirmed guest count, whichever is greater. Caterer will be prepared to accommodate _____ % over the number of guaranteed guest count. **48-hour notice is required on cancellations.**	Gratuities $ _____
	Subtotal $ _____
_____ _____	Tax $ _____
Client's Signature Date	Deposit $ _____
_____ _____	Balance Due $ _____
Caterer's Signature Date	

Catering Contract

CATERER INFORMATION

Caterer's Name _____

Address _____

City, State, Zip _____

Phone Number _____

CLIENT INFORMATION

Client's Name _____

Address _____

City, State, Zip _____

Phone Number _____

EVENT INFORMATION

Type of Function _____

Location _____

Date _____

Time _____

Number of Guests _____

A 20% deposit is due upon signing this contract. The deposit will be deducted from the total bill and the remaining balance must be paid, in full, on the date of the function. Check and credit card payments are accepted. Returned checks will be charged a $25 reprocessing fee.

In the event of cancellation, the caterer must be notified in writing 30 days prior to the date of your function. If written notice is received within that 30-day period, the deposit will be refunded and the client will receive a copy of the contract marked "cancelled." If cancellation occurs less than 30 days before the event, full prepayment will be retained. If the function is cancelled 48 hours prior to the event, 50% of the total food and beverage cost will be charged, based on the confirmed or estimated numbers.

The final menu selections must be attached to this contract. In the event that the client would like to make a change to the menu, not due to an increase or decrease in the number of guests, the caterer must have a 14-day notice and the change must be approved in writing. Upon signing of this contract, a guaranteed number of guests is required. If the guest count should increase or decrease by more than 5 guests, the caterer must be notified 3 business days prior to the event. All details relating to menu selections must be confirmed one week prior to the function.

The caterer shall not be liable for the non-performance of this contract when such non-performance is attributed to acts of God and other causes whether enumerated herein or not, which are beyond the reasonable control, preventing or interfering with caterer's performance. In such event, the caterer shall not be liable to the customer for any damages, whether actual or consequential, which may result from such non-performance.

The caterer reserves the right to make changes to your function only in the event that our quality of excellence would be compromised and client shall be notified of such changes in writing prior to the event.

Client's Signature _____ Date _____

Caterer's Signature _____ Date _____

Comprehensive Catering Checklist

Date of Event:	Time: : a.m./p.m. to : a.m./p.m.
Private or Open Event?	Name of Party:
DESCRIPTION OF EVENT:	
Approx. Covers Last Event:	Sales Last Similar Event: $
NUMBER OF GUESTS:	Approx. "Cover" Formula: Number of Seats x Number of Hours:

MENU

ENTRÉE:	PORTION PP	ORDER UNIT/PORTION #	ESTIMATED SERVINGS	AMOUNT TO ORDER
SIDE DISHES:				
BREAD OR OTHER:				
DESSERT:				
BEVERAGES:				
OTHER:				

Comprehensive Catering Checklist

KITCHEN STAFFING

STAFF MEMBER	POSITION	HOURS SCHEDULED	RATE	PRIVATE PARTY CHARGE?

KITCHEN SET-UP

	Time to Do:	Person Responsible	Retrieve Item From:	Place Item Where?
PRODUCT PREPPING:				
❑ Prep Sheet Filled Out				
❑ Prep Items Labeled				
AREA PRE-EVENT CLEAN:				
EQUIPMENT SET-UP:				
❑ Cooking Set-Up:				
❑ Tongs/#				
❑ Spatulas/#				
❑ Cold Side Dish Containers/#				
❑ Spoons for Cold Sides/#				
❑ Hot Dish Containers/#				
❑ Serving Spoons/#				
❑ Basting Brush				
❑ Condiment Containers/#				
❑ Cold Holding Set-Up (40°F)				
❑ Aprons/#				
❑ Food Handlers' Gloves				
❑ Trash Cans				

Comprehensive Catering Checklist

EVENT STAFFING

STAFF MEMBER	POSITION	HOURS SCHEDULED	RATE	PRIVATE PARTY CHARGE?

SERVICE SET-UP

	Time to Do:	Person Responsible	Retrieve Item From:	Place Item Where?
❏ Table/Chairs Placement				
❏ Tablecloths on Tables				
❏ Condiments				
❏ Beverages				
❏ Cups				
❏ Forks, Knives, Spoons				
❏ Straws, Sugar, Cut Lemons				
GUEST BRINGING CAKE?				
❏ Plates				
❏ Cake Cutter				
❏ Candles				
BAR				
❏ Set-Up Bar				
❏ Register				

FULL BAR OR WINE? ❏ Cash & Carry ❏ Host Bar ❏ Cork Fee ❏ Cost PP _____

ADDITIONAL NOTES:

Comprehensive Catering Checklist

Name _____

Organization _____

Address _____

City, State, Zip _____

Phone _____ Fax _____ E-Mail _____

EVENT SUMMARY & CHARGES

	COST	x Number of Guests	EXTENSION	
Cost of Food Per Person	$		$	= TOTAL FOOD
Cost of Alcohol Per Person	$		$	= TOTAL BAR
(maximum amount served)				
Cost of Each Staff Member	$		$	= TOTAL LABOR
SUBTOTAL			$	= SUBTOTAL
GRATUITY (18% on Subtotal)			$	= GRATUITY
TAX (on Subtotal only)	$		$	= TAX
Rental Items (linen, flowers)	$		$	= RENTAL 1
Rental Item 2:	$		$	= RENTAL 2
Rental Item 3:	$		$	= RENTAL 3
GRAND TOTAL				**TOTAL**

Date of Deposit _____ Amount of Deposit (a minimum of _____% is due to book event)

(Total amount remaining must be paid in full by _____)

AMOUNT REMAINING $_____

I understand and agree to the terms as outlined above.

I understand that my deposit is not refundable and that additional charges as outlined may apply.

GUEST NAME: _____**DATE:** _____

GUEST SIGNATURE: _____

Entertainment Contract

This contract, made this_____ day of _____, 20___, by and between

Client (list name, address and phone number) _____

_____ and

Entertainer (list name, address and phone number) _____

_____

The Client desires to purchase and the Entertainer desires to provide specified entertainment services, the parties hereby agree to the terms and conditions set forth herein.

A.   The Entertainer will provide the following entertainment services _____.
     The performance will begin at _____ (a.m./ p.m.). The location of the entertainment will be (list establishment's name and address) _____.

B.   List all equipment and services, such as sound, lighting and electrical service, the Client is required to provide:_____
     _____.

C.   List all equipment and services, such as sound, lighting and electrical service, the Entertainer is required to provide:_____
     _____.

D.   For the services to be performed by the Entertainer, the Client agrees to pay to Entertainer the sum of _____ Dollars ($_____).
     Payment must be made upon completion of the entertainment performance by check or credit card made payable to
     _____. The Client shall be responsible for any applicable amusement or sales tax.

E.   The Entertainer assumes full responsibility for payment of any and all copyright royalties due for the entertainment performance described herein. The Entertainer further agrees to assume full responsibility for any copyright infringement which occurs during the course of said performance and agrees to hold the Client harmless from any and all liabilities and damages arising out of any action for copyright infringement.

F.   The Client reserves the right to terminate or interrupt the entertainment, if during the entertainment performance, the Client determines, in its sole discretion, that such action is warranted to maintain security or compliance with federal, state or local laws. Such action shall not affect the Client's obligation for payment under the terms of this contract; however, payment may be withheld if such interruption or termination is necessary due to a failure by the Entertainer to observe policies of which it has been informed.

G.   The Entertainer shall maintain documentation for all charges against the Client under this Agreement. The books, records and documents of the Entertainer, insofar as they relate to work performed or money received under this agreement, shall be maintained for a period of two (2) full years from the date of the final payment, and shall be subject to audit, at any reasonable time and upon notice, by the Client or their duly appointed representatives.

IN WITNESS THEREOF, the parties, through their authorized representatives, have affixed their signatures below.

Client:_____   Date: _____

Entertainer:_____   Date: _____

The abovesigned agent on behalf of the Entertainer warrants that he/she has the authority to execute this agreement on behalf of the performing artists and further warrants that the performing artists have agreed to be bound by the terms and conditions stated herein.

Entertainment Contract II

CATERING COMPANY

Catering Company Name _____

Contact Name _____

Address _____

City, State, Zip _____

Phone _____ Fax _____ E-mail _____

ENTERTAINMENT

Name of Band/Entertainer(s) _____

Contact Person _____ Federal Tax ID # _____

Address _____

City, State, Zip _____

Phone _____ Fax _____ E-mail _____

EVENT INFORMATION

The band/entertainer(s) and catering company agree to the following terms and conditions set forth in this contract:

Date of Event _____ Day of the Week _____ Time _____

Location of Event _____

_____

_____

Type of Music to be Played _____

_____

_____

_____

Specifically Requested Songs_____

_____

_____

_____

Entertainers' Type of Dress _____ Guests' Type of Dress _____

Entertainment Contract II

SCHEDULE

Entertainer(s) Arrival Time _____

Start Time _____

Break Times _____

_____

Length of Breaks_____

Break Area _____

The Band/Entertainer(s) may be provided with food and beverages at break time according to the following schedule _____

_____

_____

End Time _____

REQUIREMENTS

Check all that apply:

❑ Microphones _____

❑ Stage _____

❑ Seating _____

❑ Lighting _____

❑ Electrical _____

❑ Sound System _____

❑ Other _____

During the performance, guests are allowed to:

❑ Photograph

❑ Videotape

❑ Audiotape

SPECIAL INSTRUCTIONS

AGREEMENT OF CHARGES

Date _____

Overtime charge will be billed at a rate of $ _____ per hour for each additional hour beyond contracted time.

The band/entertainer(s) further agree that no alcoholic beverages will be consumed or drugs used at the event. **30-day notice is required on cancellations.**

_____
Entertainer's Signature   Date

_____
Caterer's Signature   Date

Overtime $ _____

Subtotal $ _____

Tax $ _____

Deposit $ _____

Balance Due $ _____

Banquet Manager's Function Summary Report

Date: _____ File #: _____

Name of Organization: _____

Type of Function: _____
_____

Function Room: _____ Salesperson: _____

Did function start and end on time? ❑ Yes ❑ No Comments: _____
_____

Was the room cleaned after the function? ❑ Yes ❑ No Comments: __
_____
_____

Were the air conditioning and lights tuned off? ❑ Yes ❑ No Comments: __
_____

Guests' Comments: _____
_____
_____
_____

Articles Left in Room: _____

INCOME		COVER COUNT	
Hor d'oeuvres:		# Guaranteed:	
Other Food:		# Set:	
Beverage:		# Plated:	
Wine		# Served:	
Gratuity:		# Charged:	
Tax:			
Other:			
TOTAL		Name of manager in charge of service	

Recap of Banquet Sales

DATE: _____ DAY: _____ PREPARED BY: _____

| Name | SALES | | | OTHER | | | TIPS | | | CHARGE TO | | | | | Func. Type |
	Pub. Rooms	Food	Beverage	Explain.	Amount	Sales Tax	Food	Beverage	Totals	City Ledger	Guest Ledger	Cash	# Served	

Banquet Extra Waitstaff Payroll

DATE: _____	Food Check # _____	Amount _____	Grat. _____
DATE: _____	Food Check # _____	Amount _____	Grat. _____
DATE: _____	Bev. Check # _____	Amount _____	Grat. _____
DATE: _____	Bev. Check # _____	Amount _____	Grat. _____
	TOTAL _____	(Less 19% _____)	

Employee	Station	Base Pay	Overtime	Extra Covers	Set-Up	Clear	Total Wages	Grat.	TOTAL
Shift Average									

Banquet Solicitation Report

DATE: _____ MONTH: _____ YEAR: _____

SALESPERSON: _____

Name of Organization	Local/ Conv.	File #	New Business	Repeat Business	Date	Function Type	Size	Est. Value
TOTAL								

Number of outside calls: _____

Number of new B files this month: _____

Number of B files killed this month: _____

Number of newspaper leads followed this month: _____

_____   _____
Signature of Salesperson   Signature of Catering Director

Credit Application

Name of Company or Group: _____

Contact Name: _____

Address: _____

City, State, Zip: _____

Phone: _____ Fax: _____ E-mail: _____

❑ Organization   ❑ Profit Organization   ❑ Nonprofit Organization   ❑ Individual

CREDIT REFERENCES

Bank: _____

Address: _____

Phone: _____ Account # _____

Previous Function: _____ Date: _____

History with Hotel: _____ Date: _____

Previous Other: _____ Date: _____

Bookings: _____ Date: _____

It is my/our understanding that if granted credit, my/our account will be settled in full within thirty (30) days.

_____
Signature of Company or Group Official   Date

TO BE COMPLETED BY SALES OFFICE:

Date of Function: _____ Salesperson: _____

Event Revenue: ❑ Rooms: _____ ❑ Food: _____ ❑ Beverage: _____ **TOTAL:** _____

CREDIT DECISION:

Dun & Bradstreet Rating: _____

❑ Approved   ❑ Denied   Comments: _____

_____
Signature of Credit Manager   Date

Lost Business Report

Date: _____ File Number: _____

Group Name: _____ Contact: _____

Event Date: _____

Event Type: _____

_____

No. of Guests: _____ Estimated Value: _____

Event Location Selected: _____

Source of Lead and Dates Received:

_____

_____

_____

_____

Reason for Losing Business:

_____

_____

_____

_____

COMMENTS:

_____

_____

_____

_____

_____

Signature of Catering Director

CHAPTER 11

Hotel Management

Hotels are another vital part of the hospitality industry. From registration to proper sanitation, the forms in this chapter will help make the tasks of hotel management easier.

Registration Card

Date _____   **Folio #**_____

Name _____

Address _____

City _____ State _____ Zip _____

Phone _____ E-mail _____ Affiliation_____

Arrival Date _____   Clerk _____

Room #_____   Departure Date _____

Rate _____

Credit Card ❑ Mastercard ❑ VISA ❑ American Express ❑ Discover

Card # ☐☐☐☐–☐☐☐☐–☐☐☐☐–☐☐☐☐   Expires ☐☐☐☐

Notes _____

_____

_____

Date _____   **Folio #**_____

Name _____

Address _____

City _____ State _____ Zip _____

Phone _____ E-mail _____ Affiliation_____

Arrival Date _____   Clerk _____

Room #_____   Departure Date _____

Rate _____

Credit Card ❑ Mastercard ❑ VISA ❑ American Express ❑ Discover

Card # ☐☐☐☐–☐☐☐☐–☐☐☐☐–☐☐☐☐   Expires ☐☐☐☐

Notes _____

_____

_____

Front Office Cash Sheet

DATE: _____ PREPARED BY: _____

CASH RECEIPTS

Room #	Name	Amount
	CASH RECEIPTS TOTAL	

CASH DISBURSEMENTS—GUESTS

Room #	Name	Item	Amount
	GUEST DISBURSEMENTS SUBTOTAL		

CASH DISBURSEMENTS—HOUSE

Item	Amount
HOUSE DISBURSEMENTS SUBTOTAL	

SUMMARY

Total Receipts	
Guest Disbursements	
House Disbursements	
Total Disbursements	
subtract Total Disbursements from Total Receipts	
DEPOSIT	

Daily Transcript of Guest Ledger

DATE: _____   PREPARED BY: _____

															Folio #
															Room #
															# of Guests
															OPENING BALANCE DB (CR)
															Room
															Room Tax
															Restaurant
															Beverages
															Local Calls
															Long Distance
															Valet
															Laundry
															Misc. Charges
															Cash Disbursements
															Transfer Debit
															TOTAL DAILY CHARGES
															Cash Receipts
															Allowances
															Transfer to City Ledger
															Transfer Credit
SUBTOTAL	TOTAL					Departures	SUBTOTAL								**TOTAL CREDITS**
															CLOSING BALANCE

Full-Service Hotel Checklist

ROOM: _____ INSPECTED BY: _____

DATE: _____ ROOM ATTENDANT: _____

Clean = C   Dirty = D
Needs Repair = R   Missing = M

ENTRY

Outside/inside door
❏ C   ❏ D   ❏ R   ❏ M

Locks
❏ C   ❏ D   ❏ R   ❏ M

Chain
❏ C   ❏ D   ❏ R   ❏ M

Doorstop
❏ C   ❏ D   ❏ R   ❏ M

"Do Not Disturb" sign
❏ C   ❏ D   ❏ R   ❏ M

Emergency/evacuation chart
❏ C   ❏ D   ❏ R   ❏ M

Fire pamphlets
❏ C   ❏ D   ❏ R   ❏ M

Smoke detectors
❏ C   ❏ D   ❏ R   ❏ M

Thermostat
❏ C   ❏ D   ❏ R   ❏ M

IN CLOSET

Shelves/rods
❏ C   ❏ D   ❏ R   ❏ M

Hangers – men's (6)
❏ C   ❏ D   ❏ R   ❏ M

Hangers – women's (6)
❏ C   ❏ D   ❏ R   ❏ M

Laundry/dry cleaning price lists
❏ C   ❏ D   ❏ R   ❏ M

Luggage racks (2)
❏ C   ❏ D   ❏ R   ❏ M

BEDROOM

Carpet
❏ C   ❏ D   ❏ R   ❏ M

Under the beds
❏ C   ❏ D   ❏ R   ❏ M

Walls/ceiling
❏ C   ❏ D   ❏ R   ❏ M

Drapes/curtains
❏ C   ❏ D   ❏ R   ❏ M

Windows
❏ C   ❏ D   ❏ R   ❏ M

Windowsills/frames
❏ C   ❏ D   ❏ R   ❏ M

TV/travel host
❏ C   ❏ D   ❏ R   ❏ M

Remote control
❏ C   ❏ D   ❏ R   ❏ M

Bed frames
❏ C   ❏ D   ❏ R   ❏ M

Headboards (straight)
❏ C   ❏ D   ❏ R   ❏ M

Pictures (straight)
❏ C   ❏ D   ❏ R   ❏ M

ON NIGHTSTAND

Telephone
❏ C   ❏ D   ❏ R   ❏ M

Memo pad/pen
❏ C   ❏ D   ❏ R   ❏ M

Guest services directory
❏ C   ❏ D   ❏ R   ❏ M

Alarm clock/radio
❏ C   ❏ D   ❏ R   ❏ M

Room service menu
❏ C   ❏ D   ❏ R   ❏ M

IN NIGHTSTAND

Telephone book
❏ C   ❏ D   ❏ R   ❏ M

Bible
❏ C   ❏ D   ❏ R   ❏ M

Guest book
❏ C   ❏ D   ❏ R   ❏ M

LIGHTING

Bulbs
❏ C   ❏ D   ❏ R   ❏ M

Fixtures
❏ C   ❏ D   ❏ R   ❏ M

Lamps/shades
❏ C   ❏ D   ❏ R   ❏ M

ON DESK/DRESSER

Stationery (5)
❏ C   ❏ D   ❏ R   ❏ M

Envelopes (3)
❏ C   ❏ D   ❏ R   ❏ M

Directory
❏ C   ❏ D   ❏ R   ❏ M

Pen
❏ C   ❏ D   ❏ R   ❏ M

Postcards
❏ C   ❏ D   ❏ R   ❏ M

Brochure
❏ C   ❏ D   ❏ R   ❏ M

Ice bucket
❏ C   ❏ D   ❏ R   ❏ M

Tray
❏ C   ❏ D   ❏ R   ❏ M

Glasses w/ caps (2)
❏ C   ❏ D   ❏ R   ❏ M

Full-Service Hotel Checklist

| ROOM: _____ | INSPECTED BY: _____ |
| DATE: _____ | ROOM ATTENDANT: _____ |

ASHTRAYS

Desk table
❏ C ❏ D ❏ R ❏ M

Night stand
❏ C ❏ D ❏ R ❏ M

End table
❏ C ❏ D ❏ R ❏ M

Round table
❏ C ❏ D ❏ R ❏ M

Bathroom
❏ C ❏ D ❏ R ❏ M

LIVING ROOM

Sleeper sofa
❏ C ❏ D ❏ R ❏ M

Love seat
❏ C ❏ D ❏ R ❏ M

Desk
❏ C ❏ D ❏ R ❏ M

Desk chair
❏ C ❏ D ❏ R ❏ M

End table
❏ C ❏ D ❏ R ❏ M

Floor lamp
❏ C ❏ D ❏ R ❏ M

Dresser
❏ C ❏ D ❏ R ❏ M

Remote control TV
❏ C ❏ D ❏ R ❏ M

Coffee table
❏ C ❏ D ❏ R ❏ M

Artificial plant
❏ C ❏ D ❏ R ❏ M

Wastebaskets
❏ C ❏ D ❏ R ❏ M

LAVATORY/BATHROOM

Amenities tray
❏ C ❏ D ❏ R ❏ M

Shampoo, conditioner
❏ C ❏ D ❏ R ❏ M

Shower cap
❏ C ❏ D ❏ R ❏ M

Hand/body lotion
❏ C ❏ D ❏ R ❏ M

NOTES/AREAS OF CONCERN

_____

_____

_____

_____

_____

_____

_____

_____

_____

_____

_____

_____

_____

_____

_____

_____

_____

Laundry Control Sheet

DATE: _____ DAY: _____ PREPARED BY: _____

VOUCHER #	ROOM #	GUEST NAME	AMOUNT	NOTES
		TOTAL AMOUNT		

DATE: _____ DAY: _____ PREPARED BY: _____

VOUCHER #	ROOM #	GUEST NAME	AMOUNT	NOTES
		TOTAL AMOUNT		

Telephone Control Sheet

DATE: _____ DAY: _____ PREPARED BY: _____

VOUCHER #	ROOM #	GUEST NAME	AMOUNT	NOTES
		TOTAL AMOUNT		

DATE: _____ DAY: _____ PREPARED BY: _____

VOUCHER #	ROOM #	GUEST NAME	AMOUNT	NOTES
		TOTAL AMOUNT		

Folio Form

FOLIO #

Guest's Name _____   Room # _____

Departure Date _____   Today's Date _____   Prepared By _____

DATE					
FORWARD					
Room					
Tax					
Restaurant					
Beverages					
Telephone–Local					
Telephone–Long Dist.					
Laundry					
Valet					
Misc. Charges					
Cash Disbursements					
Transfer Debits					
TOTAL DEBITS					
Cash Received					
Allowances					
Transfer to City Ledger					
Transfer Credit					
TOTAL CREDITS					
BALANCE FORWARD					
NOTES					

Folio Bucket Balances Sheet

DATE: _____ PREPARED BY: _____

ROOM NUMBER	FOLIO CLOSING BALANCE
TOTAL	

Room & House Count Sheet

DATE: _____ DAY: _____ APPROVED BY: _____

PREPARED BY: _____

ROOM USAGE

Room Number	Number of Guests	Tax	Room Rate
TOTAL			

Room & House Count Sheet

ROOM RECONCILIATION

	Number of Rooms	Number of Persons	Room Value	Tax Value
Yesterday				
+ Arrivals				
= TOTAL				
- Departures				
= TODAY				

ROOM STATISTICS

Rooms Available		
Rooms Occupied		
House Count		
Average Rate per Occupied Room	$	
Average Rate per Guest	$	
Percentage of Occupancy		%
Average Number of Guests per Room		

NOTES/COMMENTS

Restaurant & Beverage Control Sheet

DATE: _____ DAY: _____ PREPARED BY: _____

VOUCHER #	ROOM #	GUEST NAME	AMOUNT	NOTES
		TOTAL AMOUNT		

DATE: _____ DAY: _____ PREPARED BY: _____

VOUCHER #	ROOM #	GUEST NAME	AMOUNT	NOTES
		TOTAL AMOUNT		

Sales Forecast

WEEK OF:

PREPARED BY:

	Sunday		Monday		Tuesday		Wednesday		Thursday		Friday		Saturday	
	FORE	ACT	FORE	ACT	FORE	ACT	FORE	ACT	FORE	ACT	FORE	ACT	FORE	ACT
ROOMS														
Arrivals														
Departures														
Stayovers														
Total Rooms Occupied														
Rooms on the Books														
House Count														
FOOD & BEVERAGE CATERING														
Breakfast														
Lunch														
Dinner														
Break														
Reception														
Total Catering Covers														
IN-HOUSE BANQUET														
Breakfast														
Lunch														
Dinner														
Break														
Reception														
Total In-House Banquet Covers														
Total Banquet Covers														
RESTAURANT														
Breakfast														
Lunch/Brunch														
Dinner														
Total Restaurant Covers														

Index

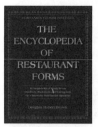

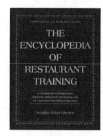